Sailing on My Own Compass

This book is a first-hand account of the inside story of what our police force has to go through on a daily basis. The pressures and tribulations, the demands and 'commands' and the variety of strategies—from diplomacy to firmness—needed to 'handle' situations that could lead to regret or satisfaction later in life. A policeman's life is not an easy one—it is a life replete with difficult choices—primarily imposed by politicians of any party. This book is an eye-opener in many ways.

—**Dr Pranoy Roy,** Co-Founder and Executive Co-Chairman, NDTV

The book is a first-person narrative of the varied experiences, spread nearly over 39 years of the author's life, who was a very successful Indian Police Service (IPS) officer. It is the story of a constantly evolving public servant whose entire career is marked with idealism and practical wisdom. From a sub-division of Delhi's police district to Government of India's corridors of power, he played several roles and all with equal aplomb, always doing what he believed to be right and not what was expedient. The book is also about leadership that inspired confidence amongst men because there was acceptance of responsibility in it and courage to face the odds with dignity. The most remarkable attribute of the author is his extraordinary power of gentle persuasion. The book is replete with instances, from dealing with hostile mobs to the highest in the political executive, where all concerned were made to see reason leading to amending the course of action already decided upon. The ability to persuade someone to one's own point of view without pressure or coercion is a rare quality. The author has it and that makes him a man for all seasons.

—**Satish Sahney,** Former Commissioner of Police, Mumbai Former DG, Maharashtra

This book narrates the story of an unassuming police officer who rose to the highest ranks in the force by sheer dint of merit, hard work and a humaneness which characterized all that he did. Normally the image of a police officer is that of a person with a tough exterior and a blunt approach, not used to softness or giving apologies. But here is the story of a police officer who was always ready to listen to the complaints of the ordinary citizen, often protecting him from the angst of not only politicians but his own force.

His wide experience not only as Inspector General of Police, Goa, and as Commissioner of Police Delhi, but also one dealing with the problem of extremists in Jammu and Kashmir (J&K) and communal situations is a must-read book for all those entering the police force. He believed in the dictum that meaningful public cooperation is the basic requirement for a successful police officer. He succeeded in his negotiations with the extremist elements in J&K because, as they said, they had 'faith' in him.

Shri Kaushal has also emphasized that a successful leader is not only the one who is posted as the head of the force, but is also the one who should have the ability and courage to protect his men when needed, even if it means that he puts his own career at risk.

This is an inspiring book not only for police officers, but also for the defence and civilian officers manning the highest posts in government.

—**Yogendra Narain,** Former Chief Secretary,
UP Former Secretary General, Rajya Sabha

The life of a police officer is never easy and it is only a small and select group of the finest who come out with flying colours such as Mr Kaushal. His memoirs portray, in fascinating ways as well as with sensitivity and wisdom, the many challenges that he faced during his remarkable journey as one of India's top cops.

There are many notable aspects of his journey such as the fact that he faced his challenges with equanimity and fortitude. This is borne out time and again as when he deftly sidestepped the unsolicited and unexpected favour of his posting in Delhi as a result of Mrs Indira Gandhi's high esteem for his work or when he dealt firmly and meaningfully with the Shahi Imam of Jama Masjid, in spite of interventions from highest political levels. All along, he enjoyed the trust and confidence of prime ministers Shri P.V. Narasimha Rao and Shri Atal Bihari Vajpayee. His administrative skills are on display time and again ranging from minor details to far reaching policy as in boldly pushing the promotions of more than 1,700 officers and men. Actually, his zeal for police welfare is truly bold and humane. I was also struck by his Holmes-like sleuthing and logic when he salvaged Mr Narasimha Rao's alibi of not having met Harshad Mehta, the notorious scamster. The gamut of his experiences is vast and his sagacity and courage are on display whether dealing with the high and mighty or when dealing with common folk as when he helped out this distraught mother, early in his career, when her schoolgoing son was mixed up in a foolish attempt at armed robbery. This is an extremely absorbing book to be enjoyed for its story-like narrative as also for the wisdom it packs.

—**Prof. Dinesh Singh** (Padma Shri Awardee),
Former Vice Chancellor, University of Delhi

I feel privileged to get a pre-publication glimpse of the memoir of my dear friend Mukund Kaushal. We met for the first time at the National Academy of Administration, Mussoorie, in 1963. It was a case of mutual liking and affection at first sight which has continued unabated for the last six decades.

A positive person as he is, he has put even the pandemic to good use by recalling memories of a life of personal and professional fulfilment. He has taken his retirement as a service condition and not the closure of his innings, and is active in serving the causes he believes in.

In his book, Kaushal highlights that for handling law and order problems dialogue with concerned parties could generally lead to solutions and in times of crisis one must first learn to manage oneself. As a civil servant under oath to the constitution, one should be politically neutral and professional. These are not mere litany of generalities; Kaushal's personal and professional life is a testimony to the real-life practice of these cardinal principles. Kaushal was commissioner of police, Delhi, under the Congress government, director general (DG), Central Reserve Police Force (CRPF) under the United Front government and secretary, Internal Security (IS), under the BJP. His interaction with Vajpayee in opposition, his defying the instructions regarding the powerful son of Prime Minister (PM) Morarji Desai and his tackling of the Shahi Imam again testified the adherence to professional ethics at great personal risk.

I'm sure this book will be read with much interest by the new generation and will help the readers in reaffirming the dharma of public service.

—**Syed Shahid Mahdi,** Former Vice Chancellor,
Jamia Millia Islamia University

I am delighted to write about *Sailing on My Own Compass*, a fascinating page-turner which provides an enthralling account of Mr Mukund Kaushal's experience in the police service. Throughout my career, I have worked closely with the police department. The collaborative modicum through which public service professionals thrive and navigate is resonated in exciting tales that Mr Kaushal has brought forward. As he writes, 'Humility is not weakness. It conveys the strength of conviction,' this book provides an insider's perspective of dealing with several challenges with conviction.

The tale of the rehriwalas [cartsellers], where he mitigated the challenges of citizens through the empathetic side of police force, is an appropriate beginning to this book as it sets the context of multiple complexities such as empathy, law and order and livelihood that civil servants have to keep in mind while dealing with challenges throughout their careers. The exciting chase of Bhagwant Singh in the antique dealer case keeps one hooked almost like to a fast-paced movie. The anecdotes around pushing promotions for the meritorious officers, upholding the prestige of the police department and the emotionally enriching tale of the apology to a junior colleague bring to light the myriad trials and tribulations that a civil servant faces through their tenure. These stories will be exciting reads for colleagues, aspirants and the common citizen who desire to demystify the workings of the Indian Police Service.

Circumstantial stories around Charan Singh coming to power, Mulayam Singh's protest rally to Delhi, the Babri Masjid–Ram Janambhoomi dispute, Harshad Mehta scam, Uttarakhand statehood movement will keep the reader deeply entrenched in the political economy of the last few decades. The story of Mr Kaushal being called to the privilege committee of the Parliament is a fascinating story which reflects the checks and balances that every civil servant has to operate under and also resonates with the value of responsibility being championed by senior officials to defend their decisions and shield their colleagues.

Sailing on My Own Compass is the culmination of a rich and rewarding career that Mr Mukund Kaushal has led. It is a must read for young civil servants who will be greatly inspired and motivated by Mr Kaushal's career. The book is a wonderful read.

—**Amitabh Kant,** CEO,
NITI Aayog

What a remarkable book by a remarkable person! I never knew or interacted with the author when he was an officer, but the book is a true reflection of his personality, the most remarkable feature of which is his humility that comes out so eloquently in his book.

The prologue provides the gist and the approach of the book. It contains the essence of what is to follow. The style is simple and anecdotes crisp and engrossing.

The book is a treatise on leadership in practice. The author's focus is on 'team effort', the essence of leadership as he calls 'trust' a magic tool. It indeed is. Unlike some of the present crop of leaders, Mr Kaushal believed in giving credit to his juniors and taking all the responsibility. This comes through in a number of episodes narrated by him. His going the distance to protect his team members earned him respect. Not allowing an SHO to be suspended was one such instance that brings forth this quality.

For Mr Kaushal, dialogue was the key to resolving issues. Whether it was the group of agitating students or lawyers, this approach not only resolved issues, but won him lifelong friends and admiration.

The author was never shy of admitting his mistakes and even expressing regret as he did when he wrongly took a junior officer to task in Goa. Only a psychologically secure person could do that.

Author's brush with prime ministers and their sons make for a very interesting read and his forthright approach in dealing with them makes it even more fascinating.

This is a book worth reading and worth keeping.

—**Anil Swarup,** Former Secretary, Ministry of Coal and
Ministry of Education, Government of India

Mukund Bihari Kaushal's book isn't a self-serving autobiography. It's a compendium, a collection of the life events of a police officer who rose to be the commissioner of Delhi Police and had an eventful four-year stint as secretary, special secretary in the Union home ministry.

The narrative is as eclectic as has been the career of Mr Kaushal, as the DG of CRPF, the Centre's point person in talks with militant/secessionist groups in Kashmir and the Northeast, whom the government had sought to mainstream albeit with limited success. In his recollections interspersed with interestingly related episodes, the author makes the reader a co-traveller in his journey as a field operative and a key player in Delhi's power corridors.

The career-travelogue, so to speak, brings his audience face to face with former prime ministers, affording a rare peep into their temperaments and their way of working. Indira Gandhi is as much part of Mr Kaushal's book as Morarji Desai, Chaudhary Charan Singh, P.V. Narasimha Rao and Atal Bihari Vajpayee. Figuring besides them in the stories told are L.K. Advani, Sanjay Gandhi, Kanti Desai and Arun Jaitley.

A chapter that held my attention the most was related to the Harshad Mehta episode of 1993* and the events that followed his allegation of graft against Narasimha Rao, then sitting PM. The ill-reputed stockbroker claimed to have delivered one crore rupees in cash at the PM's residence. What

---

*The year when Harshad Mehta held a press conference following the case.

makes the book a must-read is Mr Kaushal's version of behind-the-scene efforts which brought the controversy to a close.

Having known the author for over four decades, one can say that like Sadat Hasan Manto, who called himself a *chalta phirta* Bombay [in other words, an embodiment of Bombay, the city], Mr Kaushal is an everyday Lakhnavi Babu. The book is a testimony to that etiquette, that persona matching the culture of the city where he spent his formative years, notwithstanding the police uniform and the epaulettes he wore.

—**Vinod Sharma,** Political Editor,
Hindustan Times

In reality, I have no business to be here on this page and this book. I am just too junior to Mukund Kaushal Saheb to be writing anything as a review, comment or opinion on what he has said and written in this wonderful book which recalls poignant moments from his days in the Indian Police Service for close to 40 years. However, he requested me to do so, on the basis of some of my writings and commentaries in print and visual media. No doubt the J&K factor played up since he heard of my close association and many years spent in that state. I have been fortunate to have experienced a few turbulent conflict zones in difficult times and at all ranks, but the strongest association that Kaushal Saheb and I have is through J&K. In fact, I met him only once and that was after the fateful events at Chittisinghpura in March 2000; I was then the Colonel General Staff of the HQ Victor Force (Rashtriya Rifles) in South Kashmir and he was special secretary in the Ministry of Home Affairs directly responsible for J&K.

I read every word of this fascinating collection of narration of events in Kaushal Saheb's career. What struck me were a couple of things. First is the sheer simplicity of the narrative with no attempt at self-promotion or romanticization of the achievements. Second, his personality emerges as one who is principled, patriotic and committed. I particularly liked the reference to his spouse as a person who demanded nothing from him, leaving him to do his job with a sense of pride. Each of the short chapters is about an event which was challenging and demanded very sensitive handling. The ones which really stand out and I strongly recommend that the reader must turn to are firstly the negotiations with the Hizbul Mujahideen in August 2000 when offensive operations were ceased in J&K. Of course, it leaves the reader pining for more especially about the background and the subsequent fallout. Kaushal Saheb keeps it short, meaningful and with no unnecessary anecdotal references. That is why it is purely professional. The second narrative I enjoyed thoroughly was the one concerning the arrest of former Tamil Nadu chief minister (CM) and two central ministers in Chennai during the leadership of Prime Minister Atal Bihari Vajpayee. It's an apt story to highlight what senior government officials go through many times when orders are completely in the grey zone and they have to use their own discretion to take decisions knowing fully well that these may never be backed. However, more often than not it is the spoken reputation of a government official which carries the day. Kaushal Saheb had the distinct advantage of having a reputation of being a doer, someone who could be relied upon, was honest and had no political affiliations. His ability to serve with aplomb under governments led by different political parties and that too in crucial appointments exemplifies his professional approach with no strings attached. The chapter on his experience as police commissioner of Delhi brings out much of the necessity for a police officer to be politically neutral.

The other aspect of this book which needs mention is the presence of humanism in every facet of his professional narratives. He is obviously a great believer in 'people orientation' and has always balanced tasks with people. That is one of the reasons for his success and the maintenance of such a reputation. He is a believer in 'talking and engaging,' something I too adopted extensively as my strategy in J&K. Today's conflicts are less to do with conventional ways of war fighting. They are more about influence and sway that can be established over the people. With technology extensively supporting this, we have social media and other instruments of information and psychological operations. In all this, unless you as a leader are willing to engage with the people and conduct frequent town hall kind of meetings to assuage their sentiments, you can hardly be successful. Kaushal Saheb brought the basics of leadership to the fore. I loved his statement which I quote, 'Civil servants are not only administrators but are trustees of public interest.' It reveals his understanding of what needs to go into countering a proxy hybrid war launched against us in J&K. Our tendency for many years of relying only on kinetic operations to bring peace was obviously flawed. It's the people-oriented approach with a balance between hard kinetic operations and soft power related people centricity that wins the day.

I once again thank Kaushal Saheb for his magnanimity in asking someone many years his junior to write his impressions of this book. I will continue to remain indebted. I also hope many young people will read this book and benefit from the multifaceted experiences of Mr Mukund Kaushal—police officer extraordinaire.

—Lt Gen. Syed Ata Hasnain, Param Vishisht Seva Medal Uttam Yuddh Seva Medal, Ati Vishisht Seva Medal, Sena Medal, Vishisht Seva Medal & BAR (Retd), Former General Officer Commanding, Chinar Corps

Mukund Kaushal has written this book straight from the heart, something that he also brought to bear on his three-and-a-half decades of service. Apart from being an easy, breezy, grippy read, it's an account of an upright IPS officer who put his uniform and his people ahead of everything else, including personal glory, even promotion.

Kaushal had many important and high-profile roles, including working with India's top bureaucrats, senior ministers and prime ministers under different dispensations, but he served only one master—India's constitution. The book is peppered with interesting examples of how he handled student leaders, hardened criminals, terrorists and leaders across the political divide—he combined tact with tenacity, benevolence with bare-knuckled aggression.

This book serves as a treatise on leadership and management—many corporate executives could take a leaf out of it. It's an honest and gripping account of the life and times of Mukund Kaushal set in the backdrop of the 1970s, going all the way to the beginning of this century when he hung up his boots in 2001. It's a fascinating socio-political account of the times, replete with his brush with the high and mighty, the low and the lowly.

Mukund Kaushal will not be remembered for the glitter of the offices he has held, but for the lasting impression he's left on humankind that he served so dedicatedly and selflessly. *Sailing on My Own Compass* is a worthy read.

—**Rahul Joshi,** Managing Director and Group Editor-in Chief, Network 18, Former Editorial Director, *Economic Times*

Sailing on My Own Compass

A POLICEMAN'S DIARY

Mukund Kaushal

RUPA

First published by
Rupa Publications India Pvt. Ltd 2022
7/16, Ansari Road, Daryaganj
New Delhi 110002

Sales Centres:
Allahabad Bengaluru Chennai
Hyderabad Jaipur Kathmandu
Kolkata Mumbai

ISBN: 978-93-5520-146-1

First impression 2022

10 9 8 7 6 5 4 3 2 1

The moral right of the author has been asserted.

Dedicated

to
Maa and Pita Ji
Late Smt. Shyama Kaushal and
Late Shri Harish Chandra Kaushal
who made me what I am today

to
my life partner and soulmate Asha
who brought balance in our life and made it complete

to
God's most valuable gifts to me, my children,
Bharat, Rina, Deepam and Gauri

and

my grandchildren,
Ashwarya Nandini, Shubhankar Mihir,
Dhananjay Madhav and Aryaman Mihir
who are source of my happiness and joy

CONTENTS

FOREWORD

Mukund Kaushal belongs to that genre of police officers who possess a deep sense of duty, setting them apart from the crowd. In putting down his memoirs, he has done this profession a great service. He makes no pretence of being a superhero, but demonstrates how important values are if a policeman sets out to have a successful career. What he conveys is that, ultimately, it is an adherence to basic values that finally enables an officer to triumph over odds. This is the message one gets going through this lean volume.

The writing style mirrors the individual's personality and the series of episodes that he enumerates display a mixture of professional rectitude and humaneness. At one level, he is a popular and successful police officer, and at another, he is unbending in standing up to politicians and those in authority who think they can browbeat the police. The way he stood up to the late Sanjay Gandhi is an excellent example of this and a lesson for police officers across the country. That Mukund Kaushal finally emerged as perhaps one of the most regarded and highest-ranking police officers of his generation should give younger colleagues hope for their future.

Two events stand out as far as Mukund Kaushal's professionalism is concerned. One was his successful management of the exposition of the holy relics of St Francis Xavier when he was the chief of police in Goa, which brought India many encomiums from across the entire Catholic community. The other was his detailed exposure of the Harshad Mehta case, which at one time threatened to undermine the integrity of India's one of the most outstanding prime ministers. His meticulous detailing of police practices and sensitive handling of the situation are something that every professional policeman has a reason to be proud of.

Mukund Kaushal has had a varied career in the police department and a stint in the home ministry. More than the detailed accounts of the major events that he was privy to, it is his innate professionalism that comes through in this memoir and should be an inspiration for younger generations of policemen.

I would recommend young police professionals to read this book and take to heart the lessons that it provides.

M.K. Narayanan,
Former Director, Intelligence Bureau,
Former National Security Advisor,
Former Governor of West Bengal

PREFACE

Every new publication of bureaucratic memoirs makes me envious of those colleagues in civil service who have had the audacity to pen their memoirs. I have not been able to bring myself to publish my story yet despite the fact that two prominent publishers had approached me in this regard soon after my superannuation. There were two reasons for this. One, I doubted whether the readers of my book, if there were any, would get much out of my personal story. And two, after writing about 100 pages, I erased it because I found that there were too many 'I's' in it. In fact, it read very much like the stories of many IAS contemporaries.

Mukund Kaushal's narrative is refreshingly different.

I have known Mukund Kaushal for the last 58 years. We joined the civil services on the same day. Unlike many of our performing colleagues, Kaushal has a mind of his own. He is independent, fearless and yet stubbornly modest. He is known to have resisted the demands of his political masters and has not hesitated in saying no to their wishes. He presents his case with conviction and without any fear of consequences. The beauty lies in the fact that he does it without offending anyone. In fact, he possesses the magic of taking care of everyone's sentiments while proposing a course of action. Intriguingly, he proves right every time.

Perhaps unknown to him, he has been practising the principle of reciprocity in his dealings with his colleagues, men in uniform and the members of general public. The principle of reciprocity was developed in ancient civilizations independent of each other.

The *Babylonian Talmud* says, 'What is hateful to you, do not do to your fellow: this is the whole Torah; the rest is the explanation.'

The Padma Purana, which categorizes itself as representing goodness and purity, states, 'If the entire dharma can be said in a few words, then it is—that which is unfavourable to us, do not do that to others.'

According to the *Analects,* Zigong asked: 'Is there any one word that could guide a person throughout life?' Confucius replied: 'How about reciprocity: never impose on others what you would not choose for yourself?'

Thales of Miletus, a Greek mathematician, astronomer and pre-Socratic philosopher said, 'Avoid doing what you would blame others for doing.'

The reciprocity principle is one of the basic laws of social psychology: it says that in many social situations, we pay back what we received from others. These philosophical discussions concern the ways in which patterns and norms of reciprocity might have a role in theories of justice, stable and productive social systems, healthy personal relationships and ideals for human social life generally.

To Kaushal, reciprocity comes naturally. The empirical evidence establishes that he has avoided harming anyone even when it was obligated. Only a rare police officer like him could situate the welfare of his subordinates or the less privileged above his own.

I find his language unpretentious, devoid of the overhang of a cultivated style of narration. At times you feel that he is simply speaking to himself of the days spent in the police service. His idiom is simple and direct with hardly any contrived embellishment.

Two things stand out in his narrative: one, that he has a phenomenal memory of events and people. He would recall the date and the exact time of the incident. Once he told me, after we superannuated, that he met me for the first time in front of the administrative block of the National Academy in the afternoon and that I was wearing a pair of light brown corduroy trousers with a blue blazer. I could not contradict him because I did not remember what I was wearing 40 years ago. That he has been gifted with an incredible photographic memory can be endorsed by anyone who has come in contact with him. And the same gift is reflected in every snippet presented in the book.

His phenomenal memory is evident throughout the book. Besides the names of police constables and the accused, the woman who meets him accidentally, the victim of a crime, he even remembers names of many junior police officials, their postings and some incidents related to them.

Another quality that Kaushal does not share with many other writers of memoirs is his transparent authenticity. He believes what he says he believes in. According to researchers, genuine leadership is synonymous with being authentic. Being authentic is acting consistent with what you hold out to be to others and acting consistent with what you hold out to be to yourself. Admiration is the highest reward in the realm of governance. In making attempts to be admired, the loss of authenticity seems a small price to pay. We do not even notice that we are being inauthentic and even if we did, we are unaware that being inauthentic costs us our integrity. 'After years of studying leaders and their traits, I believe that leadership begins and ends with authenticity,' says Werner Erhard. In short, being authentic is critical to being a leader.

Despite having spent four decades in the Civil Services where appearances are supposed to be more important than the substance, Kaushal personifies authentic leadership. He does not hesitate in showing his real face always and every time. He puts it very disarmingly when he says that he sleeps well. The 'sleep well' test is acknowledged as the best test for doing what is right.

At the end of some of the chapters, Kaushal leaves useful tips for civil servants e.g., 'the force must feel assured that their leader has confidence in their abilities', or 'a well-motivated and committed force achieves amazing results', 'intrigues and misrepresentations sometimes create serious problems, but if you take the bull by the horn and put correct facts to the concerned authorities, there are very good chances of your retrieving the situation' or 'if one is functioning according to rules and is morally correct, he can afford to take a stand, but to the extent possible, avoid confrontation with authorities.' His younger colleagues would be well advised to follow his tips.

We have spent many hours together in flights between Delhi and Pune, while driving from Pune airport to Panchgani, during extended sojourns in Asia Plateau reminiscing about our time in the government. Most of the time, he talked and I listened. Since he is a brilliant storyteller with deadly recall of things, faces and events, it is always a pleasure to listen to him. What is remarkable is that you can feel that everything is neatly arranged in his mind unlike mine where things are in a tangled mess. Even when he repeats one of his stories (which is quite often), there are no contradictions.

Not every civil servant writes his/her memoirs and the world is so much better for it. But there are a lot of self-certified achievers who wash their dirty linen in public without any apparent provocation. I sometimes wonder that when we have little cause for pride as a profession, when we have collectively made a mess of things, then why do we indulge in blowing our trumpet?

I think most of the bureaucrats who have written their autobiographies should have suppressed their urge to impose their stories on us. But there are some among civil servants who should have shared their experiences and beliefs. There are some who should have written their memoirs, but were reluctant or averse to sharing their stories. It's a pity that they did not recount their trials and tribulations, victories and defeats, for others to enjoy and to learn something from.

Kaushal is one of those few. Some of them write with a lot of determination and deliberate planning, while some others do because of ennui or an accident. But for the pandemic and the insistence of many of his colleagues in the IC Centre, he would not have acquiesced to narrate his story and we would have been deprived of it.

I think he should start working on his second book of snippets.

Prabhat Kumar,
Former Cabinet Secretary
Former Governor of Jharkhand

PROLOGUE

This book is a lockdown child—a lockdown so long, it almost seemed like a dark, dusty never-ending tunnel. When I felt drained due to constantly reading newspapers (talking about whether the virus came from a Chinese native eating a bat or the Chinese Communist Party themselves!) and magazines showcasing deserted roads and marketplaces, books exploring the meaning of life, watching the blaring TV—constantly warning its viewers about death looming above them—and trying to keep myself sane by talking to loved ones on call, I was desperately looking for something to keep myself occupied, something that not just helped me pass time, but revitalized me.

The lockdown filled everyone with a strange nostalgia, a longing for the past far gone and thus extremely valuable. While trying to recollect some old incidents, I started noting down whatever I could remember and that was the starting point of this book. I never thought that I would write about my experiences of Civil Services as it made me feel like a narcissist indulging in constant self-gratification...but neither had we imagined a pandemic taking over our entire lives, changing the way we viewed not only the past but also the present and the upcoming future; this very pandemic would also make us do things we never thought we would—like me beginning to write a book. Eventually, my writing became my safe haven. An afternoon routine I found myself running back to everyday gave me sense of control in my life. At least, my pen and paper would behave the way I wanted them to.

Immediately after my retirement, I had received a letter from a well-known publisher from Delhi, requesting me to write my memoirs. He spoke to me on call, but I expressed my unwillingness. The civil society organization for which I work conducts training programmes in 'Ethics of Public Service' for serving government and public sector undertaking (PSU) officials. My colleagues, especially our president Shri Prabhat Kumar, former cabinet secretary and governor, who is also my batchmate and a very close friend, after hearing some of my experiences during my lectures, had been pressing me to record my experiences into writing, but for some reason, I kept avoiding their encouraging words. I'd written the forewords for Professor Raj Gopal's two books and his publisher, who came to see me in this connection, repeatedly motivated me to produce my own memoir. My daughter Gauri (Dr Gauri Seth) too has been consistently pressing me for years to write my memoir. What these persuasive attempts couldn't achieve, the lockdown did.

I entered IPS getting an opportunity at the age of 20 and superannuated when I reached 60. My long journey with the government has really been quite interesting—partly smooth and partly challenging, but on the whole, I enjoyed it and left highly content and proud. I saw my retirement, not as a closure of my innings, but rather as a service condition. This was my time to continue serving the society which had given me so much.

I wasn't exactly an extraordinary student, but God had

blessed me with a decent memory along with the motivation to stay studious. It took me a while to gain momentum as a student. Initially, I was not good at writing examinations, but once I picked it up, I did not look back. Since my childhood, I have wanted to read books beyond my syllabus—you may call it both, an expensive and a troublesome habit! Fiction, (both Hindi and English), poetry, magazines like *Reader's Digest, The Citizen, Dharmyug* and newspapers were my go-to companions. I was well-versed with most of our religious books since I was a young child, as I'd find myself reading them aloud to my bedridden grandmother. It was my privilege, as my grandmother would at times explain the philosophy or lessons behind some of these stories to me. Despite it being so long ago, I thank my good memory for having helped me retain a lot of her teachings and insights. This not only added to my knowledge, but also had an impact on my thinking and attitude. After all, the words you hear, read and consume as a child help shape who you become.

As I reflect upon my life, I find three major influences that continue to define who I am today. First and foremost, the contribution of my grandparents and parents in shaping my personality, including my way of thinking and my values, was immense. My grandfather had a very strong personality. Some property-related issues in our family had left him disenchanted with materialistic possessions. He, with the consent of his father, decided to donate his entire property consisting of the zamindari of two villages, a big garden and two houses in Kanpur city to Thakurdwara (a family temple). In the end, he only kept a small house for his family. Funds of this trust are currently being utilized by a new family trust, which I formed with the consent of all my family members for the education of poor but deserving children, mostly girls, in an English-medium public school. There was another aspect of my grandfather which stood out—his integrity. He had resigned from his job as a police officer when he was asked to arrest two well-known freedom fighters. However, when the British superintendent of police (under whom he was working) retired and took up a post-retirement assignment as the chief of watch and ward of Great Indian Peninsula Railways (GIPR) (later known as Central Railways), he invited him to join hands with him, which he (my grandfather) accepted. Finally, he retired from there as his second-in-command.

My father is another person I've looked up to in my life. He has always been my role model and guide. He received scholarships throughout his academic life and was awarded a gold medal at Thomason College of Civil Engineering, Roorkee (It is now known as IIT Roorkee). He had a towering personality and an unwavering presence. A man of action with strong determination, he never fought with anyone, but was extremely conscious about his self-respect. He was soft-spoken, humane and full of compassion, a perfect blend of firmness and empathy. I would fail miserably if I tried recounting the number of people my father helped and aided throughout his life. Even during personal adversities, he made sure he never let anyone suffer alone. It's quite easy to help someone else when everything is okay in your life, but true, unconditional service lies in sacrifice, in going beyond your own troubles to eradicate those of others. I remember how he once told me that the person who comes to ask for your help is not usually concerned with your problems, so you should do for them whatever you can within your capacity. At the time of my father's cremation, a lecturer in Lucknow University came and told my brother that our father gave him regular financial assistance to complete his studies. My brother was not aware of this fact. That man requested to participate in my father's last rites as a family member. This incident has stayed with me ever since. Throughout his life, my father looked after his extended family, matters concerning children's education, marriages, illnesses, you name it. He had an unshakable value system and never strayed away from his responsibilities.

My mother, daughter of a Rai Bahadur* and a government advocate, taught me two important things—first, God looks after those who share and second, one should never see another human being as inferior, irrespective of their class, colour, occupation, caste, gender or age.

And of course, my acknowledgements would be incomplete if I do not mention about my wife's contribution in making our life smooth and enjoyable. She managed the entire household and fulfilled all her commitments within the salary I'd earn, without ever complaining. She never asked me for anything and was always happy. Her contentment with whatever I could provide for her, rather than increasing my stress, always made me want to do more for her. I never discussed official matters at home, but she quietly supported me throughout my days of service, especially during times of crisis. She would advise me to do what I thought was right without fearing the consequences. While taking up higher responsibilities on a bigger canvas—where important decisions were to be taken and critical situations to be handled—the stability and positive vibes at home made it possible for me to sail through this challenging and otherwise difficult service. No amount of thanks would be enough to you, Asha, for turning my life into a pleasant and interesting journey.

---

*One of the highest honorific titles awarded to distinguished Indians in British India.

I never studied in a convent or public school. While my father's colleagues had been able to send their children to English-medium schools, my father was looking after the education of quite a few children in the family and hence had to divide his income into many halves rather than having the luxury of splurging it only on his children. All of us either studied in affordable government schools or in ordinary private schools. But studying there itself was a big education. Children of my father's subordinate staff including those of domestic help also went there. We studied and played together; in my mind, I was equal to them, there was no divide between us. Thanks to my parents, I learned to treat everyone as an equal, remained grounded and appreciated all, irrespective of their background.

Serving in the police gave me many opportunities to witness various shades of life, to study and understand people's behaviour and to deal with larger groups of people i.e., mobs. To me, it was very interesting to watch a person behave differently in different situations. To handle offenders at all levels—be it juvenile wrongdoers, hardened criminals or dehumanized terrorists—gave me an insight into the workings of the human mind. It was a lifetime experience. I saw life and people very closely. I learnt a major valuable lesson: while managing rioting mobs, especially communal riots, timely assessment of the situation and quick, firm and objective handling normally controls the situation. You cannot let your emotions cloud your decision-making. At the same time, you have to always retain human compassion and sensitivity to distinguish tough handling from abuse of power and police brutality.

For me, every incident—good, bad or ugly—was an experience and I always tried to analyse and learn from those. Even after successfully managing a serious law and order situation, I'd hold meetings to discuss and identify areas where we could have done better or where our shortcomings were not noticed. I learned two important things during my service: only teamwork can lead to success in a tough and challenging job like police. A leader should be able to establish a relationship of mutual trust with his team members. Trust works as a magic tool as it is a force multiplier and gives amazing results! And of course, this trust has to be both ways. While a leader must be able to convey to his team members that he has faith in their abilities to deliver, they must also trust their leader and understand that he has broad enough shoulders to protect them as they perform their duties, which naturally would include honest mistakes. A leader has to develop strong personal credibility and has to lead his team from the front. He must learn to give credit to his juniors and be prepared to take responsibility when things do not go as planned. Leaders who take ownership of their responsibilities make an impact on the organization and deliver results. IPS officers must learn to become part of the force/organization they are serving. Those who do it have achieved success. It is also the leader's responsibility to create leadership at different levels of the organizational hierarchy and also to build a pipeline of future leaders for it.

The other important learning was that the best way to judge the effectiveness of an organization having public dealings is to assess the level of 'public satisfaction' achieved by it at a given time. Public satisfaction is not anything abstract. There are various ways of assessing it.

During handling of law and order situations, even critical ones, I found that 'talking to people' or 'establishing a dialogue with the involved parties' could help in diffusing the tension and at times even providing the solution. Unlike Army, which mostly deals with the nation's enemies, police normally regulates, contains and controls their own people, who at times get excited, agitated and occasionally violent. They have to be dealt with a lot of tact and restraint. But whenever and wherever required, I took firm and tough action especially against hardened criminals and communal riots or terrorist activities. A leader must ensure that his actions never convey any impression of vengeance or that he is settling a score. My experience also taught me that patience and cool temperament are not only good qualities, but a professional requirement for those involved in public dealing.

While patience gives you extra time to think, the cool temperament enables you to see far and take an appropriate decision. I also felt that humility is another quality which makes a leader more acceptable. Humility is not weakness. It conveys the strength of conviction, it is accepting the truth in other person's views or listening to displeasing views with patience and not reacting with aggression. It is a kind of virtue that can pull along other virtues. Unfortunately, it is in short supply, especially at senior levels in the Civil Services. Leadership is tested in crisis. Fortunately, due to a variety of experiences in the early duration of my service, I realized that the first requirement for handling any crisis was to learn to manage yourself. Sometimes, even an ordinary situation becomes a crisis if the leader gets into panic mode.

Success is possible only if the leader has a clear vision about his organization. In simple terms, it implies that a leader, when he assumes the new role, should make an assessment where his organization stands on various parameters and where he intends to take it in a given timeframe. He must communicate his vision clearly to his team members and also what he expects from them. Wining leaders are very demanding. This would give direction to the organization and leader could then motivate and prepare them for achieving the task. Successful leader must also know that what has brought them to this level will not take them there where they aim to reach unless they keep on rediscovering or evolving themselves. A leader should always be conscious of his contribution to the force/organization, which has given him the honour to lead them.

A successful leader must earn wide acceptability among his team members without compromising on his dignity and objectivity. This implies maintaining constant touch with his team members and developing a proper understanding of their problems and their true potential. The assurance that a leader would be accessible, whenever needed and that he is concerned about them creates confidence in the team members and is a great motivator.

While I always remained a disciplined officer, I never hesitated in expressing my views, despite knowing they most probably wouldn't match with my seniors' at times. Conflict never caused me anxiety or hesitation. I always believed that I owe it to my service to convey what I thought was right. However, once a decision was taken, I accepted the orders and implemented them in letter and spirit, even if I had opposed it during discussions. Perhaps that is what led to my seniors having faith in me. A few incidents narrated in this book are its testimony. But I was always conscious of my self-respect. While I ensured I remained within the limits of discipline, I never accepted misbehaviour or maltreatment from anybody. I remember declining LG's banquet invitation for my wife and me in Goa as he had added our names at the last minute. He had earlier invited Army commandant and some secretaries of the local government who were junior to me. It was only on a second thought that he deleted someone else's name and put in mine.

The prestige of public servants lies in serving the people and completing the task entrusted to them without creating any controversy. A public servant must realize that the status and powers bestowed upon them are for successfully achieving the targets given to them and should not be mistaken as their personal powers. Generally, officials tend to do people's work as if they are doing them a favour. This is probably a legacy of the British Raj, which is unfortunately continuing till date. I also noticed that a large number of civil servants were unwilling to engage with people whom they were supposed to serve. Public servants ought to have a sense of urgency in performance of their duties. I learnt the importance of completing my tasks within a set time from my boss in the Railway Protection Force (RPF), Shri Raj Deo Singh, who later on became director of the Central Bureau of Investigation (CBI). Civil servants are not only administrators, but are 'trustees of public interest'.

Notwithstanding my personal views on the political scenario in the country, I truly remained apolitical throughout my service and served various governments of different shades with complete sincerity. All of them trusted me and assigned important responsibilities and tasks, which I completed without creating any controversy—be it handling of communal situations or preventing the massive BJP rally during the Congress' rule, the J&K elections during the United Front regime, managing various critical situations, preparing the action plan for J&K or conducting negotiations of political nature during the BJP government's tenure at the Centre. The fact that I was appointed as the commissioner of police (CP),

Delhi, by the Congress government, DG CRPF, by the United Front government and secretary, IS, by the BJP, the senior leadership of which was arrested by me quite a few times, is a testimony of how I kept all kinds of political affiliations aside during my service.

During the second half of my tenure as CP, Delhi, there was a BJP government in the national capital territory (NCT) of Delhi and Congress government at the Centre. On assuming charge of Delhi, the first and only demand of the BJP was my transfer, to which the central government did not agree. But during the complete one year for which I served after that, my relations with the NCT government remained extremely cordial. In fact, they conveyed to the central government that they wanted me to continue. The CM accepted and acted on my advice on two occasions despite Delhi Pradesh BJP's opposing directions. I worked with full sincerity and commitment for the government I was serving and enjoyed their confidence. On many occasions, I advised the government against the stand they were proposing and conveyed what I thought was correct and appropriate, and that was ultimately accepted. I thank God that my intentions were never doubted and I superannuated with a clean slate.

I always felt that God has been generously kind to me and I probably got a little more than what I deserved. There were always better people on the scene, but I got the chance, remaining ahead and eventually succeeded. I refused extension in my service as I thought it compromises both position and authority. On my superannuation, I decided that except for an honourable government assignment, I would not accept any private engagement. I am happy that I've been able to adhere to my decision so far. The only exception was that I advised the IPL management for two months in 2010 at the request of my batchmate in police and also a very close friend Shri I.S. Bindra, who was abroad at that time. No terms and conditions were settled as I agreed to undertake it at the insistence of my friend. On his return and much after my assignment was over, the IPL governing body sent me some honorarium for my services. I have also been serving some civil society organizations and Katyayani Shakti Peeth Trust (which manages Chattarpur Mandir and a few other temples in Delhi). For about four years, I worked, at the request of my friends who were the founding members, as the honorary director of the Rotary Blood Bank (RBB), New Delhi. It was a temple of service and allowed me to immerse myself in charity, which to me is invaluable. I also learned and practised the pleasure of giving. I could almost double the staff strength of the RBB, gave them an increase of about 40 per cent and left about seven and a half crore as earnings in the bank. It was a wonderful and memorable experience.

I have had more than 30 years of association with PRAYAS, a national-level non-profit, child-centric and humanitarian organization. The good work done by PRAYAS has been appreciated, both at national and international levels. The central guiding spirit behind the various landmarks PRAYAS has achieved is its general secretary Shri Amod Kanth—a police officer extraordinaire, who has made a difference in the lives of many people. He is a rare combination of an outstanding police officer who has the professionalism of the highest calibre, combined with a deeply passionate personal commitment for the betterment of society. At present, I am the president of PRAYAS. This is the second time I have assumed this responsibility. For the last six years, I have been the chairman of Jan Shikshan Sansthan, which now works under the Ministry of Skill Development and Entrepreneurship. I have also established a family trust which gives scholarships to deserving children, with a focus on girls, coming from weaker sections of society to study in English-medium public schools, which they couldn't otherwise afford. At present, 18 children are availing this scholarship. My other engagement is with IC Centre for Governance (ICCfG), a civil society organization committed to collective thinking and acting on important issues relating to public governance. I treat my association with the ICCfG as a privilege, since it allowed me to work in the area of my choice and serve the cause that is dear to my heart. I must take this opportunity to express my gratitude to my friend Shri Prabhat Kumar, president of the ICCfG, who encouraged me to share my experiences, especially the ones relating to ethical challenges and dilemmas during our programmes on ethics of public governance.

This book is not only a narration of what happened with me but also what life has taught me. I treat these incidents as opportunities to test myself and to do what I thought was correct. I owe it to various circumstances that influenced my thinking and attitude and to the incidents which helped me complete this part of my journey smoothly and to my utmost satisfaction.

Most of the facts mentioned in various incidents and other details are based on my memory except for some dates, figures and sequence of events in a few chapters. I had to rely on information available on the Internet. In some cases, my old friends, Shri Sudhir Beloria, Shri Mukund Upadhyaya and a few other friends who are still in service refreshed my memory by giving me insight into the past through their recollections. I must acknowledge the great encouragement and support provided by my family—my wife Asha, my daughters Rina and Gauri, Bharat, Deepam and my grandchildren in putting this memoir together.

I must also thanks Shri Vinod K Maurya, manager, administration, and Ms Archana Dubey, programme officer, IC Centre for Governance, for assisting me in completing this book.

My acknowledgment would not be complete unless I express my thanks to my publisher, Rupa Publications. I am personally grateful to my old friend Shri R.K. Mehra, chairman, and his son Shri Kapish Mehra, managing director, Rupa Publications, for their interest and strong support in bringing out this book. I am thankful to the senior commissioning editor Shri Rudra Narain Sharma, who was extremely helpful and demonstrated immense understanding during the entire process of the publication. My thanks are also due to Ms Sakschi Verma, the copyeditor of the book.

As long as Lord Almighty spares me, I am content and happy in doing what I am doing.

Mukund Kaushal

1

BEGINNING AS A POLICEMAN

joined the National Academy of Administration, Mussoorie, on 10 July 1963, as an IPS probationer. After completing my foundation course, I reported at Central Police Training College, Mount Abu (presently known as National Police Academy) for my basic police training. Thereafter, I spent three months at Police Training College in Phillaur, Punjab, and eventually joined the Delhi Police on 12 April 1965 for my district training.

On 6 January 1966, I took charge as sub-divisional police officer (SDPO), Shahdara, in Delhi's north district. The sub-division covered the entire trans-Jamuna area of the Union Territory (UT) and had two police stations. Except for a few middle-class localities and old markets, the entire area consisted of resettlement quarters, unauthorized colonies, markets, industrial areas, some urbanized villages and the rural area bordering Uttar Pradesh, which made my challenges a bit daunting. The area was known for illegal constructions, illicit distillations, smuggling of liquor; it was home to a large number of criminals and various other illegal activities connected with an interstate border—the real underbelly of the city that most of us do not get to witness staying in our privileged bubbles.

The first independent charge of a sub-division is generally treated as a continuation of training for young IPS officers. I was extremely privileged that I undertook my district training and first independent charge under two very outstanding police officers—Shri P.S. Shukla, IPS, Punjab, and Shri Ved Marwah, IPS, West Bengal (later shifted to UT Cadre). Shri P.S. Shukla knew the fine intricacies of the police station functioning like the back of his palm—as a committed guru, he made sure that I too learned about them thoroughly. Shri Ved Marwah was an exemplary police leader and I learned a lot by observing him. He was my role model. It was from him that I learnt to speak my mind fearlessly and with pride. He was a kind and friendly person, but a tough mentor who taught by giving responsibilities and assigning new challenges. I owe a lot to these two great policemen, who are now unfortunately no more. Yet, I'd like to believe I carry parts of them with me.

Initially, I was busy with law and order situations related to the Punjabi Suba agitation. When that mellowed down a little, I started devoting my time to routine police functioning like supervising investigations, scrutinizing case diaries, preparing inquiry reports on public complaints, listening to public grievances, patrolling (especially during the nights) and staff welfare activities like checking messes, barracks and occasionally participating in volleyball games. Every day, I was learning something new and adding to my experience. At times, I would laugh at my efforts to hide my ignorance. I smile as I recollect these good times.

Sometime in May or June 1966, I received an order from my superintendent of police (SP) that all the handcarts were to be removed from the Chotta Bazar in Shahdara as they were causing traffic jams and a lot of inconvenience to the customers, shopkeepers and residents. On checking, we found that there were more than 600 carts in that area selling vegetables, fruits, snacks, hosiery items, toys, stationery and other miscellaneous goods. Since this was going to be a forcible removal, it required substantial force, which was to be requisitioned from police headquarters.

While we were planning and jotting down the police arrangements we needed for this task, the rehriwalas came to know about it. Almost 300 of them, along with some women and children, assembled outside the police station on GT Road to protest. They shouted slogans against the police and their voices still faintly echo in my ears. The GT Road at that time was not as broad as it is today. Vehicular traffic including buses and trucks were moving at a fast pace. The kachha (unpaved) space on the roadside, where the demonstrators were standing, was quite narrow and the likelihood of any child, who had come with the demonstrators, getting injured could not be ruled out. Since the demonstration was peaceful, I asked one of my officers to go to the demonstrators and ask them to come in the front lawns within the police station premises so that I could talk to them. We also told them to stop shouting slogans. Not only my station house officer (SHO), but the protesters too were surprised on being called inside the police station premises. When the protesters learnt that they had been allowed inside the premises to protect their children from the fast-moving traffic, something within them changed. Our consideration came to them as a pleasant surprise and their anger towards the police vanished. Sometimes, instead of brute force, a mere act of kindness or consideration can be enough to persuade a person with opposing views.

During my talk with some of them, I came to know that

not only was each rehri a source of income for a family of five to six, but was also supporting one or two other families whose children were employed for delivering goods and collecting payments. They questioned me about where they were supposed to go now for ensuring their families' survival. We had no answers. When they left, I put the same question to SHO Shahdara. However, to my dismay, for the SHO, this dislocation was merely a routine exercise. He told me in a nonchalant tone that there would be no problem in removing them since they were unauthorized and it would not lead to any serious consequences. My concern, however, still remained unanswered: how would all these families earn their bread and butter? It weighed heavily on my mind, probably because I was a new entrant in the service and my sensitivity was dominating my reactions. Had I joined the service to help people or to deprive them of their livelihoods? Why were the police authorities so insensitive and not even trying to look for an alternative site? Questions such as these endlessly ricocheted in my mind. I was thinking that even if their carts were unauthorized, the rehriwalas had a right to earn their bread and butter.

The same evening, I visited Gandhi Nagar police station, which was almost a part of my daily routine. On reaching Gandhi Nagar, I saw SHO Malik Ramdas sitting in an open space in front of the police station and talking to two or three elderly gentlemen. The SHO greeted me and introduced the gentlemen to me. One of them was Shri Brijlal Goswami, a corporator and chairman of a committee of the municipal corporation for the trans-Jamuna area. He was soft-spoken and very well-known in his area. After a bit of casual conversation, I informed him about the orders I had received to remove the rehriwalas. He quite casually responded that there wouldn't be any issue as they were unauthorized... I immediately answered back that it was not the people but their carts which were unauthorized. If these carts were removed, how would they feed their families? To my surprise, Shri Goswami was both moved and impressed with my attitude and assured me that he would try to help me sort out this problem. This gave me some relief.

The next day, Shri Goswami visited my office and we surveyed a big piece of vacant land, which belonged to the municipal corporation and was located right in front of the Shahdara police station. On my request, he got this land temporarily reserved for the rehriwalas to park their carts and continue their business. I also requested him to get some street lights and a few water connections installed at the site for their convenience. Later, about 15–20 rehriwalas, along with their leader (comrade Shankar), were called to my office and their list was prepared under the supervision of the local police and the corporation staff.

The rehriwalas could not believe that they would now have their own market, where they could do their business without any fear of being uprooted! They decided to peacefully vacate the Chotta Bazar and, hence, no force was required for their removal. They went to the new place allotted to them in a procession shouting 'Delhi Police, zindabad' repeatedly. After they moved to the new place, some of their leaders, along with comrade Shankar, came to see me. I was discussing some matter with my two SHOs when the rehriwalas entered my room and sought my permission to name the new market space as 'Kaushal Market'. I told them that I only did what I thought was correct and that it would not be appropriate to name the market after me. They reluctantly agreed after a lot of persuasion. One of their leaders observed that what had surprised them was the fact that a police officer, who was ordered to remove them, had helped them get a temporary place to carry on their business and earn a livelihood. After their repeated requests, the SHO and I visited their market, which was hustling and bustling with goods, lights, laughter and chattering. I felt extremely emotional on seeing the market thrive and felt satisfied that I could contribute towards the betterment of the rehriwalas there. After about 27 years, I had a chance to pass through that area again and to my relief I found that the market continued to flourish.

This was the beginning of my career as a policeman.

2

FIRST EXPERIENCE

had taken over as SP, south district, Delhi, in July 1971. Sometime in August, I, along with S. Ramakrishnan, assistant superintendent of police (ASP), Cantt, was returning from president's route arrangements, when we got a crash message from Inspector Swaroop Singh, SHO, Rajinder Nagar, that a serious riot had broken out in which some students of Gayatri Devi Salwan College had completely vandalized a TV shop, a few nearby small stores and set on fire about 25 cycles and a motorcycle belonging to shopkeepers and residents. An altercation between a group of students and a shopkeeper dealing in electronics led to the present situation. He also informed me that more than 2,000 highly agitated residents and shopkeepers had assembled and were demanding strong action against these rowdy, volatile students. Adding to this crisis, about 400 students, who were inside the college premises, were threatening the residents from rooftops with acid bulbs and iron rods in their hands.

Inspector Swaroop Singh only had a few constables with him and needed some additional force. Both, Ramakrishnan and I, immediately rushed to the spot realizing the severity of the situation. On the way, I requested the police headquarter to provide reinforcement. While I had handled two serious riot situations as ASP, this was the first major law and order crisis, which I had faced as district SP—my first real challenge.

On reaching the Old Rajinder Nagar market where the riots had taken place, we were surrounded by an angry mob of residents and shopkeepers, who wanted us to take immediate strong action against the students who had caused such havoc. This mob included some important people like Shri Balraj Madhok, the former president of the Bharatiya Jana Sangh, a general secretary of the Delhi Pradesh Congress, some counsellors and some Resident Welfare Association (RWA) office-bearers.

The students were shouting slogans against them from within the college campus; the college gates had been thankfully closed by the local police. The SHO was standing in the middle and had only 10 policemen by his side. Since I had only a small police force at my command and the reinforcement was likely to reach only after two to three hours, I involved the people around me in a dialogue to get all possible details regarding the incident and also for hearing their complaints about these students. Meanwhile, I spotted two press reporters, Shri Shailendra from *Hindustan* (Hindi edition) and Shri Virendra Kapoor from *The Indian Express* in the crowd, both of whom were well known to me. I spoke to the two press reporters and requested them to go inside the college to find out what the students were planning and what their demands were.

After about half an hour, these reporters came back and informed me that the students had agreed to remain inside the premises, provided the SP comes alone and unarmed inside the campus to talk to them. The situation was extremely tense.

The residents and shopkeepers were gradually increasing in number and so was their rage; some of them openly expressed their desire to enter the college premises to teach them a lesson. I could not have let this happen—I immediately decided to go inside the college and talk to the students despite personal risk as the students were in a foul mood and had already indulged in arson and vandalism. Not only my officers, but quite a few residents advised me against it. But this appeared to be the only option to diffuse the situation and also to gain some time till the arrival of additional reinforcement. The assistant commissioner of police (ACP) and SHO were directed to manage the raging crowd outside. My decision of going alone inside the college had an impact on the crowd outside and their anger started decreasing. They appreciated the initiative taken by the police.

I wasn't sure what would happen when I entered. The students, some of whom were armed with iron rods and acid bulbs, glared at me aggressively. But I was confident about myself. Some student leaders met me near the gate and asked me to come inside the building. They took me to a classroom, surrounded me and bolted the room from inside. They tried shattering my courage through indecent and derogatory remarks; two to three students even threatened me. However, I kept my cool and informed them about the raging mob outside, which was pressing police for strong action against the rowdy students. With my persistent efforts, I could persuade them to discuss the way out. Finally, they agreed that if a safe passage is assured, they would disperse. Meanwhile, Shri Shanti Narain, principal of Hansraj College and dean of Students' Welfare, Delhi University and a highly respected faculty member, also reached on the spot. By this time, although I was still alone, I had assumed a dominating position. Now my main task was to convince the mob outside to peacefully disperse. After reassuring the students, I went out and started talking to the agitated mob. With reinforcement having arrived by then, I was now in a better position to deal with the situation.

While this was going on, my boss, deputy inspector general (DIG), Shri P.A. Rosha and deputy commissioner, Delhi, Shri R. Srinivasan arrived. After I briefed them about what had happened, they started talking to the residents who were still there in large numbers. They conveyed their annoyance with the college students and wanted police to take strict action against them. Some of them also mentioned that SP's going alone inside the college had diffused the situation—none of them complained against the police. I also told them that a criminal case under appropriate sections of law had been registered by the local police. The two senior officers had some discussion between themselves, after which I was called. The deputy commissioner told me that in order to assuage the sentiments of residents and shopkeepers, he and the DIG had decided to suspend the SHO. Suspending field officers without going into the merits of the case and also without hearing the officer concerned had become a practice in those days. Such decisions were normally taken by officers who were not part of the police hierarchy.

This came as a shock to me and I instantly expressed my disagreement with their decision. The deputy commissioner was surprised on hearing my response and looked towards the DIG for a reaction. This was much before the CP system was implemented in Delhi. I told them that the situation was already under control and no violence was expected from either side. To their surprise, I insisted that the SHO deserved a commendation for controlling the situation with almost negligible force, merely through his courage and persuasion. He had very tactfully separated the two fighting groups, persuaded the students to go inside the college and also managed the agitated crowd. My bold and clear stand pleased the DIG and he observed that what the SP was saying had weight. But the deputy commissioner was adamant. However, he agreed for a transfer instead of suspension, which I thought was the only option to save the SHO and I agreed reluctantly. I told the DIG that for maintaining the morale of the force, instead of sending the SHO to Police Lines, he could be posted as SHO, Cantt, who in turn can take over as SHO, Rajender Nagar. Thankfully, my suggestion was accepted by both the seniors.

What happened in the next two to three days settled the tension between the rowdy students and the residents and shopkeepers for quite some time. Some of the students, who had taken a leading part in this riot, had a fight with a DTC bus conductor. About six to seven of them had assaulted him and snatched his bag containing money. It was brought to my notice and I ordered registration of a dacoity case. When the students came to know about it, they were absolutely shaken and rushed to my office. They were very apologetic and requested me not to proceed with the case and close it. I told them that they deserved the punishment for their conduct. However, since I did not want this incident to adversely affect their lives, I told them that instead of requesting me they should go with their parents to the college principal seeking an apology and only on his nod I would consider letting them go. Thus, we were successful in settling the problem and leaving behind a good impression about the Delhi Police.

This experience gave me a lot of confidence. I earned a reputation in the force as someone who was capable of protecting his officers for their bona fide performance of duties. My tactful and calm handling of a serious riot situation was appreciated by the department; the media, too, gave a favourable coverage to the police. I also realized that even difficult law and order situations could be diffused by talking to people; patience, courage and a cool temperament are essential for officers who have to deal with people. This incident also helped me earn the confidence of my immediate boss, the DIG, which he repeatedly expressed in presence of other senior officers.

3

OUT OF THE BOX APPROACH

S ometimes, an out of the box approach has the power of changing an entire course of one's life and leads to amazing results. If I remember correctly, it was a late afternoon in early 1972 when an SHO (naming the police station is being deliberately avoided to protect the identity) informed me about a sensational daylight robbery. He also said that both accused had been arrested and were being interrogated. On reaching the police station, I learned that these two young accused had entered a flat, threatened the housewife with a revolver, gagged her by putting a tape across her mouth and also tied her with rope. After committing the robbery, they tried to escape. The woman, in the meantime, managed to free herself and started shouting for help. Some milkmen caught hold of the robbers and gave them a good beating. Meanwhile, the local police had arrived, arrested the robbers and brought them to the police station.

The interrogation revealed that these two young men were planning a big robbery for which they needed a lot of money. To pursue their bigger objective, they had committed a few thefts like lifting briefcases from cars in Connaught

Place and crowded areas in Karol Bagh market. Encouraged by their initial success, they committed this daylight robbery, not expecting they would be caught red-handed. They had been aware that the victim would be alone in the house at that time; they gagged her with a tape, the way they had seen in the movie *The Anderson Tapes*, they revealed. An alarming aspect of the case was that they had managed to modify a toy revolver and fitted a device that could fire a .22 cartridge! After giving instructions for obtaining their remand and to work out all other crimes committed by them, I left for my office.

On coming to work the next morning, I found a woman waiting to see me. In her late 40s, the woman looked well-educated and from a well-to-do family. She told me that she was the mother of one of the accused who had been arrested. She had come to request that the boys be allowed to appear in the examinations which were scheduled to start the next day. My first reaction was what would these boys—having such a criminal bent of mind—do in the examinations? However, the woman was persistent with her request and had brought her son's academic record including earlier examination results to convince me. I was surprised looking at the brilliant academic records of the boy; I wondered how a young and capable boy with such intelligence had become a violent robber? What had led him away from the normal path?

I realized that the boy had the potential to become a big criminal. Allowing him to sit for his examinations was probably all that could help him redeem himself. I thought that a good academic result might change the course of his life. Considering his young age, his good school records and the fact that he had a very sharp mind, I decided to take this chance. I must admit that I was quite impressed by his mother's confidence and persistence. I advised the SHO that while applying for police remand, we may request the court that we intend on allowing the boy to appear in the examinations—something very unusual for a police investigative agency to do. My SHO was also surprised, but complied with my orders.

The boy's mother came to see me after a few months. She told me that despite being beaten up after he was caught and appearing for examinations in police custody, her son had scored well. She was anxious to know how the police planned to proceed in the case. I told her that police had enough evidence and would be filing the charge sheet shortly. Though this was the correct course of action, owing to her unconditional motherly love, she looked disappointed. She pleaded that considering his young age, her son should be given an opportunity to change the course of his life. While appreciating her sentiments, I told her that the police will not be able to do much and she could approach the Delhi administration for withdrawal of the criminal case against her son. She, thereafter, approached the chief secretary with a petition, who spoke to me on call and asked about my views in the case. I confirmed that the facts mentioned in her petition were correct and that the police would be filing the charge sheet. I also conveyed my apprehension: in case he was convicted (which was almost certain) and sent to jail, he might turn into a big criminal. When the chief secretary mentioned about the withdrawal of the criminal charges against the boys, I told him that, in this case, the police could not move for withdrawal of the case. However, I added that if the Delhi administration asked for our comments regarding withdrawal, we would have no objection, given the special background of the case.

Thereafter nothing happened for some time and I was transferred as Inspector General of Police (IGP) Goa. On my return to Delhi after three years, I was on deputation in the railways for a short period and then made my return to the Delhi Police. In April 1980, I was promoted as additional commissioner of police, New Delhi Range. Sometime in the mid-1980s, returning from my office one day, I saw an elderly woman and a young man waiting for me in the verandah of my Lodi Estate residence. I immediately recognized the woman as the mother of the boy who had been arrested in the robbery case almost eight to nine years ago. The young man touched my feet and the mother thanked me profusely for what I had done for them. She told me that the robbery incident had completely transformed the boy and he had thereafter totally devoted himself to studies. He completed his master's degree with first division and started teaching in a Delhi University college! Who would have thought? I was extremely delighted to see the transformation of the young man, who could have otherwise become a criminal. I was happy that I took an out of the box decision at the appropriate time. The young man had now qualified for the Civil Services, but was now apprehensive about the police verification report. They had come to me for help.

The young man's transformation, which looked like a film story, had an impact on me. I decided to help them and assured that I would make all efforts to ensure that a fair verification report goes to the concerned authorities. I pursued this matter persistently and notwithstanding some initial difference of opinion, a fair and correct verification report was sent by the police department. The young man eventually got his appointment for one of the central services, to my delight.

He met me occasionally. During his service, he was considered an efficient officer and held some important positions in his department. He ultimately superannuated in the rank of additional secretary to the Government of India. I couldn't believe that this was the same young man willing to gag a woman to rob her cash. Sometimes sympathetic appreciations of the events really do have the power to transform someone.

When I look back and analyse the transformation of this young man and who all contributed to it, I unequivocally give major credit to his mother, whose single-minded determination, persistence and love for her son played a major role in building his new life. My out of the box approach and extra initiative in handling the case—including withdrawal of criminal charges against the young man and ensuring that a fair verification report was sent—also contributed substantially and I take immense pride in that. But most importantly, it was the young man himself who put in extra efforts to reconstruct his life. Ultimately, it was the blessings of Lord Almighty that saved a life from going astray. I learnt the importance of sympathetic understanding and forgiveness

4

THE SENSATIONAL ABDUCTION OF AN ANTIQUE DEALER

little before midnight on 11 October 1971, I got a crash message from my south district police control room about the abduction of one Subhash Kapoor, aged 20 years, resident of Kailash Colony. He was the owner of Kangra Art Gallery, an antique shop in NDSE Part II Market. While Kalkaji police station started the investigation, the central police control room alerted all its vans, various police checkpoints and pickets. I issued instructions to all patrol parties of the district to check all vehicles and directed SDPOs of Hauz Khas, Lajpat Nagar, Lodi colony and SHOs of Hauz Khas, Defence Colony, Lajpat Nagar, Kalkaji and inspector, special staff, to reach my office housed on the first floor of Defence Colony police station.

By the time I reached my office, the preliminary inquiries made by the local police had revealed that four to five people had arrived in a jeep and after abducting had moved towards Nehru Place. Immediately, all police parties were instructed to track the information by following the probable route of the kidnappers. An old woman who sold peanuts at the junction of Greater Kailash-Sant Nagar crossing (outside Tanzanian Embassy) made a major contribution to our enquires by informing the search party that four to five men in a jeep had stopped there to ask her a few questions before leaving. She revealed that they were talking in Punjabi and were probably Sikhs. She saw them holding someone forcefully and also informed us that the jeep was a little higher in size than the police jeeps. After about an hour later, the central police control room informed us that some criminals in a Jonga had broken through police barricades on GT Road near Alipur. They fired shots at the police on being stopped for questioning. The police also tried firing back, but the offenders fled. Our PCR flashed messages to the control rooms of the neighbouring state, Haryana. Inquiries with the victim's family unfortunately didn't reveal much. I decided to form a special team for investigating the case and for the recovery of victim Subhash Kapoor. An FIR number 696/71 under Section 364/34 of the Indian Penal Code (IPC) was registered at Kalkaji police station. This sensational abduction received a lot of coverage in the media.

Since our special team had no information barring the fact that the accused probably used a Jonga, I called Sub-Inspector (SI) Chaudhary Gian Chand for consultation. He had worked with me in the anti-corruption branch. He was a storehouse of criminal intelligence—an encyclopaedia of criminals in Delhi and neighbouring states—and an outstanding investigating officer. After hearing all the facts and whatever little information we had gathered, his immediate reaction was that the Jonga would help us trace this fast-moving criminal gang.

SI Gian Chand knew a few criminal gangs who owned

a Jonga, but needed a day's time to provide full information on this. The very next day, he gave us a list of eight criminals who owned a Jonga. He suggested that our investigation teams should monitor the whereabouts and the present locations of these vehicles, which might give us important clues and information. The field inquiries regarding these vehicles took us four to five days, but it did not reveal any useful information—two or three of them were in workshops for quite some time and the movements of the other remaining vehicles were not suspicious.

SI Gian Chand advised me that since the vehicle involved in the crime had gone towards Punjab and that some Sikhs were noticed in that vehicle, the possibility of the involvement of an old, hardened criminal Bhagwant Singh, who owned a Jonga, could also be looked into. He was earlier known to be operating at the Delhi-UP border with his gang, but was now reported to be residing in Ropar, where he had obtained an excise licence. I was surprised at how quick and well-informed SI Gian Chand was with the whereabouts of all these criminals. He later on told me that he was maintaining diaries regarding all interrogations conducted by him.

Anyhow, since we had no other clue and no ransom note to rely on, we decided to act on whatever information we had. A police party under Hauz Khas SHO, Inspector T.R. Anand—a very tactful and experienced police officer—was sent to Ropar to locate Bhagwant Singh. Our team succeeded in tracking the suspect and he was made to join the investigation. In the beginning, his interrogation did not yield any meaningful information. We questioned him on the basis of the information we had and confronted him with the other cases he had been involved with. Bhagwant Singh kept on denying any role in this crime. We eventually had to bring in his adopted sister. She was the widow of another criminal—his close friend—whom he had been helping financially. On seeing her, he broke down, admitted the crime adding that he had planned the entire abduction.

Bhagwant Singh told us that one of his old gang members had told him that the victim was quite rich and this led to the idea of his abduction for ransom. He had collected detailed information about the victim's movements and his daily routine. Thereafter, Bhagwant Singh had planned the abduction. It was also decided that they would first take the victim to Punjab and thereafter shift him to Suratgarh in Rajasthan, where he had many relatives and associates to aid their venture and protect them from the view of the police. This was a smart move to mislead us, if we tried to locate the abductors by tracing their route.

On the decided day, they abducted the antique dealer Subhash Kapoor. They first went towards Nehru Place, then moved to Dhaula Kuan and eventually took the Ring Road to take the GT Road leading towards Ropar, Punjab. Kapoor had been forcefully sedated through an injection in case he tried jumping out of the vehicle or screaming for help. He was then shifted to a safe location in Suratgarh, Rajasthan, as planned.

Anticipating resistance at Suratgarh during the rescue operation, as it was the stronghold of the accused and also far away from Delhi, a strong police party—under the leadership of ACP Ambrik Singh and Inspector T.R. Anand—was sent to Suratgarh. Accused Bhagwant Singh, who had been arrested, also accompanied the police team. I kept a close watch on the developments. The next afternoon, a message was received from ACP Ambrik Singh informing that the victim had been rescued and the police party had left for Delhi. During the operation, our team had kept Bhagwant Singh in the front to avoid any resistance. Besides Bhagwant Singh, four other accused, including Singh's informers from Suratgarh, Patiala and Delhi were arrested.

After the safe arrival of the police party, along with victim and the accused persons in Delhi, a press conference was held at my office, where I briefed the media regarding the complete details of the case. The press gave very detailed and positive coverage to the story and complimented Delhi Police for their investigating capabilities and for safely rescuing the victim within a short time. Subhash Kapoor, who had lost all hopes of reuniting with his family, was overjoyed and told everyone during the press conference how grateful he was to Delhi Police for being safely rescued and that too without any ransom.

It was a matter of great satisfaction for me. My team had done a great job.

5

DIALOGUE IS ALWAYS
A BETTER OPTION

The experience of handling a riot, involving a large number of students, shopkeepers and residents in Rajinder Nagar in 1971, however complex and difficult, proved to be very handy. This experience equipped me with the courage and conviction needed to deal with agitations and volatile situations, especially created by university students in other colleges. This was a regular feature in the first three to four months of every academic year, especially in the university colleges situated in South Delhi. Barring three to four colleges, most of the students in these colleges were the ones who could not get admission in north campus due to low percentage. A common issue was the shortage of 'university special buses' which were being provided by the Delhi Transport Undertaking to students on concessional rates. However unacceptable their means of protest were, I admit that to some extent the students' problems were genuine.

Their agitations, which had the potential to turn into full-fledged riots, generally resulted in major traffic jams on roads requiring diversions, causing a lot of inconvenience to commuters, damage to government and private property with occasional incidents of assault on the public servants on duty. These agitations also became very time consuming for the local police. On an average, more than half of a working day of police station staff was spent in dealing with these situations. Their preoccupation with these duties was delaying the investigation of cases, inquiries into public complaints and also affecting regular beat-patrolling necessary to keep a proper watch on hooligans and other activities in sensitive areas. I realized the problem and started looking for a solution before the start of the next academic session. I was also aware that the Delhi Transport Corporation (DTC) would not be able to provide sufficient additional buses in the near future to meet the requirements of students. The only possible way out was to arrive at an understanding with the students by winning their trust and providing some ad-hoc mechanism consisting of local police, field supervisors of DTC and the students' representatives to manage these day-to-day problems. This was needed at four to five places in the district due to the widely spread-out locations of the colleges.

While I was still waiting for an opportunity to translate my possible solution to a reality, I was informed by the SDPO, Lajpat Nagar, Sardar Ambrik Singh, about a riot on Ring Road falling under the jurisdiction of Sriniwaspuri police station, where the students of PGDAV College had hijacked a DTC bus. They had damaged a lot of other buses, private cars and injured some people by pelting stones. The traffic on the ring road had stopped. The local police had resorted to some mild baton charge and were successful in pushing the students inside the college premises. At this point, I reached the spot. The students were still pelting stones and the DTC bus was still within their reach and could have been damaged. We decided to push the students further inside the college premises and I ordered the use of tear gas. This action had the desired effect and we were able to bring back the bus on the Ring Road in the next half an hour. With the agitating students inside the college, the situation was coming back to normal.

I thought that this was the right time to talk to the students about a possible solution to their perennial problems and also to provide some relief to the local police so that they could get back to their routine. Since I was in uniform, I took off my cap and left it in the car. I then told the SDPO and SHO about my intention to go inside the college for talking to the students. SDPO Ambrik Singh, who was a very experienced police officer, advised me against it as he felt that the students at that point of time were very annoyed with police and might indulge in some mischief which might include hurting me. However, I was quite confident about myself and was not prepared to miss the opportunity. I had already done this before at Salwan College, Rajender Nagar in 1971.

After giving the required instructions to my officers, I entered the college campus alone and unarmed. The college building, where students had assembled, was at a little distance from the main gate. The students were surprised to see me alone and shouted slogans like 'student unity zindabad', 'Delhi Police *hai hai*'. Anyway, when I reached near the college building, they started asking me in a very offensive tone as to why I had come there after beating the students with lathis and tear-gassing them. I spoke to some union leaders, who had come forward, telling them that I wanted to talk to them about their problem. Somebody among the students shouted that we should take him inside the college building. This, of course, hinted at some risk, but I took the chance. My experience was that in all such mobs, there was always a saner element. Howsoever small it may be, it plays an important role in diffusing the situation. We went inside a lecture room, where mobs of students circled me. As expected, they made some indecent remarks, but I kept quiet. One of them shouted that since I had ordered for lathi charge and releasing tear gas on the students, now was the time to settle their score with me.

I realized that this could be the starting point of my dialogue with them. Maintaining my composure, I told them that they were absolutely right and were definitely in a position to physically harm me for I was alone and unarmed. I further explained that when I ordered for the lathi charge and tear-gassing on the students, I along with my team were merely performing our professional duty of maintaining order, controlling a rioting mob, preventing damage to public and private property and protecting people moving on the road. I added that if they now decide to assault a public servant on duty, they would be committing a grave and non-bailable offence, but if they still desired to settle their score with me, they could go ahead. All this was said keeping my tone mild and friendly, but full of confidence. This was when the saner elements among the students intervened, took charge of the situation and silenced the rowdy ones. They wanted to know what the possible solution to their problem could be. I told them that since there was no immediate possibility of the DTC management providing additional buses for university specials, we might work out some ad-hoc arrangements with the help of area DTC supervisors, local police and student representatives. On my suggestion, they went outside and invited my SDPO, local SHO and some DTC officials to work out a solution. With a little tact, patience and confident approach, an otherwise serious and threatening situation was converted into a friendly gathering deliberating on a possible solution for the students' perennial problem.

A new relationship had developed between the students and the south district police. I started getting invitations from student unions of different colleges to be the chief or special guest in their events. In an annual function of one of the colleges, noticing the huge clapping on my arrival, the vice chancellor, Shri Sarup Singh (who was the chief guest) conveyed to me that I was very popular with the students, which according to him was quite unusual for a police officer who had to ensure the maintenance of law and order.

Meanwhile, on 27 January 1973, I was transferred as IGP, Goa, Daman and Diu, and local newspapers carried this news. Around two to three days after I handed over the charge and was busy in making arrangements for transporting my household goods to Goa, I was told that some student leaders had come to visit me. When I went out, I was pleasantly surprised to see Shri Sher Singh Dagar, secretary of Delhi University Students Union, along with some student union leaders of south Delhi colleges. They had come to invite me for a function organized by the Union to bid me farewell. They had already printed the invitation cards and were distributing them. They informed me that Vice Chancellor Shri Sarup Singh had agreed to preside over the function. During the farewell function, the student leaders said that while I ordered for lathi charge and use of tear gas on them on many occasions, I was their 'best friend' and had always a good understanding of their problems. The vice chancellor observed that this was probably the first farewell of a police officer organized by the university students' union and was full of appreciation. I was also moved by this gesture of the students. I don't know whether any such farewell was organized thereafter. This was the pleasant end of my tenure in the south district after which I moved to Goa.

6

LEFT FOR GOA, DESPITE OPPORTUNITIES TO STAY BACK

On 27 January 1973, I got a call from the police headquarters informing me that I had been transferred and posted as IGP Goa, Daman and Diu, and formal orders had been dispatched. I immediately called my head clerk, signed the handing-over documents and told him to fill all the important details. The deputy superintendent of police (DSP), headquarter, was told that while I had signed the handing-over papers, I would be available on call till the arrival of my successor. To my wife's surprise, I reached my residence much earlier than my usual time. Before she could ask me anything, I informed her that I had been transferred to Goa and she should start packing and winding up things.

At that time, I was facing a lot of difficulties on domestic front and this transfer had further aggravated the situation. Only a month ago, I had lost my father-in-law, Dr Hari Shanker Budhwar, a very popular and successful medical practitioner in Kanpur. He was just 51, and was survived by his wife, two sons and a college-going young daughter. The two elder daughters were married. Being the eldest, the responsibility of taking care of the family naturally fell upon me. I needed some time to settle the things including the 'death duty case' of my father-in-law. My wife was also expecting and the delivery date was due by the end of February. Since I knew Shri Bishan Tandon, who was an IAS officer and a powerful bureaucrat posted as joint secretary in the Prime Minister's Office at that time, I decided to meet him. He was well known to my father and during my posting in Delhi, I had met him quite often and he, too, had visited my house a couple of times. I recall telling him about the difficulties that my family was facing and requested him to get my transfer deferred by six months. However, to my disappointment, he looked quite indifferent and did not give me any assurance. As I did not know anyone else in the Ministry of Home Affairs (MHA), I decided to proceed with this transfer.

If I remember correctly, It was either 29 or 30 January that I got a call from PM's office that Chote Saheb (as late Shri Sanjay Gandhi was known) wanted to see me at 6.00 p.m. Shri Sanjay Gandhi had become a power centre in the PM's establishment at that time. While I was nowhere in his close circle, he had known me for sometime as I had done some work for him in a very effective manner without creating any controversy. Once he had also dropped in my office and given me a round in the prototype of a car which he was planning to manufacture. I did not know why I was called, as I was not holding any charge at that time. When I reached 1, Safdarjung Road (PM's residence), a security officer who was waiting for me at the gate, took me to Shri Dhawan's room. While I was talking to Shri Dhawan, Shri Sanjay Gandhi entered the room and straight away told me, 'Kaushal Saheb, your transfer orders are being cancelled and you would again take over the same charge (SP South). After you join, you should get Chopra arrested and suspend the two police officers who had not obeyed my orders.' This was a one-sided conversation and after directing Shri Dhawan to do the needful, he left the room without waiting for my response. All this happened in under five minutes. Shri Dhawan congratulated me for the cancellation of my transfer order and also for Sanjay Gandhi's faith in me. But this had put me in a dilemma as I could not have implemented either of the two oral instructions. I very politely explained my position to Shri Dhawan.

The background was that Chopra, a known civil contractor, who had a contract to build Safdarjung Flyover was also building Sanjay Gandhi's car factory and had asked for some payment from him, which had led to this unpleasant development. An old woman labour was killed at the site of Safdarjung Flyover due to a pulley falling on her and the local police had registered a criminal case of negligence against the sub-contractor. The pulley belonged to Chopra's sub-contractor and the criminal liability could not be stretched to arrest him. The SHO and the head constable were not at fault as I had instructed them not to arrest Chopra as no criminal case was made out against him.

Incidentally, I had neither seen Chopra, nor I knew him. I only knew that I could not comply with these oral instructions. I didn't know who asked Sanjay Gandhi to call me. Probably he had developed some faith in me. This is corroborated by the fact that in 1975, he again got my transfer order issued, without any request from me, posting me back to Delhi. Shri Om Mehta, (the then minister of state, MHA), told me about it in November 1975, when he visited Goa and requested the Goa government to relieve me immediately. However, I left Goa only in February 1976 since the CM was reluctant to relieve me.

I came home and told my wife briefly about what had happened in the meeting and she was happy that I did the right thing. Throughout my service and beyond it, she has been a great support and had always advised me to do what I think is right. I realized my transfer to Goa, which I wanted to postpone due to personal reasons, could become a controversy and that would not be good for me. So, after dispatching our household goods to Goa and getting air bookings done for my family and myself for the morning of 12 February, we left for Lucknow, my hometown, to avail the remaining joining time with my parents. I returned to Delhi with my family on February 10 without knowing a big surprise was waiting for me. When I reached my residence at 69, Lodi Estate, which now houses the office of the World Bank and the IIC Annexe, I was surprised to see Shri B.N. Mehra, SP, security, walking up and down in my lawns. He informed me that he had been sent by PM Smt. Indira Gandhi to convey that my transfer to Goa was being cancelled and I would be going on transfer only after five to six months following my wife's delivery. He also mentioned that I would be again taking over as SP, south district, where my successor had already taken over. This was like a shock. I did not know who informed the PM that my wife was expecting and the bigger surprise was that she had chosen to intervene in a small matter like an SP's transfer. I was supposed to take over my old charge. I had neither requested her, nor approached anybody close to her for getting my transfer cancelled. This remains an unresolved mystery till date.

The fact was that Smt. Indira Gandhi knew me only as a district SP posted with Delhi Police. In fact, that too, was a mere coincidence. Once a young girl had jumped in front of her car and on being asked why, she complained about her maternal uncles who were trying to outrage her modesty. Mrs

Gandhi asked Shri Dhawan to find out the facts from police and ask the SP concerned to meet her with report on the same day when she comes back for lunch. Since I was the concerned SP at that time, Shri Dhawan conveyed the instructions to me. I immediately made inquiries and gave her a detailed report at lunchtime. Thereafter, on two or three occasions, on different matters relating to Delhi Police, irrespective of whether they pertained to my area or not, she told Shri Dhawan to instruct Kaushal to find out the facts and report to her. I did this as part of my duty. Besides this, I had no other connection with Smt. Gandhi or her family. I did not know anyone else among the people close to the PM.

I do not know how wisdom dawned upon me at that moment that if my transfer orders were deferred and I was reposted as SP South, I would be treated as a 'khalifa' (a person who could do anything) in Delhi Police! Even my officers would not judge me on merit. I would be treated like an influential officer close to the PM. At that time, I had completed only nine years of service and this would not be good for my career. I requested Shri B.N. Mehra to help me. But he insisted that he had been deputed by PM and his duty was only to convey her orders to me. It took some time but I convinced Mehraji that any change in my transfer orders at this stage would become a liability for my future career and since I would be flying to Goa the day after morning, I would be grateful if he could report that he could not meet me. Shri Mehra accepted my request very reluctantly.

On 12 February 1973, I left for Goa along with my family. To this very day I am not aware who advised Shri Sanjay Gandhi to call me and who informed Smt. Gandhi about my wife's pregnancy. If I had made any effort for this, I could have taken advantage of this situation and stayed back. Both Shri

Sanjay Gandhi and Smt. Indira Gandhi had clearly conveyed their desire to retain me in Delhi and that even suited me for my personal reasons. However, I wanted to work like a normal civil servant and did not deliberately avail the two opportunities. I was happy with what I did and in course of time I forgot about it.

But the matter did not really end there. Sometime in 2006 or 2007, my batchmate and a close friend, Shri Ramesh Sharma, former director, CBI, called me and said that he was surprised to know about my proximity with the Gandhi family. He knew the Gandhi family at a personal level due to his Kashmiri connections. Failing to make any sense out of what he said, I asked him to clarify his remarks. He told me that he had just gone through Shri Bishan Tandon's recently published book *PMO Diary—Prelude to the Emergency*, whose author had devoted an entire page and a half to my transfer from Delhi to Goa in February 1973! I got the book from Ramesh and went through the relevant portion. Shri Tandon had made four points relating to this matter. Firstly, that Smt. Indira Gandhi had very clearly told her Principal Secretary Mr Dhar that I should be retained as SP in Delhi. Second, that Mr Dhar asked him to find out about where I was; third, he made several attempts to contact me and my family in Lucknow and Kanpur, but did not succeed. Fourth, the coterie in the PM's house had taken up my case and the PM got interested in the matter.

While I do not know who informed Smt. Indira Gandhi about my wife's pregnancy as told to me by Shri B.N. Mehra (SP Security) and what led her to instruct her principal secretary to postpone my transfer, but Shri Tandon's allegation that I had approached the coterie in the PM house to take up my case was absolutely incorrect. If that was so, I should have stayed in Delhi after Shri B.N. Mehra conveyed PM's direction to me. But I chose to proceed with the transfer. Similarly, Shri Tandon's assertion that he tried to contact me was also incorrect as no message or information was received by me neither at Lucknow, nor at Kanpur. The fact was that the only official person I contacted in Delhi for the postponement of my transfer was Shri Bishan Tandon and in spite of my informing him about the problems that my family was facing, his response was not positive.

However, it is an old matter now and I have forgotten about it. Life has moved on, just as it always does. I met Bishan Bhai quite a few times after that, but this matter was never discussed. Incidentally, my posting in Goa as IGP became a landmark point in my career. Maybe everything happens for a reason, even if we don't understand that reason immediately.

7

THE POWER OF 'SORRY'

believe that only people with courage apologize for the mistakes they commit during the course of their lives. Normally the tendency is to ignore the mistakes if they have not been noticed. But such persons forget that while others may not have noticed it, they cannot hide it from themselves and continue to live in guilt. It will always remain in their subconscious mind and if they repeatedly do it, it may adversely affect their ability to distinguish between right and wrong. Those who commit mistakes and feel apologetic earn respect from others. If they happen to be part of leadership in any organization, they not only get the respect but also earn the trust of their team members.

In February 1973, I took over as IGP Goa, Daman and Diu. After working in the Delhi Police for quiet sometime, including a tenure as a district superintendent of police, I found the functioning of Goa Police lacking in many ways. The police stations were not functioning at night and there was no system of ensuring a round-the-clock police presence. To start with, I established a police control room at Panjim and attached a vehicle for twenty-four-seven patrolling in the city.

An educated head constable was made in-charge of the PCR van. It started well and was appreciated by the people and the media. If I remember correctly, within a month of starting this new project, CM Bhausaheb Bandodkar (he knew very little English and Hindi) told me on call that the head constable in-charge of the PCR van should be immediately suspended as he had found him on checking a complete drunkard with red eyes and a heavy, wavering voice. Bhausaheb was a very good person but a feudal type of administrator.

The next day, I called the head constable and he almost matched the description given by the CM. In Goa Police, drinking was quite common and a part of the local culture. I told head constable D'Souza about the CM's observations and placed him under suspension. He did not react and left my room without saying much.

After I passed any order, normally I had the habit to look for its reaction. I spoke to SP Shri Ramakrishnan about it. What he told me was utterly shocking. D'Souza was a teetotaller; the changes in his eyes and voice were a result of the shock after his 21-year-old son drowned in the river Mandovi. I felt the ground beneath me whisk away. This was a huge slap on my face. I was ashamed that I had taken such a drastic action against the head constable merely on the oral orders of the CM without verifying the facts. By placing him under suspension, I had also damaged his reputation among his colleagues, family members, friends and relatives. I felt so miserable that I immediately decided to rectify the mistake and told the SP about it.

The next morning after reaching the police headquarters, I called a meeting, which was attended by the SP, all deputy SPs, inspectors and the two office superintendents. Head constable D'Souza was also present. I openly admitted that I had committed a big mistake by suspending him and was filled with guilt and regret. Had I properly inquired into the matter, this could have been avoided. Admitting that I was at fault, I apologized to him for causing him undue humiliation and damaging his reputation. The head constable was reinstated immediately. He broke down as he hadn't expected that he would receive any apology, let alone his old position. There was pin-drop silence in the meeting. With my apology, I felt that I had shed a heavy burden from my mind.

By this time, I knew that there were some back biters in the meeting, who would misrepresent the facts to the CM. I said so in the meeting, but still this happened. I got a call from the CM who wanted to know the reason behind what happened in the meeting. I informed him that the entire story of the head constable's suspension—which happened following his orders, had reached the press who also knew about his son's death. I added that before the media could have played up the news embarrassing the CM, I had settled the matter. The CM was satisfied.

The facts of this incident became known to almost everyone in the force due to Goa being a small place. Some officials in the government and people in the media also came to know about it and conveyed their appreciation. But it had a far-reaching impact on my force. They developed a faith in my leadership and a relationship of trust was created between us. This proved to be an asset throughout my posting in Goa.

As a result of this incident, admitting to my mistakes and apologizing on having caused any pain or inconvenience to anyone became a part of my nature, both in my personal and professional life. This helped me in keeping my mind free of any burden and sleep better at night.

A similar incident took place sometime in 1980–81 when

I was posted as additional commissioner, New Delhi Range in Delhi Police. I was attending a dinner at the residence of my old friend Shri O.P. Vaish, an eminent citizen and a famous tax consultant. As I was talking to some guests, I overheard two people discussing the mishandling of a murder case by the Delhi Police. I was sure that they were not aware of my presence. One of them mentioned that the Lajpat Nagar Police had very casually investigated a case of bride burning against his close friend who was working as a deputy manager in Food Corporation of India. The investigating officer was not prepared to listen to his friend's pleas. This was quite disturbing.

The police station Lajpat Nagar was in my range and I felt a sense of responsibility towards it. I left the party a little early with my wife. After reaching my residence, I contacted DCP South and spoke to him about the case to find out the complete facts. Investigation in such cases was normally finalized at the DCP level and was not sent to additional commissioner of police unless called for. He told me that the case had perhaps been approved for challan and the charge sheet was being prepared. I directed him to come to my office the next day along with the ACP, SHO Lajpat Nagar and also bring the case file. The DCP naturally wanted to know the reason why I'd called for the case file and the officers; I avoided revealing much considering that the field staff might indulge in some manipulation. I learnt that the accused was out on bail. I told my personal assistant SI Kamal Sapra to call the accused and put him in an inner chamber in his office so that he was not seen by the district officials when they came to see me.

The DCP, along with his officers and the case files, reached my office. The case files were examined. I asked them whether the plea of the accused—of not using the oil stove, which was alleged to be the weapon of offense—was verified properly. In fact, it turned out that they were using an LPG gas connection! The investigating officer had just gone by the allegations made by the father-in-law of the accused without checking the facts. I directed the DCP to verify this aspect of the evidence again within two to three hours. The ACP, who was deputed to verify the facts, reported back that the plea of the accused was correct and that the investigating officer of the case had committed a major blunder. Since the case file had not gone to the prosecution branch with the challan yet, I decided that the case should be closed and a final report be sent to the court, along with a request to discharge the accused.

After giving these instructions, the accused person was called. When he entered my chamber, his face reflected a lot of fear and anxiety He didn't understand why he had been called by the additional commissioner of police when his challan had been finalized. I told him that the case of murder was registered against him on the complaint of his father-in-law, who had accused him of burning his daughter. However, during the investigation, the police committed negligence and did not verify the evidence thoroughly. I told him that no case was made out against him and I had decided to close the case; he was now free. He was also informed that we would be requesting the court to discharge him. You cannot possibly imagine the joy in this man's eyes unless you saw it! He fell on the floor, crying as he repeatedly chanted God's name and thanked him. This was nothing short of a miracle for him. When he calmed down, I told him that due to the negligence of my officers, a lot of harassment and loss of reputation had been caused to him for which I sincerely apologized on behalf of the Delhi Police as well as on my own behalf. But he kept on repeatedly saying that 'Sir, you are like a God to me. You have given me a new life. You need not apologize for anything!' He added that he had never expected to be free again and he touched my feet. He was very eager to give this unexpected happy news to his family and left after taking permission. I was feeling very relieved and happy with what I did.

A little bit of alertness and prompt action saved a person who had been wrongly accused of murder from further harassment of court trial and loss of social standing. Apologizing for the mistakes you've committed not only rectifies the wrong that's been done, but also establishes the reputation of the person doing it as a strong person capable of accepting his mistakes and creates a special relationship between him and his team members. Even his peers and other senior persons in the organization appreciate his ethical stand.

8

MAINTAINING POLICE PRESTIGE

I n the Union Territory administration (except Delhi), the local politicians—including that of the ruling party— generally indulged in petty politics. Even small incidents were viewed microscopically. Except for senior officers, the entire gazetted and non-gazetted staff consisted of local people. Most of them had developed connections with political leaders, especially of the ruling party, for personal gains. They were providing information regarding their departments and also about their officers to their political connections. This had made the functioning quite difficult for senior officers, especially of those working in departments dealing with the public. Adding to their plight were the local newspapers. Although Goa was a small place, it had a large number of daily and weekly newspapers in different languages i.e., English, Marathi, Konkani and Portuguese. Since nothing important was happening, even small incidents and rumours were getting undue publicity. Any news or rumour involving a senior officer was bound to get a lot of publicity. The ruling party had a lot of say with the media as the latter depended heavily on advertisements given by the local government. For some time, I had been a victim of this malicious publicity, when I had refused to carry out the CM's oral orders which were against the rules and also ethically incorrect.

Sometime towards the end of 1973 and the beginning of 1974, an occasional newspaper named *Voice of Goa* started getting published from Vasco. Its editor Vitthal Nawelkar had the support of the CM for reasons best known to them. Shri Vasant Joshi, a local car dealer and a successful businessman was an important MLA of the ruling Maharashtrawadi Gomantak Party from Vasco. It was being mentioned by some people including the press that the CM probably wanted to create a parallel power centre in Vasco and hence was encouraging Vitthal Nawelkar.

I do not remember the date and month, but sometime in 1974, inspector Alex Rasquinha (in-charge of Vasco police station) arrested two criminals. In fact, they were called a day before the arrest for questioning and were sent back. The arrest took place on the next day. These alleged criminals were Nawelkar's men. He started pressurizing the police inspector for their immediate release. When the inspector refused to do it, Nawelkar threatened him and said that he would come with his supporters to get them released forcibly. The police inspector had informed him that the next day they were to be produced in the court, but Nawelkar was adamant and probably thought that this was an opportunity to establish his influence in the entire Vasco town.

When information regarding these developments reached police headquarters, I directed SP Shri S. Ramakrishnan to proceed to Vasco, along with a platoon of the Goa Reserve Police, to take charge of the situation. Meanwhile, the CM also came to know about this. Without considering the merits of the case or even consulting me, she spoke first to the chief secretary and then to the lieutenant governor (LG). She told them that a serious law and order situation had surfaced at Vasco and IGP had sent reinforcement there. Her intention was to protect Vitthal Nawelkar. Knowing my tough stand on the matter, she told the chief secretary and the LG that there was a possibility of police resorting to firing without mentioning anything about Nawelkar's threat of forcible release of the alleged criminals from police custody. The CM did not speak to me deliberately. I got a call from the chief secretary to meet him immediately. By this time, Shri Ramakrishnan had informed me about the developments at Vasco. Nawelkar was collecting his supporters about 400 yards away from the police station and had declared his intention to march up to the police station to get his men released. I told the chief secretary that since the situation had taken a serious turn, I had decided to proceed to Vasco. When I went to see him on my way to Vasco, I clearly told him that under no circumstances would I allow these ruffians to criminally trespass into the police station, and possibility of using fire arms also could not be ruled out. The chief secretary agreed with me, but suggested that I should meet the LG before proceeding to Vasco. I told him that the situation at Vasco was quite grim. My men needed me at that very moment and since I had very little time at my disposal, I requested him that he should allow me to go and inform LG about it. He agreed and I rushed to Vasco.

When I reached Vasco police station, I noticed that a mob of around 1,500 persons had assembled nearby. They were shouting anti-police slogans. Vitthal Nawelkar was inciting them and telling them that he would get his people released forcibly from police custody. I had a discussion with my officers—SP Shri Ramakrishnan, DSP Shri V.R. Kadam and inspector Rasquinha—about the proposed action. The reinforcement from Panjim and the local police were deployed for the protection of the police station building. A reserve was kept as a 'quick reaction team.' I directed the SP to place a firing squad with an SI on the vacant road outside the police station facing the Nawelkar supporters. Thereafter, we first gave a warning on the microphone to disperse the mob and in case of non-compliance declared that the police would be forced to take action. Nothing happened for some time outside the police station, but within two to three hours that followed, I got about 10 phone calls from the LG, who kept on asking me about the developments without giving any positive direction. I told him that while I was avoiding any strong action against the demonstrators, I was clear that in my presence, I would not allow this mob to criminally trespass into the police station. I also told him that in that eventuality, the police would have to resort to firing to ensure that 'the rule of law' and the dignity of the government were maintained. The LG gave no guidance. The chief secretary also spoke to me and agreed with my stand. I informed him about the LG's frantic calls to me. He was ringing me up repeatedly under pressure from the CM.

All this while, the stand-off was going on and the mob had not dispersed. I asked the SP to stand with the firing squad and thereafter I proceeded towards the unruly mob along with my personal security officer and a wireless operator. I spoke to Nawelkar in a very firm and loud tone so that others could hear that whatever he was proposing to do was an absolutely illegal act that could not be permitted. I told him that we were determined to enforce the law and if necessary, we would use firearms. In case they tried to do any mischief with me, the SP had the instructions to open fire. Neither Nawelkar nor his supporters expected this firm and bold action from the police. They had probably anticipated that the police would agree to make some kind of compromise under pressure. But were thoroughly disappointed. Shri Joshi, the local MLA, sensing that police was quite determined to enforce the law, also advised Nawelkar to disperse his supporters and wait for the court orders the next day. Nawelkar's plan to establish his leadership had fallen flat and he had no option except to disperse. This established the reputation of Goa Police as a force capable of implementing its decisions.

Before I returned to Panjim late in the evening, I had deployed a fresh platoon of Goa Reserve Police at the police station. I instructed the DSP and the inspector to remain present there. I reported the whole matter to the chief secretary and requested him to inform the CM and LG about it. The CM never spoke to me about this incident.

I was satisfied that I could protect the prestige of the police and the government and that 'the rule of law' had been enforced.

9

FIGHTING FOR MY TEAM MEMBERS

Serving in a small administration like that of a Union Territory is quite difficult and challenging at times. Everything about you and your official functioning is known all over the town and there is lot of interference from the local government. While your good work may be ignored, your mistakes would always be taken seriously. Since the subordinate staff are mainly local and permanently based there, they gain access to local politicians, sometimes even to CM. It is quite difficult to break this linkage. The key to survival and success lies in acting within the framework of rules and in not seeking personal favours from the political set-up at any cost.

I joined as IGP Goa, Daman and Diu, in February 1973 and remained there till February 1976. The senior officers in Goa Police were from IPS (Union Territories Cadre) and DSP rank officers were either from the Goa Police Cadre or on deputation. The remaining force had come up through local recruitment. Sometime in 1974–75, three vacancies came up in the rank of DSP. As there was a huge stagnation in the rank of inspectors, I saw this as a great opportunity to give local promotions to my officers. After discussing it with the chief secretary, I submitted a formal proposal to the government and requested for constituting a Departmental Promotion Committee (DPC). The DPC approved by the government included me (IGP) as the chairman and my SP, along with a joint secretary, GAD, as members.

After thoroughly examining the records of eligible officers in order of their seniority, the DPC recommended the names of three senior-most inspectors for promotion to the rank of DSP. The recommendations were according to the rules and based on merit. The proceedings of the DPC were submitted to the chief secretary for the government's approval. After about three weeks, when I checked, I was informed that the file was with the CM. This became an endless wait. The chief secretary informally told me that the CM was interested in the promotion of inspector at Serial No. 4. I then showed the records of the officers to the chief secretary—a very seasoned, helpful and god-fearing bureaucrat—and told him that the recommended officers were not only senior in service, but their records were also much better than that of the inspector at Sr. No. 4. The decision was kept pending and after sometime it was conveyed that another DPC may be formed as the file containing the earlier proceedings was not traceable. This was very unusual as DPC files are handled with lot of care.

The new DPC was formed with the expectation that the recommendations would be changed. The joint secretary from the GAD told me that the CM was interested in the inspector at Sr. No. 4, but I told him that as head of the force, I couldn't supersede the claims of his seniors without any proper justification. I completed the formalities again and notwithstanding the pressure, I sent the same recommendations once again. I couldn't let this pressure distract me from the right course of action.

This was the beginning of trouble for me. A well-orchestrated media campaign maligning me and my family was started in some selected newspapers at the instance of CM. The government had a lot of influence with the media. This was the same media which was going gaga over me in January 1975 for the excellent handling of overall arrangements for the 'Exposition of St Francis Xavier's Relics', which attracted a lot of tourists including international visitors. The government had appointed me as Exposition Commissioner for this event, in addition to my normal duties.

During this adverse media coverage, some of my colleagues advised me to file defamation suit, but I deliberately did not react; I wanted to avoid any confrontation. The chief secretary was well aware of this mischief and silently agreed with my approach—I'd say he was my main moral support. While I was trying to ignore it, the then speaker and the leader of opposition in the assembly, who met me at an official function at Rajniwas, told me that they knew the complete facts behind this malicious campaign and were also aware of who was doing it and why... They wanted to take up this matter in the assembly and embarrass the government. But I did not encourage them as I was keen on avoiding any politicization of this matter. I knew that in such situations, unlike government servants, politicians always have an upper hand because they have an open platform where they can speak to the media. During my discussion with the chief secretary on this subject, I told him that notwithstanding this malicious and damaging media campaign against me, it was not possible for me to ignore the rightful claims of the three senior inspectors. This would have been morally incorrect. I also told him that if the government was so keen to promote the officer at Sr. No. 4, they could create an additional post, but I would not change my recommendations as it would certainly affect my moral authority as a force leader.

There was a stalemate for a month or two. Then all of a sudden, the recommendations of the DPC were approved and promotion orders of the three senior inspectors were issued. The chief secretary could convince the CM that she should avoid the controversy and send her approval. He also mentioned to her that in spite of adverse propaganda in the media, IGP had maintained a strategic silence during the entire controversy in the interest of the administration. He also told her that since he had taken over as IGP, he had kept the law and order situation under control, and also was solely responsible for the extremely successful completion of the 'exposition arrangements' which had earned massive goodwill for the state government. He had also not given any opportunity to the opposition party in the assembly to embarrass the government. Eventually, the CM was persuaded and also appreciated my stand.

After a few months when I was transferred from Goa after completing my tenure, the CM invited me and my wife for a farewell dinner at her residence. We maintained good relations thereafter.

This incident only reconfirmed my faith that if you follow rules and are ethically correct, you can afford to take a stand on a right issue and normally it should work. Standing by what's right not only gives you a lot of self-satisfaction and peace, but also earns you respect, trust and goodwill among your team members and peers. However, my advice is to avoid any confrontation with authorities and also not allow any politicization of the matter.

10

TAMING A GIANT
TRADE UNION LEADER

On 12 February 1973, when I landed along with my family at Dabolim Airport, Goa, on transfer from Delhi, SP S. Ramakrishnan introduced me to two well-known personalities of Goa—Mrs Cecilia Menezes, wife of a local industrialist Shri David Menezes and a very pleasant, sophisticated and dignified lady, and Shri Mohan Nair, a very tall, heavy built man with a long flowing beard, wearing a white khadi safari suit. Shri Ramakrishnan told me that Mohan Nair was a powerful trade union leader who controlled all labour unions operating at the port including Goa Shipyard. We exchanged some pleasantries and parted with a social promise to meet soon.

I think four months after I took over as the IGP, there was a labour strike in a big factory in north Goa where some of the agitators indulged in arson and vandalized the factory's property. The local police controlled the situation and some persons suspected to be involved were arrested. I also visited the spot. The factory owner, who had a link with the ruling party, tried to pressurize us into taking strong action against the labour force to teach them a lesson. But I ensured that only appropriate effective action was taken against those who were actually involved in the crime. A Left leader, Gerald Pereira, was controlling the trade union at the factory. He came to meet me with a request that no undue harassment should be caused to the labour force due to the influence of the factory owner. But when he found that police had already acted objectively and no innocent person had been targeted, he left the place thanking me. This was the beginning of a new relationship of trust between the trade union leaders and the police.

All this while, Mohan Nair was having a gala time. His real strength was the labour force from eastern Uttar Pradesh (UP), mainly from Jaunpur and its neighbouring districts, which formed the major chunk of the total labour force at the Vasco Port and the Goa Shipyard. He used to walk with authority, travelled in a chauffeur-driven car and always used embossed letterheads for correspondence. He was in full control of the trade unions and was capable of bringing all activities of the port to a total halt. The labour department had reconciled to his influence and control on the different trade unions. The industrialists and mine owners (whose goods were being transported through the port) considered it proper to keep him in good humour. This led to his prosperity and influence in the port town. He had put up big framed photographs of Hindu gods and goddesses in his office since his main union members were Hindu labourers from eastern UP. He had managed to capture a photograph of him talking with Smt. Indira Gandhi, which he would occasionally use to influence those who were of value to him. Somehow, I was not convinced about Mohan Nair and had a suspicion about his background. My initial informal enquiries revealed that nobody in Goa knew when he came there and what his background was. All this created a doubt in my mind.

I picked up Inspector L. Gracious of the Special Branch, CID. I briefed him in detail about the task and deputed him to visit Kerala for discreet inquiries to collect all possible information about Mohan Nair. Inspector Gracious was a low profile, extremely competent and a hard-working officer who had a knack for collecting good intelligence. He was a committed professional, who started from the rank of assistant constable and superannuated as DSP. He visited Mohan Nair's village, the school where he studied and met a few persons who knew him. To our surprise, it was found that he was not a Brahmin as he claimed, but was a Roman Catholic Christian and that his original name was something else! People in his village had no knowledge of where he had gone, except for one or two persons who mentioned that he perhaps had gone to Goa or Bombay for a job. Gracious had brought some photographs and documents with him as well. Prima facie, these did not constitute any criminal offence. But the value of this information was a total bombshell. If revealed properly, this could have demolished Mohan Nair's image and influence over all the trade unions. I thought I could use it for my official purpose and keep his activities under check.

A message was informally conveyed to Mohan Nair to see me as and when he visited Panjim next. He could not control his anxiety and came to my office the very next day. I offered him tea and gave him an envelope containing all the information, photographs and documents collected by Gracious. I told him that since I was busy finalizing an important report, which was to be sent to the chief secretary, I would be talking to him after a while. He hurriedly saw all of them with utter disbelief; he must have wondered how had I managed to uncover a past he'd so successfully hidden. He glanced through some of these documents and started fretting; his eyes started tearing up. He got up from his chair trembling and touched my feet with a request that I should not make it public as it would wreak havoc for him. He would not be able to stay at Vasco. I also knew that Mohan Nair was diabetic and suffered from high blood pressure. So, to avoid any harm to his health, I assured that this information about his background was only known to me and I had no intention to damage his reputation. When he felt a little assured, I told him that I had no objection to his trade union activities as long as he was fighting for the genuine demands of the workers. I added that he must assure me that he would not bring the port activities to a total halt to blackmail the industrialists and mine owners as this caused heavy losses to the government. He nodded in agreement and kept his word. Thereafter there was no major strike at the port.

As mentioned before, Mohan Nair was also controlling the trade union at the Goa Shipyard—a public undertaking and a subsidiary of Mazgaon Dock, Bombay. Sometime in 1975, Mohan Nair's Union at Goa Shipyard gave a call for a strike to protest against the malpractices of their MD Commodore Paradkar. The union had made serious allegations of corruption, malpractices and victimization against Commodore Paradkar. The union demanded an impartial high-level inquiry. I had informed the chief secretary about the developments and also told him that as per our intelligence reports, Paradkar enjoyed a very bad reputation.

A week later, Admiral Kuruvilla, chairman of Mazgaon Docks, visited Panjim to meet the LG and sought his intervention in the matter. Our LG, as I'd noticed earlier as well, had a weakness for siding with the defence service officials. Admiral Kuruvilla briefed the LG that the strike at Goa Shipyard, which was causing a lot of loss to the government, was a doing of trade union leader Mohan Nair, who was trying to blackmail Commodore Paradkar. This was totally false. But LG believed it and on the advice of Admiral Kuruvilla directed the chief secretary to immediately detain Mohan Nair. When the chief secretary called me to convey LG's direction, I vehemently opposed it. I told the chief secretary that both the LG and Admiral were not aware of the ground realities and had gone by the one-sided version of Commodore Paradkar, against whom there were serious allegations. LG was so overawed by the Admiral that he did not consider it proper to consult his own police chief in a matter which had law and order implications. I told the chief secretary that it was with a lot of efforts that I could control Mohan Nair's activities and also that he had not created any trouble in almost two years. I informed him about my inquiries at Kerala with a request not to share them with anybody. I added that if we detain Mohan Nair, he would suddenly become a big hero and would capitalize on this opportunity to regain his old position. The chief secretary, on my request, again spoke to LG, but he remained adamant and the detention orders were issued nonetheless. I deputed SP to go to Vasco with some force to detain Mohan Nair. But at the last moment, I decided to go to Vasco to ensure that there was no slip in implementing the government orders. As I had opposed the detention, I was not prepared to take any chance, else I would have been misunderstood.

I recall it was raining cats and dogs and it was difficult to move on the Panaji/ Vasco Road. The roads/streets were filled with the scent of mud and grey mist. Mohan Nair was brought to Panaji and after providing him all required medicines as requested by him, he was detained and sent to Aquada prison. Later on, he was moved to Yerawada Jail in Pune.

Mohan Nair's detention, as expected, had very serious repercussions and the labour union called for an indefinite strike. I was not aware of what all efforts were made by the Goa Shipyard management to deal with the strike, but the stalemate continued. On the thirty-sixth day of the strike, Shri S.S. Bhatnagar (special secretary at the Department of Defence Production), came to Goa for a meeting with the chief secretary regarding the strike at the Goa Shipyard. Shri Bhatnagar had worked with my father and was aware of my posting at Goa. The chief secretary called me for the meeting. I told Shri Bhatnagar very clearly that the strike is a result of the mishandling of the matter by Admiral Kuruvilla and that the uncalled-for detention of Mohan Nair had created this situation.

On being asked to suggest a way out, I advised that the allegations against the commodore were serious and, therefore, he should either be shifted or a high-level inquiry be ordered against him. I added that as per our intelligence reports, the workers would be prepared to resume their duties if they were assured that there would be no victimization of their leaders and would also accept wages for the strike period as per the prevailing labour laws. They only wanted fair treatment and that there should be no witch-hunt.

While we were still in the meeting, an unexpected development took place. Personal secretary to the chief secretary came inside and informed that a labour delegation headed by Mohan Nair's deputy wanted to see him. After consulting us, the chief secretary called them inside. Our Special Branch had no information about the arrival of this labour delegation. They wanted to convey a message from

Mohan Nair that their leader had full faith in the IGP as he had always been fair to the labour unions. Whatever solution was suggested by him would be acceptable to him and the union. This had shocked everybody, including me. I, in my remotest imagination couldn't have anticipated this. At that moment, the chief secretary observed that this had happened because of IGP's fair treatment of the labour unions in the past and that he had not allowed any pressure to prejudice his action. Shri Bhatnagar obviously felt relieved since he saw the possibility of finding a solution to his problem. I was feeling a little awkward, but fortunately, I had already suggested the way out to Shri Bhatnagar before the arrival of this labour delegation. He wanted me to speak to the labour delegation once again and advise them to resume the work. He also said that the required assurance regarding no victimization and the due payment of wages could be given to the workers. After getting the nod from the chief secretary, I called the union leaders inside and asked them how early they could resume the work. They informed us that since workers stay in different villages, it would take at least two days to inform everybody, but they would definitely resume the work in two days. I also informed them about the assurances. In regard to their leader Mohan Nair's detention, I informed them that his detention involved a legal process and it might take a week or 10 days for his release. The strike at Goa Shipyard was over; my fair and objective handling of the trade unions during my tenure had paid the dividends.

Both Mr Bhatnagar and the chief secretary appreciated my handling of this difficult situation and complimented me for my empathetic understanding of the people and the events.

11

EXPOSITION COMMISSIONER

After I assumed the charge as IGP Goa, Daman and Diu, in February 1973, I took some time to settle in. Both the people and the place were new; the language and the culture were different from what I was familiar with. I had to understand the prevailing official culture, various equations, a dominating CM (whose functioning style was quite authoritative), the nature and capabilities of officers and men who constituted the police force, the people and of course, the press. The only significant event in the first six months was the sad demise of the CM Shri Dayanand Bandodkar or Bhausaheb as he was popularly known. His cremation, which was attended by a large number of people, was an emotional moment and testimony of his popularity among the local population.

Probably towards the end of the year or beginning of the new year, I was called by the chief secretary Shri T. Kipgin to be informed that the government had decided to appoint me as exposition commissioner for the exposition of the holy relics of St Francis Xavier, Apostle of the East and Patron Saint of Goa, Daman and Diu, which comes after a decade. The event was to start from 23 November 1974 and go on till 5 January 1975, covering a period of 44 days. The UT administration had decided to make it a mega event, which would be attracting Catholic devotees, not only from all over the country but from different countries, and thus it served as a big opportunity to present Goa as an international tourist destination. I had to undertake this responsibility in addition to my existing assignment as IGP.

I knew this was going to be a very challenging assignment and I had no past experience of organizing such events. But I accepted this challenge as an opportunity to learn; challenges always excited me as they pushed me beyond my comfort zone. Later on, I was told that the LG agreed on my name as both the CM Smt. Shashikala Kakodkar and the chief secretary had insisted on it and had suggested only one name.

Among the Christian missionaries who came to India, St Francis held a unique place. He was the son of a privy councillor of a king, but preferred to be a teacher of Aristotelian philosophy before coming to India. After meeting Ignatius of Loyola, he became a tireless missionary spreading the message of Jesus throughout the Orient.

This exposition was important because of the changes the Union Territory had undergone in the last decade. The last exposition was held two years after the liberation of the former Portuguese colony in 1964. Due to the non-availability of infrastructure and other resources, it was celebrated on a very small scale. Over the years, the Union Territory's population had increased. The social, economic, political and religious spheres had witnessed vast changes. With faster communication available and the corresponding increase in the tourist traffic, this exposition was expected to attract more than half a million pilgrims besides other tourists from various states of India and different countries. This called for a special effort on the part of the Union Territory administration.

During my meeting with the chief secretary, I explained to him that besides maintaining law and order during the exposition, my task as the Exposition Commissioner included the safe arrival of tourists in Goa through road, rail, air and by sea; I also had to ensure the accommodation for their comfortable stay, facilitation to pay homage to their saint at Old Goa, availability of medical assistance at different places, adequate local transport, the opening of tourist information centres at different points and the adequate publicity of tourists facilities, for which I needed support from different government departments like transport, health, education, tourism, publicity, etc. Since this was a grand and prestigious event, I requested that these departments should depute their senior officers, preferably the number two in their hierarchy, for coordinating and working with me. The chief secretary agreed with my proposal and the government issued an order not only placing the number two senior officers of these departments under my operational control but also putting their exposition budget with me.

This order of the government created an interesting situation. In the Goa administration, there were about 11 IAS officers and two IPS officers. Seven or eight senior IAS officers went in a group to the chief secretary to protest against my appointment as exposition commissioner. Their first plea was that since they were available, this important responsibility should have been given to one of them and second, that I was already handling the heavy responsibility of law and order and, therefore, I should not have been given this additional burden. The chief secretary patiently heard them and then observed that after considering all these factors, the government had found IGP as the most suitable choice for this appointment. This was the first attempt made by these officers to dislodge me. The chief secretary himself narrated the incident to me.

Before calling the first coordination meeting of the representatives from different departments, I created a special cell in my office as a nodal point to record, pursue and monitor all decisions, developments and other activities. If I remember correctly, Shri Pinto, one of the office superintendents at the police headquarter and an enthusiastic worker, was made in-charge of this cell. The first coordination meeting was held in which a decision was taken to construct an overall picture of the total tasks relating to the exposition and then to list out different issues relating to them. I also directed them to prioritize these issues within a rough time frame to be indicated along with the name of the department and the officer. I decided to replan my daily working schedule as well; I kept the first half of the day for police work—when things on the law and order front were normal—and entrusted the routine office work and general supervision to the SP. Afternoons till late evening were reserved for exposition work.

Among the major priorities was arranging accommodation for about six lakh pilgrims and tourists, who were expected to be in Goa during the 44 days of the Exposition of Relics. The existing hotels and inns were clearly inadequate. They were also beyond the means of ordinary pilgrims. We, therefore, thought to utilize school buildings for this purpose and started their inspection to assess what additional improvements and alterations would be required to make them comfortable for the pilgrims of different categories. Since the accommodation was needed from mid-November 1974 to the second week of January 1975, when the schools were normally open and some of them had examinations, we proposed to modify the academic calendar by readjusting their holidays and examinations. After initial reluctance, the government agreed to our proposal as there was no other suitable alternative. This enabled us to establish pilgrim camps in Panjim, Madgaon, Old Goa and other neighbouring areas. We made arrangements on the presumption that on an average, a pilgrim or tourist would stay in Goa for about four days. The accommodation was also categorized in different classes depending on the facilities. The rent started from ₹1 per day to ₹10 per day. In the highest category, we provided beds and linens. Approximately out of seven to eight lakh visitors a little more than one lakh availed our facilities. The director of tourism, Shri Mahajan, supervised these arrangements with the assistance of our exposition control room and the local police officers helped them whenever required. Later on, we appointed camp in-charges, shift managers and also provided locker facilities in each camp. While transport was made available at each camp, medical assistance was arranged at nearby convenient points. Information regarding all facilities was made available at the central exposition control room, local control rooms, police stations, information centres and with the officers in-charge of the camps. This was given wide publicity in the media making Goa a star attraction for the tourists.

The second big issue was organizing transport for the movement of pilgrims and tourists within Goa, especially for their visit to Old Goa from their place of stay and to visit other tourist attractions. The existing fleet of buses in Goa was just sufficient to meet the daily local needs. We made requests to both Maharashtra and Karnataka governments to provide extra buses. Our deputy director, transport, Shri Ingle (who was part of my team), had worked out a total requirement for the exposition as around 350 additional buses. This was a large number! But when I met Karnataka transport commissioner in the meeting at chief secretary's chamber, he turned out to be my batchmate! He told the chief secretary that we were batchmates and he would meet our entire requirement of buses from Karnataka. A big issue was solved just due to personal relationship. I told our deputy director of transport to identify various routes for the pilgrims as well as parking lots for the additional buses. He was also told to plan special tours for the entertainment of the tourists with the help of director tourism. These tours had proved to be extremely popular with visitors. In all, a whopping 552 tours were organized covering about 24,000 tourists. This was in addition to their various visits to Old Goa, the main venue of the exposition.

A series of meetings were also held with the church authorities to know about their calendar—details of religious ceremonies starting from moving of the holy relics from Basilica of Bom Jesus to Se Cathedral, where devotees and faithful would be paying their homage, the dates of various festive days when special ceremonies would be held and the closing ceremony when the holy relics would be returned to Bom Jesus Basilica. All these occasions required extra police and security arrangements to regulate and control the large crowds and to ensure the sanctity of the ceremonies. With God's blessings, everything happened according to the schedule, with a lot of grace and dignity.

We opened tourist information centres in all towns, including the main venue at Old Goa. They were also established at airports, bus stations, ship jetty and railway stations. Tourist information literature was also sent to tourism departments of different states, from where tourists were expected. Some of this literature was also sent to major tourist centres abroad.

Since a large number of tourists and pilgrims were to assemble every day at Old Goa to pay homage and were likely to spend the whole day there, arrangements had to be made to open eateries, bars, bakeries, general stores, medical stores and entertainment stalls. To meet this requirement, a temporary shopping complex of about 600 shops was planned at Old Goa and it turned out to be a massive hit.

At that time, the roads in Goa were good but very narrow, especially the road between Panjim and Old Goa—the venue of the main ceremony. This road did not have the capacity to take the traffic load during the exposition period and since there was no scope for widening it, we had to look for an alternative. There was a huge hillock starting from the outskirts of Panjim up to Old Goa, which had a nearly flat top. The local villagers were occasionally using it. I surveyed the area along with PWD engineers and to everybody's surprise, we discovered remnants of an old road going across the hillock! The archaeological authorities informed us that this road was built during the rule of the Kadamba dynasty, which ruled Goa before the Portuguese occupied it. The discovery of this road was a pleasant surprise to the locals. The road was repaired and used as a return route from Old Goa to Panjim, dispelling all apprehensions about possible traffic jams and ensuring the smooth flow of vehicles.

The old monuments at Old Goa, including the Se Cathedral and Basilica of Bom Jesus needed repairs and maintenance. The precious paintings on the ceilings of these buildings had to be revived. This was to be handled by some experts. A meeting was held with the officers of the Archaeological Survey of India (ASI) to undertake this work on priority basis so that it could be completed before the start of the exposition. The revival of ceiling paintings was extremely tedious and time-consuming, but on our request and persuasion, it was fortunately completed within the given time. This also required regular coordination with the church authorities, which could be achieved with the help of Father George, who was stationed at Old Goa.

There was an apprehension in the minds of Goans that this huge influx of pilgrims/tourists during the exposition would create various shortages in Goa—the shortage of food items, vegetables, milk and other basic essentials. They also thought that this shortage of essential items would result in a price rise. They feared that there might be chaotic traffic jams on their already narrow roads. All these apprehensions were reported in local newspapers and had caused panic amongst the locals. After making adequate arrangements to ensure regular supply of these items on normal prevailing rates, I issued a press statement assuring the locals that their normal life would go on smoothly.

During a meeting related to the exposition arrangements, it was proposed that this opportunity should be utilized to organize a large-scale exhibition at Panjim as an added attraction for the tourists. The responsibility for this was entrusted to the industries department. But after a few weeks, the industry minister Shri Usgaonkar expressed his inability to organize the exhibition as his director of industries had raised his hands. He informed the CM about this and thereafter, the CM called the chief secretary and me for a meeting and told me that while the government was fully aware that IGP's hands were full, they would be relieved if I could also accept the additional responsibility of organizing the exhibition.

Now, this subject was absolutely unknown to me but there was no other option. After consulting some friends in Bombay who were dealing in the publicity and advertising business,

I got the names of a few professionals who could help me in organizing the exhibition. We invited them to Goa and after a brief consultation with the CM and the chief secretary, the work was entrusted to Shri Talashilkar. He gave a presentation and after incorporating changes suggested by us, his proposal was approved by the government. Of course, on my advice, the local government wrote to various state governments to direct their industry departments to send their stalls for the exhibition. Similarly, the Central Cottage Industries Department of the Government of India was approached for their participation. The 'Expo 74', as this exhibition was named, was organized at Campal Ground, Panjim. It unexpectedly became a big show and attracted more than 90,000 visitors in the very first five days. The Goans had never seen such a large and glamorous extravaganza.

Sometime in August or September 1974, when almost all arrangements except for the exhibition had been made, my colleagues in the other service, made another desperate attempt—this time through the LG—to take over the charge of the post of Exposition Commissioner on the ground that I was already under great pressure due to my heavy responsibilities. They suggested that I should not take the additional burden of exposition on my 'already burdened' shoulders. The chief secretary informed the LG that I had already made all arrangements for the exposition and it would be unfair to replace me at this stage. He also mentioned that since everything was going as scheduled, this change wasn't really required. The LG insisted that the chief secretary should take it in writing from me that the additional charge would not affect my performance as the IGP. When the chief secretary informed me about it, I was shocked and conveyed my resentment... After all, till that very date, the

LG had not bothered to even find out what arrangements were being made for the exposition. He had not called me for any meeting to acquaint himself with the progress of the exposition arrangements. I couldn't really understand how my written undertaking would add to his confidence. I told the chief secretary that the government should have considered all this before entrusting this task to me. There had been no change in the situation and all the arrangements were almost complete. Somehow, the chief secretary managed the situation and convinced the LG that I should not be asked to give this undertaking. The second attempt of my colleagues to dislodge me also failed.

Since the exposition required a round-the-clock massive police arrangement, our force requirement was substantial. The strength of our own reserve police was quite less. We decided to request the Maharashtra government for the additional force. After the CM spoke to Shri Sharad Pawar, who was then Minister of State (MoS) for Home in Maharashtra, I went to Bombay and met him. He almost took no time to agree to meet our total requirements. Shri T.B. Spadigam, SP training, was given responsibility of looking after the logistics and deployment of the outside force.

Since all arrangements had been made, I decided to hold a press conference to inform people about all aspects of the arrangements. The representatives from Bombay Press and other national dailies (in addition to our local press) attended this press conference. Written briefs had been prepared for the convenience of the press.

An interesting incident happened during the press conference: Shri Diego Silvera and Shri B.G. Koshy representing a Bombay magazine and a newspaper, respectively, raised a question—if on the opening day when Holy Casket would be opened and if the holy relics were found missing, what would Exposition Commissioner do? Since this was asked in a lighter vein, I smiled friendly and immediately said that both of them would be detained for interrogation. The press conference concluded on a highly satisfactory note. All the possible doubts had been clarified and we were geared up for the exposition.

The first day of exposition attracted a very large crowd, which first witnessed and then joined the procession carrying the holy relics from Basilica of Bom Jesus to Se Cathedral. Thereafter, they lined up to pay their homage to the holy relics. The first day passed off peacefully and thereafter our arrangements at Old Goa, the venue of the holy ceremony, went like a clock. As far as the arrival of tourists and pilgrims were concerned, I can only compliment my team members, who managed reception, transport and accommodation of these tourist groups, varying from 100–800 people by working tirelessly, days and nights alike. Quite a few big groups arrived at a very short notice. But fortunately, they were comfortably managed by our officers. The pilgrims arrived not only through road rail and air, but also by ship from Bombay and Kerala including a luxury liner, Jupiter, which also brought foreign tourists. Our team members at headquarter were such a committed lot, that irrespective of the departments they belonged to, they took responsibility for all situations and completed their tasks wonderfully well. In the first 15 days, the number of pilgrims who visited Old Goa had crossed three lakh and by the end of December 1974, the number had exceeded six lakh. The first five days of January 1975, which was the last week of the exposition, witnessed a huge inflow of tourists and pilgrims. On the last day, i.e., 5 January, about 66,000 devotees paid homage to the holy relics. Approximately seven to eight lakh pilgrims and tourists visited Goa during this period. The pilgrims came not only from India, but also from foreign countries like the US, Europe, Tanzania and Ethiopia. Portuguese foreign minister Mário Soares, who was of Goanese origin and Indian ministers Dr S.D. Sharma and Shri Raj Bahadur also visited Goa during this period. The last ceremony was taking back the holy relics to Basilica of Bom Jesus in a procession, which took place as planned. The entire function and ceremony of Exposition of Saint Francis Xavier's Relics was completed with dignity and grace.

The Goan press was all praise for the arrangements made for the exposition and among the national dailies, *The Times of India* and *Deccan Herald* gave extensive positive coverage to the exposition, complimenting the Goa government. The local English daily, *The Navhind Times*, wrote an editorial titled 'A Difficult Job Well Done'. I still remember what it read:

> [F]ears about the possible repercussions about the pilgrim influx during the exposition proved wrong. As to the arrangements at Old Goa, those who had visited earlier expositions are all praise for the present arrangements; pilgrims had excellent and easy opportunity to pay their homage to the Saint's relics. On the whole, the Goa government and the Exposition Commissioner and his staff, in particular, can take legitimate credit for having done a difficult job well!

A Bombay weekly, *Current*, complimented the Exposition Commissioner for the perfect arrangements and gave a headline in their paper which read: 'Expo Ends, Kaushal can get some sleep now!'

12

WHEN I CHOSE TO BE INDISCREET

t was sometime in 1978 that the then Prime Minister's personal security officer (PSO), an ACP rank officer, reported to me that the PM's son Shri Kanti Lal Desai had given oral orders that his friends coming to the PM house to meet him and their cars should be allowed to come inside without any checking or frisking. He had also instructed that the briefcases or bags carried by them should also not be checked. These oral directions were against the standing instructions on the security of VVIPs and the provisions contained in the Blue Book for the prime minister's security. It could have resulted in some serious incident. Shri Kanti Lal's room was adjacent to PM's room, but had an independent entry from one side of the house. At that time, as per the existing instructions, visitors including ministers were not allowed to bring their vehicles inside the PM House and frisking and checking of bags etc., was being strictly followed. The PSO had done his job by reporting the matter to me and now it was for me to take appropriate action. Shri Morarji Desai was the prime minister at the time and I was heading the VIP security unit of Delhi Police, which was responsible for the security of the president, vice president, prime minister, visiting foreign dignitaries (heads of state and government), home minister and other VIPs. There was no Special Protection Group (SPG) at that time.

It was a very difficult situation requiring immediate action. I was in a dilemma. Enforcement of the existing mandatory security instructions would have annoyed the PM's son and knowing him from my Goa days, the unpleasant reaction was a certainty. Ignoring it was also almost impossible as any untoward incident involving the PM's security would have been disastrous for the Delhi Police and also for my career. Only a few years back, a brother and sister duo (Jagotas) had gained unauthorized entry into the PM house after breaking through the gate and had taken two rounds in their car before they could be stopped and arrested. It was, later on, found that they were undergoing psychological treatment. No serious action was taken as Shri B.N. Mehra, the then head of the security unit, was very close to the Nehru-Gandhi family. I immediately brought it to the notice of my seniors, i.e., ACP and CP, who told me that they would be taking it up—but no guidance or instructions came for the next two days. It was hanging like a Damocles sword over me. I must mention that while under pressure, I remained composed—probably due to my unflinching faith in Lord Almighty. During this period, my wife was a big support to me. Normally I never discussed my office matters at home. But seeing me quiet and worried, my wife insisted on knowing the problem. While briefly informing her about the problem and the action which I was proposing to take, I told her that it might lead to my transfer from Delhi to some remote destination like Andaman or Laccadive Islands and we would have to vacate our bungalow at Ashoka Road and withdraw our children from their schools. She advised me that I should do what I considered right and should not bother so much about the consequences. We would manage the situation as and when it comes.

After PSO had brought it to my knowledge, the ball was then in my court. I did not receive any direction from my seniors after reporting the matter to them. Now I had two options—either to maintain the status quo, which was against the provisions of the Blue Book and in case of any serious incident, i.e., any attempt on PM's life, get myself permanently branded as a professionally incompetent officer or be called indiscreet by taking up the matter in writing. In both cases, the risk was entirely mine. After giving thorough consideration to all aspects of the issue, I decided to put it in writing and addressed DO letters to my immediate seniors with a copy to the concerned officer in the MHA in-charge of the VVIP security. The letter clearly mentioned the oral instructions given by Shri Kanti Lal Desai, son of the prime minister, which was in violation of the provisions contained in the Blue Book, the huge risk involved to VVIP security and requested guidance and direction in the matter. I was convinced that what I was doing was right and according to the rules.

My seniors' immediate reactions were not very happy. They almost bombarded me. In fact, it was conveyed to me that they always considered me a very cool and mature officer and did not expect that I could be so indiscreet as to make a complaint in writing against the PM's son. I also knew very well that no decision could be taken by the official hierarchy since it involved the PM's son and required his intervention. I was, therefore, sure that this letter or its content would be reported to the PM. I was keeping my fingers crossed and had prepared myself to face the consequences. It so happened that my letter was put up before the PM the very next morning and as per his PSO's version, he read it twice and a smile came on his face. Hats off to the gentleman (Shri Desai) for his quick and right decision. It was conveyed to us that 'rules must be observed'. Thereafter we had no problem. Even minor requests for some deviation by personal staff were not permitted. With my experience of VVIP security, I can say with a lot of sense of responsibility that very few VVIPs could have reacted like this especially when the complaint was against their own son. My immediate seniors, who had admonished me only a day before, congratulated me for taking a bold and correct step.

A little later when I analysed the incident, I realized that probably I could muster the courage to take up in writing this important issue relating to PM's security involving the conduct of his own son because on two earlier occasions also I had not exactly implemented his (PM) observations about his security arrangements as they were against the prescribed security instructions. This was during the time when I was trying to understand the VVIP's (PM) attitude towards his security arrangements and his expectations from us.

Notwithstanding whatever is mentioned above and a few more similar incidents, he (the then PM) was gracious enough to have conveyed in writing to my commissioner, at the time of his departure, his detailed and specific appreciation of my performance as deputy commissioner in-charge of the VVIP security.

It was a great experience and education. I realized that confidence and courage to adhere to the rules and to what you think is correct normally saves the situation.

13

SPEAKING STRAIGHT

On 15 July 1979, Shri Morarji Desai, prime minister of India submitted his resignation to the president due to intense infighting among different factions of the Janta Party. Both Babu Jagjivan Ram and Ch. Charan Singh had staked their claims. The morning of the day the leadership issue was to be decided, word spread that Babu Jagjivan Ram's name had been finalized. Lots of his supporters and some important political persons including media people gathered at his residence on Krishna Menon Marg. I had made adequate security arrangements at the place and also visited the venue for supervision. However, by evening things changed, since Ch. Charan Singh succeeded in mobilizing more support and submitted his claim to form the government. Immediately after the announcement, a good number of his (Ch. Charan Singh's) supporters, important political personalities including some former ministers and media men assembled at his residence, ie., 12 Tughlaq Road. Supporters from neighbouring districts of western UP also started arriving in buses and trucks

It was interesting to watch that quite a few persons, who were expressing their joy and conveying their proximity with

Babu Jagjivan Ram in the morning and calling him '*Apne Babuji*', were now at Ch. Charan Singh's residence showing the same joy and addressing him as '*Hamare Chaudhary Saheb*'. I recognized many of them. There was nothing surprising in this as such things do happen in and around power centres.

The PM elect expressed his desire to address his well-wishers and supporters. My team, with the help of the available Central Public Works Department (CPWD) staff, prepared a makeshift stage by putting together the office tables lying in the annexe and provided a public address system. Few additional mega lights were also arranged. Since the parametre wall was very low, we immediately deployed uniformed armed policemen around the outer cordon and the inner security cordon was created by heavy deployment of security personnel including Ring Round teams from my unit. Some screening and checking/frisking arrangements were also put in place at the entry points of the bungalow and the residence. Ch. Charan Singh spoke to his supporters and media and thanked them. On our advice, he thereafter went inside the house, which had been reasonably secured by that time.

Ch. Charan Singh was sworn in as prime minister on 28 July 1979. At that time, he was staying at 12, Tughlaq Road, which was very vulnerable from the point of view of VVIP security, especially for the prime minister of India. It had very low boundary walls with no tin sheets or any other fitting which could be used as view cutters. The main residence was also very close to the main road with good traffic frequency. The residential building also needed complete overhaul to meet the minimum security requirements, even if it was a temporary residence for the PM. I was working out what all was needed to be done and prioritizing accordingly.

While I was performing my duties, I was under great mental pressure since my father, who had been a chief engineer in UP Irrigation, had very strained relations with Ch. Charan Singh, when he was irrigation minister in the UP government. My father had passed away in February 1975. The fact of this unpleasant relationship was not known, as far as I know, to anyone in Delhi. But the possibility of the PM coming to know about it through somebody else was always there. The tussle in my mind was whether I should tell the PM about it and wait for his reaction or avoid it for the time being and face the things as they develop. The second option was against my nature. I always believed that there should be complete trust in relationship between you and the person, under whom you are serving. According to me, hiding any information, especially of this nature, amounts to cheating. In this case it was all the more important, as I was responsible for his security, which was an extremely important and sensitive matter requiring total trust. I also knew that Ch. Charan Singh did not trust people easily. I, therefore, decided that I would personally meet the PM and inform him of the facts.

Next day early morning I reached the PM's residence and sent a request through his old PSO Inspector Kartar Singh that I wanted to see him. I was immediately called in. The PM was sitting on the floor on a dari in the back verandah of his house and shaving. I introduced myself and told him that I was in-charge of his security. I further informed him that ad hoc security arrangements had been made at his residences, which were being further strengthened at war footing. I also told him about the vulnerability of his present residence and that while I would be keeping him informed about whatever I would be doing in this regard, he might like to give some instructions. He observed that he was satisfied with the arrangements made so far and I could go ahead with my work. At this stage I requested him that if permitted, I would like to make a submission. After getting his nod, I told him that I am late Shri H.C. Kaushal's son. All this while he was shaving, but upon hearing this he suddenly turned towards me and said, '*Accha aap engineer saheb ke bete hain* [Oh, you're engineer saheb's son]'. He smiled and then asked me why I was telling him about it. I told him that since I was responsible for his security, I thought he must know. I then asked him what were the instructions for me; he after a pause said that I should continue my work and keep him informed of the developments. He also instructed me to send an immediate note to the secretary, Urban Development, to inform him of the changes and any additional fittings etc., that I needed to get done at the house. Thereafter, I left, but I was happy and relieved that I had shed a big burden from my mind. After this, even if I had been transferred, it would not have bothered me. Total trust was very important for my functioning; and I never looked back. Ch. Charan Singh trusted me on very sensitive issues like sharing his apprehensions relating to his security, restrictions relating to the entry of his relatives in the house, what type of persons should be a part of his security team, etc.

My straight speaking, I think, was responsible for me continuing in that important assignment.

14

STRENGTH OF FORGIVENESS

My father helped a lot of people during his life. Even when he was facing some really difficult times, he never refused help. He would do whatever was possible for him at the time. Once when I was talking to him regarding this, he told me that 'if somebody comes to you for help assess his problem and help him according to your means. You should not consider whether the person concerned had not helped you in the past when you needed it or has hurt you or anyone close to you'. His logic was that the concerned person who has come to seek your help is fully aware of what he has done to you and is still requesting you for help, that is his punishment. He also said that when you help anyone, do not expect anything from him. You should do it only because you feel happy doing it. I tried to follow his advice to the extent I could.

During my different postings in Delhi Police, engineers of UP Irrigation Department posted at Okhla, Delhi, would occasionally come to me whenever they had any problem or issue with Delhi Police. Since my father had served the Irrigation Department of UP throughout his life, they found it easy to approach me. I must admit that I had a soft corner for them and always responded to their requests. Sometime in 1980, when I was posted as additional commissioner, New Delhi Range, an assistant engineer of UP Irrigation Department came to me with a request for an appointment for his chief engineer (CE). Since he knew me for quite some time, he also told me that initially, his chief was reluctant to come to me after hearing my name, but finally agreed when he could not find any other connection in Delhi Police. I did not deliberately discuss this subject with him but gave an appointment to his CE.

The CE came to see me at the appointed time and date. By this time, I had come to know about him from my mother and younger brother who were staying at Lucknow. Since it would not be appropriate, I am not mentioning his name. The CE's problem was quite serious. His daughter, who was married to an Airforce officer, was the accused in a theft case and the Airforce police had recovered a lot of stolen property from her possession. At their instance, the local police had registered a criminal case against her and they were now pressurizing Police for her arrest. The CE informed me that his daughter was a patient of sleepwalking and she was not aware of what she was doing in her sleep. She had a long history of treatment for this disease. She could not tell the investigation officer how she came in possession of the stolen property recovered from her house. During our conversation, I was addressing the CE as Uncle, considering that he was a junior colleague of my father when he was in service. He requested me not to proceed further with the investigation since she was suffering from sleepwalking. I assured him that I would be looking into the case and would come back to him after discussing it with the concerned officers.

The investigating officer and the ACP who was supervising the case told me that there were many instances of her committing these thefts and the victim families were pressurizing police for action against her as they thought that she did it knowingly and her disease was not that serious. The Airforce Police was also in favour of legal action against her. I asked my officers to contact their senior officers and explain to them that all this had happened due to her medical condition for which she was under regular treatment. During this time the CE came to see me three to four times and I informed him about the developments and my efforts. In one of the meetings, he mentioned that my father was a great gentleman but for some reason, his relationship with him was not very good for which he always felt bad. In fact, I was aware that he had worked against my father and tried to bring him harm, but I asked him to just forget the past.

I knew that I could close the case on the grounds of her medical condition and send a final report to the court. The recovered property could be returned to the rightful owners after obtaining the court orders. But my only consideration was that the local hierarchy of the Airforce wanted action against the accused. I, therefore, met the Air Vice Marshal of Western Air Command and explained to him the entire background of the case. He was convinced and agreed with me. I came back to my office and directed the DCP to close the case and send a final report to the court.

The CE came to know about the developments and immediately reached Delhi. When he came to see me, he was full of tears and thanked me profusely. He was very excited and emotional and was finding it very hard to express himself. I offered him tea. Suddenly he said that he must confess that his relations with my father were not good. To his surprise, I informed him that right from the beginning I was fully aware of all the facts and also about his relations with my father. I also told him that I had spent quite some time with my father during his last days in the hospital and he neither said anything against anyone nor asked me to settle any score. I could not have acted in any other way except as I had.

I closed the conversation by saying that I did exactly what my father would have done had he been there in my place. My father would have never refused to help his daughter. When the CE left my room, he was feeling extremely grateful and said he did not know what to say. He was full of tears and gave me a lot of blessings. I was happy and satisfied with what I did.

Forgiveness gives strength!

15

PAY REVISION OF RPF

During my deputation to the railway ministry (RPF), I was nominated for a 12-week training programme in 'International Personnel Management' at the Royal Institute of Public Administration (RIPA) in London. On my return from training and a short holiday, when I was entering Rail Bhawan to rejoin my duties, I asked the RPF sentry at the gate, as was my habit, how he had been. And he instantly said that all of them were waiting for my return. The guard in-charge, who was standing next to him told me that the Pay Commission report had been released and the RPF had suffered the most. In short, he informed me that while they had not been given the higher pay grades given to other armed forces of the Union, they were deprived of the certain benefits which they were getting earlier as railway employees. I directed him to see me in my office after half an hour. After some preliminary discussions with him and the concerned office superintendent, I called on the DG, Shri S.P. Banerjee. I spoke to him about the grievances of the RPF personnel relating to the Pay Commission's recommendations and wanted to know about what could be done and how we should proceed. The DG observed that he was very concerned about it as there was a lot of resentment in the force on this issue and he was waiting for my return so that the issue could be taken up with the railway minister. I requested three days to study the matter.

After studying the recommendations of the 5th Pay Commission regarding the pay scales of Armed Forces of the Union (AFU), other benefits including ration money given to them and also going through what railways had done for the RPF on the recommendations of the Pay Commission, I prepared a proposal for the pay revision of the RPF personnel containing new pay scales for the different non-gazetted ranks of the RPF (constables to inspectors) and mentioned some important facts about the performance of the force— especially the crucial role and sacrifices made by them during the violent agitation in Assam and handling of current militancy in Punjab. Since Punjab police, due to their heavy commitment regarding controlling militancy in the state, was not in a position to protect railways, our Railway Protection Special Force (RPSF) were deployed for station protection, train escorting and track patrolling duties, which they were performing very effectively.

The DG took an appointment with Shri Madhavrao Scindia, minister for railways, and both of us, along with member traffic and our member in-charge, appeared before the minister and drew his attention to the injustice done to the force in the implementation of the Pay Commission recommendations. The minister also called the finance commissioner (FC) of the Railway Board to join the meeting. Since I knew the FC at a personal level, I had already discussed the issue with him and had prepared my proposal on the lines suggested by him. During the meeting, the DG asked me to present the case and I explained in detail the recommendations of the Pay Commission regarding revision of pay scales of AFU, including other benefits like ration money, etc., which were given to them. I also informed the meeting that when the RPF was converted to an Armed Force of the Union in 1985, the procedure required the concurrence of the Ministry of Home Affairs and during a discussion in the MHA on the subject (incidentally, the proposal for conversion of RPF into AFU was drafted and dealt by me), it was recorded that any change of pay scales of AFU working under MHA would automatically be extended to the RPF. After our meeting at the MHA, a DO letter to this effect was sent by me to the MHA. The railway ministry did not take all these facts into consideration while implementing the Pay Commission's recommendations in respect of the RPF. Since I was abroad on training, the case of pay revision of RPF was not put up in a proper perspective. I also brought it to the notice of the meeting that the RPF has been made an Armed Force of the Union only two years back and its powerful association had been dissolved. Any disparity in the pay scale with the other armed forces might be treated as injustice with the force and could give them grounds to revive their activities as had happened in 1979.

After a prolonged discussion, I was asked to prepare a formal proposal for the consideration of the Railway Board and the railway minister. However, there was a clear indication that Railway Minister Shri Madhavrao Scindia was favourably inclined towards our case. I requested the minister to allow me a week to prepare the case; as the revision of the pay scale would affect the entire force for the next 10 years, I thought it would be appropriate to have an informal consultation with the members of the force in this regard, which was agreed. The objective was to create a sense of participation in the force.

I called a staff meeting inviting two representatives representing different ranks from each railway including the three workshops at Chittaranjan, Benaras, Parambore and RPSF units. The force personnel, who had come for the meeting, were very happy and excited that the force headquarters had considered it proper to consult them. I explained the details of my proposal, which implied the revision of their pay scales to the level of the other Armed Forces of the Union. As regards the ration money, the Pay Commission had given two scales—one for BSF, CRPF and ITBP and the other for CISF, which had slightly different nature of duties. Since there was a similarity between the nature of duties between CISF and RPF, I proposed that we should get our ration money linked with the CISF. Any change in the ration money scale of the CISF would automatically be extended to RPF. After some discussions and clarifications, everybody unanimously agreed to my proposal. Thereafter, I prepared a formal proposal for the consideration and approval of the Railway Board and the minister.

During the staff meeting, an RPF personnel from some railway observed that their experience with the Railway Board was not very good and they apprehended that the Board might make some substantial cuts in the proposal. I told them that during our meeting with the minister, where DG RPF, member traffic and financial commissioner were present, they had informally indicated their approval of my proposal, but to reassure them I told the meeting that till the time they get the proposed revised scale, I would also not draw my pay in the new revised scale. I continued to draw my pay in the old scale for the next five to six months till our revised proposal for the force was approved by the ministry.

At that time, the railway ministry used to have its own

budget and was competent to sanction and implement the proposed revised scales, which were in line with the pay scales given to the other Armed Forces of the Union. We had also linked our ration money proposal with the CISF, another Armed Force of the Union. Therefore, the Railway Board had no difficulty in approving it. It took the Railway Board about five to six months to process and sanction the pay revision of the RPF. I consistently pursued the case at each stage.

Once the policy of parity in the pay scales for the RPF with the other Armed Forces of the Union was established in this case, it was followed in the future also, i.e., after the 5th Pay Commission in 1996 and thereafter. The force acknowledged the efforts made by senior officers in this regard and repeatedly mentioned it in various Sampark Sabhas which were held afterwards. It also deprived any leverage to the sympathizers and supporters of the dissolved RPF Association, which they were looking for in this opportunity.

All Force personnel, including members of any organization, want to feel assured that their leader(s) are concerned about them and will make efforts for the betterment of their service conditions.

16

PROTECTING PUBLIC INTEREST

t was sometime in mid-1992, about three or four months after I had taken over as CP Delhi, that our Special Branch received the information that Socialist Party leader Shri Mulayam Singh Yadav would be coming to Delhi next day with a large number of party workers for a protest rally at Boat Club on Rajpath. I immediately called the concerned officers for discussion to finalize the arrangements for the rally.

Meanwhile, our SP Branch and District Police had collected more information about it. It was learned that the protest rally of the Socialist Party was not for any public cause, but to lodge protest against the detention of a notorious criminal by us under NSA, who was also an important MLA of the Socialist Party in UP Assembly. Madan Bhaiya, as the MLA was known as, was a dreaded criminal and extortionist, who was operating both in UP and Delhi and had a large number of heinous crime cases including those of murder, attempt to murder, extortion, kidnapping for ransom and Arms Act against him. The proposed protest rally was expected to bring about 30,000–40,000 people, including all party MLAs and some prominent party leaders of UP led by Shri Mulayam Singh

Yadav. The organizers had also not obtained any permission for the rally—which was a legal requirement.

Any rally, especially a protest rally, had a lot of implications for the area where it takes place and also for the area through which it moves. It totally disrupts the normal life of people, students, especially the girls, with many finding it difficult to go to their schools; shopkeepers anticipating mischief and damage put down their shutters, vendors get either looted or not paid for their goods, usual traffic almost comes to a halt. The area gets dirty and littered with various items left behind by protesters. The organizers of the rally or procession, which obtain permission, are told to follow a prescribed route, a schedule; the number of participants is also approximately indicated and other conditions are imposed according to the prevailing situation in the area—none of these conditions were followed in this case. The protest rally was not for any issue of public interest. It was solely to put pressure for the release of a notorious criminal, who was detained by Delhi Police following the due procedure of law. By permitting this protest march to enter Delhi, we would allow them to cause immense inconvenience to people and the possibility of disturbing the peace in the affected area could not be ruled out. I also felt that it was the responsibility of the state to maintain order and ensure a normal peaceful life for its citizens, where they can carry out their legal activities as they desire. The state discharges this responsibility mainly through police. After consulting my senior officers, including additional commissioners, Special Branch and the district DCP, I decided to stop the protest march at the Delhi-UP border.

The organizers of the protest march, including Shri Mulayam Singh Yadav never expected to be not allowed to enter Delhi. We had blocked all entry points on the Delhi-UP border and heavy deployment of force was ensured to prevent any attempt of forcible entry. DCP Northeast, Shri Ranjit Narain, a very cool-headed and mature officer, informed them that commissioner of police, Delhi, had issued orders prohibiting their entry in Delhi. The organizers were in a panic.

Shri Mulayam Singh Yadav contacted Shri Chandra Shekhar, Member of Parliament and a very senior public leader, who later became PM. He immediately rang me up. He was visibly quite annoyed and very angrily told me that police could not prevent people from exercising their democratic right. He also told me that I should allow the protest march and their leaders to enter Delhi and hold a rally. I knew Shri Chandra Shekhar personally. I very politely told him that this protest rally, which would disturb the normal life in the area is not for any public cause, but only for the release of a notorious criminal, who had been detained by the Delhi Police. I expressed my inability to change my orders. As expected, he was not satisfied with my reply and rang up the prime minister, who in turn asked his principal secretary, Shri Amarnath Verma to speak to me on the matter. Incidentally, Shri Amarnath Verma had taught me at university. I explained to him in detail the background of the issue and our reasons for not allowing the rally. At one stage during our discussion on the phone, Shri Verma asked me whether I could release the detained MLA. I told him that his detention had been approved by the Delhi High Court and would need their approval. On Shri Verma's insistence to find a way out, I told him that I could permit four to five of their representatives to go in a police vehicle to the PM's office to hand over their memorandum, and then we would drop them back. Given our justified stand, this was accepted.

This firm and successful handling of the matter enhanced

the prestige of Delhi Police and gave the right signals to the organizers of such rallies/protests that Delhi Police implements its decisions effectively and could handle the pressure. It was appreciated by the ministry and was given positive coverage in the press. The residents of the area also expressed their happiness. The real benefit was that the force started having confidence in their leadership. And it was just the beginning.

17

TAKING RESPONSIBILITY FOR MY ORAL ORDERS

When I took over as CP Delhi in February 1992, the communal situation was very fragile, and provocative speeches by political and religious leaders from both sides were further vitiating the atmosphere. The unresolved Babri Masjid–Ram Janambhoomi dispute was at the root of this prevailing communal tension in Delhi and UP, especially in Ayodhya and the possibility of a serious communal riot at any time could not be ruled out. The backchannel negotiations between senior government functionaries, including senior ministers and communal leaders were going on. In this context, the Shahi Imam of Delhi's Jama Masjid, Abdulla Bokhari, had gained a lot of importance. After prayers (namaz), every Friday, he was making highly provocative speeches before a big congregation and further fuelling the communal tension.

My immediate task was to keep the communal situation under control and prepare Delhi Police, as quickly as possible, to effectively deal with any serious communal riot in the city.

I held a meeting with the senior officers of the field and intelligence branch. Additional CP, Old Delhi Range, and District DCPs of Central and North Districts were asked to study all communal riots, which had taken place in the last 10–15 years to identify the difficulties faced by the police in handling the situation and suggest measures, which were required to be taken in the future. Instructions were also given that even a minor incident, which had any communal overtone, should be promptly dealt with and reported to senior officers. In a few weeks, we were ready with our scheme to effectively tackle a serious law and order situation, including a big communal riot.

Our scrutiny of intelligence reports also revealed that in recent years, Shahi Imam of Jama Masjid had emerged as a religious leader responsible for creating and permanently fuelling the communal tension in the city, and since no planned efforts were made to check his activities, his influence in his community and in the area gradually increased. Senior political leaders were meeting him quite often, which further added to his importance. He needed to be checked and required special handling. I called the then additional CP, DCP Central district, DCP intelligence, ACP and SHO Jama Masjid and instructed them that in the future no senior officer would be meeting the Shahi Imam and only SHO Jama Masjid should deal with him. In case he tried to contact any senior officer on phone, he should be very politely told to speak to the SHO. Fortunately, SHO Jama Masjid, Inspector Ved Pal Rathi, was a professionally competent and a very mature officer. He was confident, daring and a man of action. I conveyed to him, in presence of his immediate senior officers, that I had full faith in his abilities to complete the task entrusted to him. He was given clear instructions to keep a close watch on the activities of the Imam and ensure that no extra importance was given to him. It really proved effective and very soon the Shahi Imam started feeling uncomfortable. Some persons with a criminal background, who were closely known to him, were arrested for their nefarious activities. Since no senior officer was responding to the Imam, he approached a Union minister, who was conducting backchannnel negotiations with him, for the transfer of the SHO. Through PMO, a message was sent to LG Delhi to get the SHO transferred. LG discussed the matter with me. I explained to him the fact that the SHO was only doing what I had asked him to do. I also told him that it was part of our strategy to contain the Shahi Imam, which is necessary to keep the situation under control. I must admit that the LG appreciated our stand and no further action was taken.

Meanwhile, SHO Jama Masjid conducted a raid in the area of Kala Mahal, where the Shahi Imam's house was located and recovered a large quantity of stolen property from the locality. The accused persons, who were known to the Imam, were arrested. No police raid had been conducted in the locality in the recent past. Naturally, the Shahi Imam was quite upset and felt that this might adversely affect his influence in the area. He again pressurized the government through his channel for the transfer of the SHO. I was called by the then Union Home secretary, who wanted to understand the matter and also to know as to why I was keen to retain the SHO in his present posting. I am not sure, but my guess was that probably the LG had spoken to him in this regard. I told the home secretary that whatever SHO Jama Masjid was doing was under my instruction and was part of our strategy to handle the Shahi Imam, who had otherwise been indulging in very objectionable activities, including inciting communal tension in Delhi. In fact, our strategy had proved quite effective and was showing results. The home secretary agreed with me and did not give any further direction. Later on, I learned that when the home minister was approached in this regard, the home secretary had advised him that the stand taken by the CP in this matter was correct and they should not interfere. SHO Jama Masjid continued in his posting.

During this period, Inspector Ved Pal Rathi appeared before me with his senior officers and requested that while he was grateful to me for the stand I had taken in this matter, he was afraid that it might be detrimental to me and therefore he could be transferred out. I told him that I appreciate his concern for me, but I had taken this stand on principle. If any officer was acting under my instruction, then it was incumbent on me to ensure that he was not punished for it. I closed the matter by telling him that he was doing very useful work and should not bother about anything else.

I think two to three weeks after this, when I was at the Boat House Club Police Post, discussing some proposed protest rally with additional CP and DCP, New Delhi, the police post in-charge SI Om Prakash informed me that there was a telephone call from the PMO and personal secretary (PS) to the PM wanted to speak to me. I immediately attended the phone and the PS asked me to speak to the PM. I had just no inkling of the matter about which the PM wished to speak to me, the least being the transfer of an SHO. Before I could think any further, the PM Shri Narasimha Rao was on the line. He, in his usual polite manner, asked me about the matter relating to the transfer of SHO Jama Masjid. I was shocked as I had not expected a telephone call on this issue from the PM himself. I told him that I would be carrying out his orders in this regard, but if permitted I would like to submit two points—one that whatever SHO Jama Masjid was doing was under my instructions and was part of our strategy to control the nefarious activities of the Shahi Imam of Jama Masjid and reduce his undesirable influence. Secondly, this SHO had been successful in putting an effective check on Shahi Imam's provocative activities and for the last few months, he could not create any trouble as the SHO kept him occupied in one or the other thing. I also mustered the courage to tell the PM that while I would be transferring him on that day itself, since he was an outstanding officer and was only sincerely carrying out instructions of his senior officers, I should be permitted to post him to another police station in the walled city, to which he agreed.

I came back to my office and directed my staff officer to call Inspector Ved Pal Rathi, SHO Jama Masjid, and his immediate senior officers, i.e., additional CP and DCP Central. The officers were surprised that a small issue like an SHO's transfer could reach and be discussed at PM's level. I told them that the stand was taken not for an individual, but on principle. The impact of these developments on the officers could be noticed on their faces and they felt very confident and inspired.

The details of these developments gradually spread in the force and it had a huge impact. The force developed faith in their leadership and felt very inspired and motivated, which gave amazing results in times to come. An additional benefit was that after this, nobody during my remaining tenure made any recommendation to me about transfer and postings of officers.

18

DEFENDING MY OFFICERS— APPEARANCE BEFORE THE PRIVILEGE COMMITTEE OF THE LOK SABHA

The demolition of Babri Masjid on 6 December 1992 was followed by serious communal riots in different parts of the country except in Delhi, where a riot took place only in a limited area in a trans-Jamuna district (Northeast Delhi) which was effectively controlled in about two to three days. After the Babri masjid demolition, BJP supporters had become a little more aggressive and were indulging in making provocative speeches. The other community was also responding in the same manner. Sometime in January 1993, the BJP gave a call for a rally on 25 February 1993 at Boat House Club lawns on Rajpath to be addressed by their popular national leaders Shri L.K. Advani and Shri Atal Bihari Vajpayee. They mentioned in their application that they would be mobilizing about 10 lakh BJP supporters from all over the country for this rally. The party had put up a lot of posters in Delhi and in other important cities in the country to create a buzz.

While in the second fortnight of January Delhi Police was, as usual, busy with the police arrangements for the Republic Day Parade and other related events, I held a meeting with my senior officers, including district DCPs to consider various options about the proposed rally—whether it should be allowed or not and what would be our strategy in either case. We also discussed the pros and cons of both the options and the consensus was that the rally should not be permitted under the prevailing communal atmosphere in the country. The possibility of such a big rally, if allowed, resulting in serious law and order situation in the current environment could not be ruled out. After briefing the LG, I requested the home secretary to call a meeting so that a final view could be taken. I was informed that the meeting had been fixed for 31 January at the PMO.

The meeting, which was held in the afternoon of 31 January 1993, was presided over by the PM and besides the home minister and two ministers from the home ministry, it was attended by the LG Delhi, principal secretary to the PM, home secretary director IB, secretary R&AW and a few other senior officers. On my request, I was allowed to speak after everybody had spoken. There was a view, not very emphatically put, that the rally might be allowed and Delhi Police should make appropriate arrangements to contain and regulate it. However, it was very clear that even with all possible restrictions, the BJP would be able to muster at least five lakh supporters from Delhi and neighbouring states. I further told the meeting that in view of the current communal environment in the country, the possibility of a rally of this size going berserk for some planned or frivolous reason and turning into a serious riot could not be ruled out. In that eventuality, senior political leaders of the organizing party would not be able to control the situation and it would be ultimately a confrontation between the police and the rioters. The possibility of use of firearms by police for controlling the situation could not be ruled out. Since we would be completely sealing the areas north and south of Rajpath, including Raisina Hills, the protesters would be pushed towards the Pragati Maidan side. The likelihood of an old masjid (Zabta Ganj Mosque) on Rajpath lawns behind the hutments, near the back of VP House, getting substantially damaged was also to be kept in mind. I therefore emphatically advised that we should not allow the rally at all. After briefly consulting the ministers, LG and other senior officers, the PM observed that he agreed with the views of CP Delhi and the meeting was closed.

While I was asked to go ahead with my planning of police arrangements for preventing the rally and giving my requirements for the additional force to the MHA, instructions were also issued to the concerned ministries to provide all assistance required by me in connection with the rally. The organizers of the BJP rally were informed in writing that their permissions for the proposed rally had been denied. I issued prohibitory orders covering the entire UT of Delhi. Our information was that the BJP would be collecting supporters at different places in Delhi.

In one of the review meetings at the PMO where home minister, both minister for state, home secretary and LG were present, Shri Rajesh Pilot MOS (IS) told me that the PM felt that after the Babri Masjid demolition, people's perception is that there was no government and we had to prove that government was effective and capable of implementing its decision. I told the meeting that I could assure them of my best efforts.

We completely sealed the entire Rajpath with heavy-duty

barricading, tin sheets and concertina wires. Heavy traffic inside the Ring Road was not allowed, rail traffic coming towards and going from Delhi were stopped, including circular rail movement; road traffic from neighbouring states was not allowed to cross the Delhi border, all central government offices on both sides of Rajpath were closed and all VIPs, including members of Parliament staying in the south of Rajpath were advised in writing not to cross the Rajpath and use Willingdon Crescent to go to Parliament and other places in the north of Rajpath. The Speaker of Lok Sabha and the vice chairman of Rajya Sabha were informed and their permission obtained.

Around 9.00 a.m. on 25 February, some BJP MPs and their supporters gathered at Vithalbhai Patel House and, despite police warning, made efforts to move towards the Parliament House violating the prohibitory orders and were arrested along with Shri Murli Manohar Joshi, Member of Parliament. Similar attempts to violate the prohibitory orders were made at Shanker Road near Rajinder Nagar, at Pragati Maidan, at Paharganj near New Delhi Railway Station and quite a few other places. If I remember correctly, in all 118 BJP MPs, including Shri Atal Bihari Vajpayee, Shri L.K. Advani and Shri M.M. Joshi were arrested. Shri Shanta Kumar, Madan Lal Khurana, Vijay Kumar Malhotra, Kedar Nath Sahni and some other prominent BJP leaders, along with a number of their supporters, were also arrested/detained by Delhi Police. Not even one person was allowed to enter or cross the Rajpath. However, an attempt was made by seven to eight non-BJP MPs to cross Vijay Chowk from the South Fountains side, but they were stopped. This included Shri. I.K. Gujral, Shri. S.S. Ahluwalia, Shri Sompal and three to four other MPs. Their argument that they were from a different political party was not accepted as the prohibitory orders were for everybody. We finally allowed them only after getting directions from the Speaker of the Lok Sabha.

The rally had been successfully prevented and no serious injury was caused to any BJP protester during the police action in different parts of Delhi. I accompanied the PM when he visited senior BJP leaders Shri Atal Bihari Vajpayee and Shri L.K. Advani on the same evening to find out about their welfare.

It was a great day for Delhi Police. We were very happy that we effectively discharged the responsibility entrusted to us by the government and that too without causing any controversy. The PM expressed his happiness to me. The home minister, both MOS, home secretary and LG personally congratulated me and Delhi Police. The remarkable job done by Delhi Police in successfully preventing the BJP's mammoth rally was possible mainly due to the great effort put in by my officers and men, especially Shri S. Ramakrishnan, P.R.S. Brar, Gurucharan Singh, Rampal Singh, Y.S. Dadwal, R. Tewari, Kanwaljit Deol, Dharmendra Kumar, Maxwell Peirera, Alok Verma, Purshottam Agarwal, Bhimsen Bassi, Deepak Mishra, Deepchand, Qamar Ahmed, U.N.B. Rao, M.A. Sayyad, Mukund Upadhyay, Sumdari Nanda, Ujjwal Mishra, Pranab Nanda, S.N. Srivastava, Prabhat Singh, Rajesh Malik, Mahabir Singh and many others. But little did we know that the real challenge was yet to come.

Sometime in late March/early April, I got the first notice from the Parliament secretariat relating to the breach of privilege, directing me to explain my conduct regarding the allegations mentioned in the notice. This was only a start. Thereafter, I received a series of notices from the Parliament secretariat. In all 34 notices came to me. While I figured in all the notices, in about six or seven notices my officers i.e., one additional CP (IG rank) and four or five deputy commissioners were also included by name. The fact that 34 privilege motion notices for one incident were served to one officer, was unheard of. I did not check the Guinness World Records. We immediately started preparing our replies and a team headed by a senior officer was deputed to complete the task in consultation with constitutional experts. We knew that the privilege committee of Parliament was like a court and could recommend appropriate action against persons found guilty of breach of parliamentary privileges. The normal practice had been for the government to accept the recommendations and the follow-up action taken. It was a very sensitive matter and needed meticulous preparations and consultation with experts to prepare an appropriate response.

However, after a few days, I got a phone call (I do not remember the date) from Lok Sabha Speaker Shri. Shivraj Patil asking me to appear before the privilege committee that afternoon. I requested him that my appearance needed a lot of preparations and I should be given time, which was the normal practice. But he was very adamant and insisted that the committee meeting had been fixed and I should appear before the committee in the afternoon. He also asked me to bring my officers that were named in the notices. Since the Speaker was very insistent, I had no other option. I reached the Parliament House, along with my officers. Some of my officers were slightly nervous, but I told them that they need not worry, since I was there with them to face the committee. While I was maintaining a very brave face and assuring my officers, the fact was that I was under great pressure. This was my first appearance before a privilege committee and I had also learned that unlike courts, they do not follow a definite procedure. A lot depends on the mood of the members of the committee which made it all the more unpredictable. Secondly, I thought that while I had still eight years of service left, had reached a certain level (DG rank) in my service, the officers, who were called along with me, had many years to go. In fact, some of them had put in only 10 or 12 years of service. I thought that it was my responsibility to protect them for their bona fide performance of duty and ensure that their careers were not jeopardized in any way.

I, therefore, decided that I would appear alone before the committee and try to convince them that since I, as the head of Delhi Police, had appeared before them, they need not call other junior officers, as I was responsible for their conduct. The officers were instructed to wait in the Speaker's visitors' chamber and were told to come inside only if I were to call them.

I appeared alone before the committee, which was being presided over by Smt. Vijay Raje Scindia, MP and senior vice president of the BJP; the remaining members of the committee were other women MPs of the Lok Sabha. The committee was to consider only 11 out of the 34 notices. Naturally, the first question was where my other officers for whom notices had also been issued were. I requested the committee that I should be allowed to make a submission in this regard. But before I could speak, the other members started expressing their grievances. Their tone was very aggressive and they were full of anger. I heard them patiently. Thereafter, with the permission of the chairperson, I started making my submission. The first point I made was that the order prohibiting the rally was issued by me after very careful consideration and I was convinced about its legality and appropriateness. Secondly, my officers only implemented my orders and did not exceed the scope of these orders in any way. On this, the chairperson intervened and observed that how could I say this, since the police were taking action against the demonstrators at different places in Delhi and I could not be at all the places at once. I informed her that my officers were continuously informing me about the developments in different places and the actions taken by them. In all cases, suitable instructions were issued by me. This could be proved through our control room records. Meanwhile one of the committee members mentioned that the policeman who misbehaved with her was from Punjab Police and not Delhi Police. I immediately told the chairperson that while police forces from different states and CPOs were deployed that day, they were acting under our banner and their conduct was our responsibility. I told the committee that since as head of the force I was responsible for the conduct and performance of my officers and was prepared to take this responsibility, my officers need not be asked to appear before the committee. The chairperson asked me to wait for a while and started discussing the matter with the other members.

Somehow, I felt that I had not been able to convince the committee and therefore, I got up and requested the chairperson that I needed a sheet of paper, which was ordered. But she asked me why I required the paper. I very politely submitted that probably I had not been able to convince the committee about what I had said and therefore I wanted to give in writing that for all alleged omissions and commissions of Delhi Police in handling the demonstration on 25 February 1993, I am personally and totally responsible and that all actions were taken as per my orders. There was a pin-drop silence and then the chairperson observed that I need not give anything in writing and I should wait for a while.

I sat down on a sofa, which was lying a little away from the place of the meeting. I could not hear the discussion, which took place among the members. After about 10 minutes, the chairperson called me and gracefully observed that they were very happy and satisfied with my reply. The committee felt that while I could not be at all places of action, since I had owned the responsibility for all the actions of the police for the said day, they had decided to drop all 11 privilege notices against me and my officers.

I could not believe what had just happened. Since the committee members were mostly from the Opposition and appeared quite annoyed in the beginning, I was expecting some adverse observations against me and my officers. I profusely thanked the chairperson and other members of the committee. All of them appeared to be satisfied with my explanation.

In the course of time, the remaining privilege committee notices were also resolved.

The crisis created by the Privilege Committee notices had been sorted out without any damage to Delhi Police and to my officers. I heaved a sigh of relief.

19

PREVENTING A POTENTIAL COMMUNAL RIOT

After the demolition of the Babri Masjid, in 1992, communal riots broke out in different parts of the country. The people and media expected serious communal riots, including arson, looting and vandalism in Delhi, especially in the walled city area. But detailed advance planning, strategic deployment of force in communally sensitive areas, effective preventive action, timely enforcement of curfew in affected areas and round-the-clock, heavy police patrolling under the supervision of senior police officers kept the situation under total control and not even a stone was pelted in the walled city during this period. We had opposed induction of Army for handling the situation and requested that Delhi Police should be trusted and given a fair chance. It was accepted by the government. When this news spread in the force, it invoked their sense of honour. My officers and men took it as a challenge and ensured that the situation remain under control. The fact that the walled city of Delhi remained totally peaceful was not only a pleasant surprise for the government, but also for the media and the people. On 7 December, which was a day after the Babri Masjid demolition, both national and international media, print and electronic, had assembled in the old city area near Jama Masjid—the expected place for trouble. But alert Delhi Police officers and men were successful in maintaining peace and did not allow any untoward incident to occur. We maintained high level of preventive patrolling and deployment of pickets at strategic locations. The intelligence unit was also keeping a close watch on the developments and movements of people, especially communal leaders. Even minor rumours were being looked into. We ensured that the 'sarafa market' (one of the biggest in the country) at Dariba Kalan, Chandni Chowk, remained open and functional throughout this highly charged period. It was a strategic confidence building measure. After about 10 days, we started relaxing the police arrangements in phases. While it took about a month to resume normal policing, special pickets were placed at sensitive points and striking reserve force was kept at some police stations in central and north districts as a precautionary measure. The walled city, centre of all communal tensions and riots in the past, remained completely peaceful for next 50 days after the demolition of Babri Masjid.

On 27 January, around noon, three communal incidents of very serious nature with potential to turn into a big riot took place in the area of police stations of Dariyaganj and Jama Masjid in central district. All three venues were quite close to each other. It all started with an Imam of a masjid, located near Tiraha Bairam Khan, alleging that some miscreants had torn the pages of the holy Quran kept in an open shelf in the masjid. A crowd of about a thousand agitated people from the affected community gathered there and started shouting provocative slogans. This area was located behind Golcha cinema. The second incident took place in Kucha Chehlan where some miscreants had vandalized a temple and damaged four to five idols kept there. In the thirdincident, a few shops in Bazaar Chitli Qabar area belonging to Hindus were burnt. Agitated crowd of one community along with some local leaders had gathered at these two places. While the police had managed to keep the city peaceful, the communal situation in the county was still quite tense. The BJP's call for a massive rally at the Boat Club (Rajpath) in Delhi had further fuelled it. The police were already under pressure due to Republic Day celebrations which were scheduled till 29 January. The situation needed to be dealt and controlled quickly and effectively as both communities had their reasons to be agitated and were capable of showcasing their anger in any way.

While special police arrangements made in the aftermath of Babri demolition had been withdrawn to a great extent, the entire police force was still in 'action mode' and without any loss of time our reserve forces from different locations and the local police stations staff moved to the spot. Additional CP Shri P.R.S. Brar reached the first spot and DCP Central covered the second and third spot which were adjacent to each other. I had just reached Le Meridien Hotel for a wedding lunch of a friend's son. Before I could get down from my car, I got a crash message from the control room regarding these incidents and I left the place for Jama Masjid police station. On my way, I was given the location of Kucha Chehlan, where the mandir had been vandalized. DCP Central Shri Purshottam Agarwal was already there. I directed him to disperse the agitated crowd collected there and instructed my staff to immediately remove the broken idols with the help of the pujari. They were taken to police station in our vehicles. The trustees of the temple were advised to reinstall the new idols in the next two days. The continued presence of broken idols at the site was source of provocation. We spotted Naib Imam of Jama Masjid coming towards the site along with some followers. Immediately, a police officer was sent to firmly advise him to go back, which he accepted. The first incident had been very tactfully handled by the Additional CP Shri Brar although he had a very small force at that time at his disposal. The crowd there had tried to indulge in some stone pelting, but the firm and quick action by Shri Brar did not allow the situation to escalate. Later on, it was found that probably a monkey, who was looking for some eatables, had torn the holy Quran.

The quick response of local police, fast movement of reserves, initiatives exhibited by the officers at the spot, leadership displayed by DCP Central Shri Purushottam Agarwal and the Additional CP Shri P.R.S. Brar were a matter of great satisfaction to me. The force was now fully geared to handle critical situations at their own level. The hard work of our team and the detailed planning were yielding results. Nothing could be more satisfying for a police chief than this. I spoke to LG, Union home secretary and the home minister and apprised them about the quick response of the Delhi Police and the initiative taken by my officers. A potential serious communal riot was successfully averted in time and situation was brought under control.

The Delhi Police had done its job well, yet again.

20

SAVING THE GOVERNMENT FROM EMBARRASSMENT—ALLEGATIONS OF HARSHAD MEHTA

Harshad Mehta's name, a well-known stockbroker from Bombay (now Mumbai), who was charged with numerous financial crimes during the investigation of 1992 security scam, is now well known thanks to TV shows and a film documenting his life. I thought that it is my duty to put the correct facts in front of people, since I played an important role in sorting out this very sensational controversy.

In June 1993, Harshad Mehta made a sensational disclosure during a press conference that he had paid ₹1 crore to Prime Minister Shri Narsimha Rao at his official residence on 4 November 1991, at 10.45 a.m. He also mentioned that the meeting was arranged by Shri Satpal Mittal, a powerful MP known for his influential contacts, and his son Shri Sunil Mittal, who also accompanied him for this meeting. Their car, which was checked twice after entering the premises, was allowed to go inside up to Shri R.K. Khandekar's (PS to PM) office. In Shri Khandekar's office, he shifted the money which he was carrying in two bags into one big suitcase and took it to the PM's chamber. After a while, PM Shri Narsihma Rao came there and blessed them. The meeting had been a short one.

The disclosure by Harshad Mehta at the press conference was potentially explosive. He also mentioned his cash withdrawals of big amounts from banks before proceeding to Delhi. There had never been such a spate of withdrawals of large amounts earlier from his bank accounts. Harshad also claimed that the PM was present at the meeting, that the Cabinet Committee on Political Affairs (CCPA) meeting ended at 10.30 a.m. and the Pakistani delegation met the PM at 11.15 a.m. This implied that the PM was so desperate to get the money that in between he dashed home, collected the cash and dashed back to his office. Later on, Harshad also released a tape containing a telephonic conversation between him and Sunil Mittal (Satpal Mittal's son) in which he had asked Sunil to go to Shri Khandekar's house and remind him about their meeting on 4 November 1991. Meanwhile, Shri Ram Jethmalani, Harshad Mehta's formidable lawyer, known for his dramatic flourish, demanded confiscation of the visitors' book from the PM's house as well as the records of telephone calls. The SPG, which was in charge of security at the PM's residence, informed that the visitors book is only kept for two months as they didn't have the infrastructure to store it. I had handled VVIP security for a long time and at different stages of my service, therefore, I felt that this was not a professionally convincing statement.

It was stated on the PM's behalf that his schedule on that day, i.e., 4 November 1991 included a customary Monday meeting with the then president, Shri R. Venkatraman. This was a breakfast meeting at 9.15 a.m., followed by a meeting of CCPA at 10 a.m., a meeting with a Pakistani delegation around 10.45 a.m., and a series of other official appointments thereafter. Harshad's counsel Shri Mahesh Jethmalani said that there was no official record of these meetings. This was not correct, as record of the CCPA meetings is kept both in the PM's secretariat and at the Cabinet secretary's office. The engagement with Pakistani delegation had been corroborated by former foreign minister of Pakistan, Mr Agha Shahi, who had attended the meeting. The prime minister publicly denied the allegation and said that no money was handed over to him. 'I will emerge out of this trial by fire in the same manner as Sita did,' he declared. However, Harshad's account of the meeting and the details he provided in the affidavit seemed, on the face of it, quite authentic. A Joint Committee of Parliament (JPC) had been announced to probe the matter and was asked to give its report by a date in July.

While as CP Delhi I was not directly concerned with this matter, I was quite intrigued by the fact that there was no authentic record of the PM's movements on 4 November. This was beyond my understanding. The fact that the SPG could not produce the visitors' book for the relevant date was also not convincing. I had worked for almost three years as DCP Security in the Delhi Police. At that time there was no SPG and the PM's entire security, i.e., at the residence, office, functions and on the route was the responsibility of my unit and therefore I was fully aware of the system in this regard. The position changed in 1985 when the SPG was created and the security of PM at his residence, office and the proximate security was taken over by the SPG. But the route and the security of the outer cordon were still with local police, in this case, Delhi Police. The security unit, Traffic Branch, district police and the Central Police Control Room were involved in the route arrangements. All movements of the PM and his carcade were announced at the wireless network of different units of Delhi Police and were meticulously recorded. This practice had been followed during my tenure as DCP security also. So, I asked Shri Mukund Upadhyaya, DCP police control room, and Shri K.P. John, DCP police communication, to check the records of the PM's movements on 4 November, and prepare a chart giving details of his movements supported by entries in the logbooks.

So far, the evidence produced by Harshad Mehta in his affidavit and subsequent statements was only circumstantial. The key witnesses, who he claimed were present at the meeting with the PM at 7, Race Course Road, were either dead—as in the case of Shri Satpal Mittal, MP—or had denied any involvement. He had not been able to provide any other evidence showing the involvement of the PM. But doubt had been created about the integrity of the PM. The JPC was looking into it and was tasked to give its report in a time-bound manner.

DCP Shri Upadhyaya prepared his report tracing the PM's movements on 4 November, supported by the relevant entries in the concerned logbooks of different police units. The log was as under—

9.12 a.m.: Left residence for Rashtrapati (RP) Bhawan
9.16 a.m.: Reached RP Bhawan
9.55 a.m.: Left RP Bhawan for office (South Block)
9.56 a.m.: Reached office (South Block)
1.12 p.m.: Left office for residence
1.16 p.m.: Reached residence
4.50 p.m.: Left residence for office (South Block)
4.55 p.m.: Reached office (South Block)
8.27 p.m.: Left office for residence

We had collected these entries from 15 different points, where it was recorded. This had definitely and conclusively proved the PM's movements on that day. He was present in his office at 10.45 a.m. on that day and was nowhere near 7, Race Course Road, where Harshad Mehta had alleged that he had paid the money contained in a suitcase to the PM in the presence of Shri Satpal Mittal, his son Shri Sunil Mittal and Shri Khandekar. This also disproved the allegation of Shri Mahesh Jethmalani and Harshad Mehta that there was no record of the PM's meeting on that day implying that he could have dashed off to his residence during that time. Had it been so, the PM's movements from his office and back would have been on record of various control rooms of Delhi Police. The evidence produced by us had established the presence of the PM at his office, at the relevant time, beyond doubt.

I took the entire record with me to the MHA and met Shri N.N. Vohra, the then home secretary. Initially, he could not believe what I told him, but when I showed him the various entries in the logbooks he was convinced. He immediately took me to Shri Rajesh Pilot, MOS, IS, who took no time to realize the importance of this evidence. It was decided to go to the PM along with the home minister. At the PM's residence, the whole evidence collected through various running logbooks was shown to him. He was satisfied and naturally happy. Thereafter, we returned. The entire records were still with me.

The same day, in the late evening, the PM's PS visited my residence and requested me to accompany him to meet the PM. I once again explained all the evidence to the PM and showed various supporting entries in the logbooks. I also told him that these are running documents and their authenticity cannot be doubted. The logs are maintained at so many different places that it is virtually impossible to tamper with them. In face of this evidence, the entire story of Harshad Mehta fell flat. The PM was very happy and looked relieved.

It was decided that a statement on behalf of the PM should be prepared for submission before the JPC. It should not only deny the allegation, but should clearly mention that at the alleged time of the transaction on that date, the PM was not at his residence, but was busy with his official programmes and engagements at the Rashtrapati Bhawan and then at his office in South Block. The statement, along with evidence, was duly submitted to the JPC, which after carefully considering the evidence closed the matter. PM Shri Narsihma Rao was given a clean chit. After JPC closed the matter, I took an appointment with the PM and carried the entire case record to his residence. I told him that he might like to keep the record in his custody considering its value. As per police rules, it could be destroyed. PM, in the presence of his PS, told me that he trusts me and I should keep the records with me. The PM's trust in me made me feel really happy.

The whole controversy involving a VVIP of international importance was resolved by the initiative of a person, who was neither asked to do it nor was it his direct concern.

21

MAINTAINING DIGNITY OF CONSTITUTIONAL INSTITUTIONS

The role and responsibility of the police force under 'commissioner of police system'* is much wider and undivided as compared to police set-ups in areas where this system is not in practice. This empowers the police to take its own view and initiative on various public issues having implications on 'public order'. Besides its conventional responsibilities of maintaining law and order and controlling crime, the police has to play a very important role in assisting the state in ensuring normal peaceful life to its citizens, creating environment where various government departments can carry out their normal functioning, maintaining dignity and sanctity of constitutional institutions, etc.

It was sometime in 1994 that our special branch (intelligence unit) got information from UP Police that Shri Kalyan Singh, an important BJP leader and former CM of UP, would be reaching Delhi by train along with his followers

---

*This refers to police commissionerate system.

(a little more than 2,000 people) to protest in front of the Supreme Court. In fact, this information was received in the morning, when Shri Kalyan Singh and his supporters were to arrive. They wanted to demonstrate and protest in front of the Supreme Court against some adverse observations, which the Hon'ble Court had made against the former CM of UP in a matter relating to the demolition of Babri Masjid at Ayodhya.

As usual, the New Delhi district police started planning arrangements for regulating the protest procession/rally and at the venue of the demonstration. I spoke to additional CP, New Delhi range, and asked him whether there had been any such demonstration or a protest rally in front of the Supreme Court in the past. He was not aware. An experienced ACP, Shri Tarlochan Singh Bhalla, who had spent a lot of time in New Delhi district, also confirmed that he could not recall any such event in the last few years. I told my officers that while people have democratic right to demonstrate/protest and express their grievances against executive authorities, political or bureaucratic, elected representative, private establishments, etc., this could not be allowed in the case of a judicial institution like the Supreme Court or the high court. If somebody was not satisfied with their decision, there was a well laid legal procedure for its redressal. Any such demonstration or rally is absolutely futile. It is the responsibility of the state to maintain the dignity of the constitutional institution like the Supreme Court and high courts, which is to be discharged through the state police.

I immediately conveyed my decision to disallow the rally and ordered my officers to stop it. By this time, Shri Kalyan Singh and his supporters were already proceeding on Barakhamba Road. The police stopped them at Mandi House Chowk and conveyed my decision. Shri Kalyan Singh was quite surprised and after arguing for some time with police officers on the spot, he started contacting local BJP leaders. After a while, I got a phone call from a very senior national leader of the BJP, Shri L.K. Advani, who objected to the police action. He contended that Shri Kalyan Singh's supporters had a democratic right to demonstrate and to convey their grievances to the court. It took some time to convince him about the correct position. But I was absolutely firm on my stand. I also told him that I would not have objected had they come to demonstrate against any executive authority. We were thus successful in persuading the BJP leaders and their supporters to peacefully disperse.

This had given a clear message to political parties that Delhi Police would not permit in future any demonstration or protest rally in front of the Supreme Court or high court. We could thus maintain and protect the dignity of a constitutional institution.

22

UTTARAKHAND RALLY AND A MISCHIEVOUS INCIDENT THAT FOLLOWED

The movement for the statehood of Uttarakhand was in its most volatile phase in 1994 when it touched its high point. The issue of reservation for OBCs acted as a precipitating factor and for the first time, this agitation crystallized into a mass movement. On 29 September 1994, a big rally was organized at Dehradun and approximately 70,000 people participated in the rally. A similar rally was held at Almora too.

Uttarakhand Sanyukt Sangharsh Samiti (USSS) called for a rally at the Boat Club, Rajpath, Delhi, on 2 October 1994. Thousands of activists from all parts of Uttarakhand left for Delhi on the evening of 1 October. The activists from the Kumaon region reached Delhi without being held up anywhere by the police. But the protesters from Garhwal were stopped by UP Provincial Armed Constabulary (PAC) near Rampur Bypass at Hardwar-Muzaffarnagar Road on the pretext of checking for arms. The protesters tried to break the police cordon several times, as they were being harassed unnecessarily by the police. The tussle lasted for a few hours. It was also alleged that the women participants were dragged out of the buses and beaten up with rifle butts. Some women were allegedly molested and raped. Thereafter, the police started firing, killing around eight persons and seriously injuring more than a 100 demonstrators. The news of this incident created a lot of anxiety and concern in Delhi, especially, because of the proposed rally by Uttarakhand activists on the same day, i.e., 2 October. Since we had banned the holding of rallies/demonstrations at the Boat Club, we decided to stop the rally on the Ring Road behind the Red Fort. The organizers were informed and they reluctantly accepted.

At about 10.00 a.m., on 2 October, when I was getting ready to leave for reviewing the police arrangements behind the Red Fort, I got a call from the PM's PS on my RAX. The PM expressed his concern about the proposed rally. He was especially worried because of the mishandling of protesters at Muzaffarnagar and about the alleged incidents of rapes and killings in police firing. He wanted me to keep these facts in mind and ensure that the rally was handled with tact and caution. I told him that I was aware of what had happened at Muzaffarnagar and was, therefore, leaving for supervising the police arrangements. The PM immediately observed that 'if you are going yourself, then I would not like to say anything further'. He expressed his full confidence in my ability to handle the agitation which was a matter of great satisfaction for me.

About 30,000–35,000 people collected for the rally behind the Red Fort. They were shocked to learn about the happenings at Muzaffarnagar, where some women were molested and raped and few demonstrators were killed in the police firing. This had changed the mood of the crowd. They were hurt and annoyed and became very aggressive. We had closed and barricaded all roads and lanes connecting the Ring Road to the town and the agitators had no other option except to assemble behind the Red Fort. We had not deployed any police force inside this enclosed area, but had very strong police arrangements all around the barricades. Some police parties were posted on the top of the fort walls with tear gas to keep the demonstrators under check. They were initially aggressive and violent. They set on fire a vacant traffic police kiosk and tried to pelt stones at some police vehicles, which was controlled. At the site, various factions of the demonstrators clashed with each other to occupy central stage. They also tried to break the police cordon at several places, but did not succeed.

One of the factions gave a call to march towards Parliament House to gherao it. The police used tear gas shell and lathi-charged to control them and finally finding it not possible to proceed further and enter the town, the rallyists started dispersing. Delhi Police had been successful in controlling and containing the agitation within the designated area without causing any serious injury to anyone and also without creating any controversy. Thereafter, I left for my office with instructions to DCPs (north and central district) to ensure peaceful dispersal of demonstrators. I gave a detailed report on call to LG Delhi and to the Union home secretary and then I briefed the press.

Around 8.00 p.m., I got a phone call from the PM on my RAX. Uttarakhand movement leader Maj. Gen. (Retd) B.G. Khanduri had complained to the PM that Delhi Police had fired on the demonstrators behind the Red Fort. On my informing him that nothing like this had happened, the PM wanted me to speak to Maj. Gen. Khanduri and clarify the matter. I spoke to Khanduri Ji and told him that I had been at the spot of the demonstration throughout and I had neither heard any firing, nor did anyone report any firing to me. Probably firing of some tear gas shells from the Red Fort wall had created this confusion. Khanduri Ji had nothing concrete to support his allegation. I told him to speak to PM. I also informed the PMO that clarification had been given and the allegation of firing was incorrect. At about 9.30 p.m., the PM again spoke to me on RAX and told me that some news agency had informed him about a very damaging statement made by UP CM Shri Mulayam Singh Yadav blaming Delhi Police for mishandling the Uttarakhand agitations in UP. He desired that I should find out more about this and give the required clarification to the press. He also wanted me to report to him after doing the needful. I spoke to some news agencies and a few press representatives and clarifications giving the correct position were issued. The PM was informed.

On that day, PM spoke to me 10 times on RAX. I was naturally feeling happy that the PM trusted me and thought that I could deliver the results. But I could not anticipate that this would create a serious problem for me.

The next day morning, I wanted to inform the home minister about previous night's happenings, i.e., the PM's directions regarding an allegation of firing made by Maj. Gen. (Retd) Khanduri, follow-up action taken by me and clarifications given to press regarding an allegation made by UP CM Shri Mulayam Singh Yadav. I tried to contact the home minister's office, but I was told that he was not free. This was a little unusual. Meanwhile, Shri V.K. Jain, special secretary, rang me up and wanted me to come urgently to MHA. When I met him, he informed me that the home minister was very annoyed with me since I had been talking directly with the PM and had not kept him informed. I told him the whole story about what happened including the fact that all the 10 calls were made by the PM and not me. I also told him that I was aware that the home minister retires for the night around 9.00 p.m. and did not like to be disturbed after that. Since all this happened between 9.00 p.m. and a few minutes past 11.00 p.m., and the matter had been settled, I thought I would inform the home minister in the morning. While I was in Shri Jain's room, the home secretary called me and informed me about the home minister's unhappiness. I explained the facts to him also. But I was surprised that none of the two senior officers took initiative to get the matter sorted out after knowing the facts. The home minister's personal secretary also told me that the home minister did not wish to meet me.

I was intrigued as to how the home minister had learned about the PM's calls to me. Meanwhile, I obtained the details of RAX calls between the PM and myself indicating the details about who had been the caller. The RAX exchange records made it clear that all calls had been made by the PM and not me. Meanwhile, somebody from the home minister's residential staff rang me up to say that on the relevant night, Shri Matang Singh, MOS in the Union Cabinet had met the home minister late in the night and he had heard that he was mentioning my name during the conversation. Now things were absolutely clear to me. Shri Matang Singh, who had a very controversial reputation, was very unhappy with me since I had refused to accept his recommendations regarding the posting of SHOs. My information was that he was taking money for this. I took the details of the call records given to me by the RAX exchange and went to see the home minister. Without waiting for the home minister's permission, I entered his chamber. He was quite surprised, but before he could say anything I told him that both special secretary and home minister conveyed to me that the home minister was very unhappy with me because I had spoken to the PM directly and had not kept him in the loop. I told him that this was wrong and showed him the call records given by the RAX exchange. It was now clear that all the calls had been made by the PM. I further told him that since that day the matter had been settled and it was late in the night, I thought that instead of disturbing him at odd hours, I would inform him the next morning. I also informed him that I was aware of Shri Matang Singh having misrepresented the facts to him and also explained to him the reasons for Shri Matang Singh's unhappiness.

The misunderstanding was cleared and the home minister was satisfied. Thereafter our relations normalized and business as usual started. I informed both special secretary, IS, and home secretary about it. A few years back, I learned that Shri Matang Singh was arrested by Assam Police on serious criminal charges and was sent to jail. I was not surprised.

Intrigues and misrepresentation of facts by unscrupulous persons can sometimes create serious problems, but if you take the bull by the horn and put the correct facts in front of the concerned authority, the chances of you retrieving the situation are very high.

23

BUMPER PROMOTIONS

When I took over as commissioner of police, Delhi, in February 1992, Delhi Police was facing difficult times. Islamic terrorists and Sikh militants were disturbing the peace in the city, land mafias aided by UP gangsters were threatening ordinary citizens and a series of dacoities-cum-murders by criminals of Padhi and Bawaria tribes had created a scare among the people. The unresolved Babri Masjid dispute had vitiated the communal environment in the country, especially in UP and Delhi.

The morale of the force was at its lowest and it had lost faith in its leadership. But due to some daring initiative exhibited by my officers and men and their exemplary performance in a short span, we were substantially successful in controlling the situation and restoring the confidence of the people in their police. The force also started having faith in their leadership. Their good work was being appropriately rewarded including 'out of turn promotions' in deserving cases.

Toning up Delhi Police

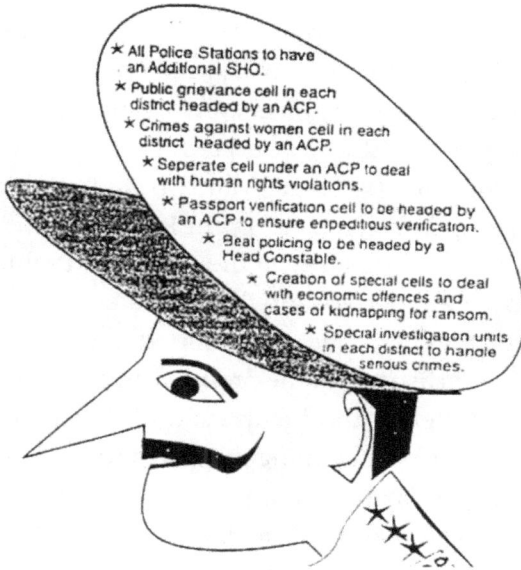

* All Police Stations to have an Additional SHO.
* Public grievance cell in each district headed by an ACP.
* Crimes against women cell in each district headed by an ACP.
* Seperate cell under an ACP to deal with human rights violations.
* Passport verification cell to be headed by an ACP to ensure enpeditious verification.
* Beat policing to be headed by a Head Constable.
* Creation of special cells to deal with economic offences and cases of kidnapping for ransom.
* Special investigation units in each district to handle serious crimes.

Reprinted from The Indian Express, *New Delhi, 9 June 1994*

During my visits to the police stations and occasional night rounds, I had an opportunity to interact with my field officers like SHOs and SIs/ASIs of the police stations and to understand their perception regarding various aspects of policing including their operational problems. I found that most of them were overworked and were going to their residences only once in three to four days. This was likely to adversely affect their personality. Those who visit their family and spend time with them were likely to retain their human touch. Officers staying alone in the police stations were more prone to acquiring wrong habits.

I also observed that except for those who had the opportunity to show some good work, the majority were lacking enthusiasm and had very little desire to take initiative or perform. On my insistence, some of them mentioned stagnation and lack of promotional prospects. They quoted examples of other states and central police organizations, where people in similar ranks were getting promotions in time. I thought that this was a serious matter and needed immediate consideration on a priority basis for improving the efficiency and performance of Delhi Police.

I discussed this matter with the concerned senior officers in the police headquarters and then deputed Shri U.N.B. Rao, the then DCP HQs, an officer committed to the welfare of the force, to study all aspects of the problem and submit his report at the earliest. Before the finalization of the report, we had quite a few discussions among ourselves to examine various possibilities. Shri U.N.B. Rao produced a very well deliberated report, covering all aspects of the issue including a set of convincing arguments in support of the proposal. Once the final draft was ready, I took an appointment with the Union home secretary to discuss our proposal before its formal submission. Shri Madhav Godbole, the then home secretary, was quite happy with the performance of Delhi Police and indicated his willingness to support our proposals, which would improve the professional efficiency and welfare of the force. The home secretary, who also had experience working in the finance department, saw the proposal and observed that he did not anticipate any problem in its approval. He advised me to submit it through the government of NCT of Delhi.

The main features of our proposal were as follows:

- The pyramidal structure of the rank and file got distorted due to haphazard sanctions of posts. The number of the posts at the higher level was not increased corresponding to the augmentation in the lower ranks, resulting in acute stagnation in the feeder line and also created problems in ensuring the needed supervisory control.

- There were growing frustrations among different ranks, i.e., constable, SIs and inspectors, for not having proper promotional avenues. It was being felt all the more because the neighbouring states and Central Police Organizations were offering better promotional opportunities. In Delhi Police, we had SIs with 18 years of service, inspectors with 10 years of service and constables with 25 years of service not yet promoted. This was adversely affecting the morale, performance and output of the Delhi Police, which was responsible for policing the National Capital—having a variety of its special problems.

- The proposed upgradation envisaged the creation of 1,150 posts of head constables in place of 1,150 constables, 390 posts of inspectors instead of an equal number of posts of SIs and 120 posts of assistant commissioners of police in place of 120 inspectors. About 50 posts of women SIs were also upgraded to the rank of inspectors. This would considerably improve the pyramidal structure of command and control in the force. It also fulfilled some related recommendations of the National Police Commission.

- It was also mentioned that similar upgradation had been approved by the government for the Personnel and Training Department, Ministry of Railways and the Intelligence Bureau.

- While preparing the upgradation proposal, every care was taken not to have any big financial burden on the state exchequer. In fact, this was the real strength of our proposal. In police, pay scales had not much variation from rank to rank as compared to the civilian posts. In all these cases, while higher ranks were given to officers and men, the financial costs were only admissible for two increments at the time of fixation of pay in the higher scale. The additional cost was so minimal that it could be met within the existing salary budget of the Delhi Police.

When I met the chief secretary, Delhi government, in connection with our proposal, he told me that his 'experience was that it needed a lot of efforts and persuasion to get even one post of gazetted rank sanctioned from the finance ministry and Delhi Police was proposing 120 new posts of ACPs'. According to him, there was very little chance of getting it approved. I explained to him that since our upgradation proposal was not putting any additional financial burden on the Delhi Government, they should recommend and forward it to the central government. Despite my persistent efforts, the Delhi government took almost a year to forward it to the central government. I had deputed a team of my officers to chase the proposal at every stage. I personally met the expenditure secretary and the then finance minister, Dr Manmohan Singh. The finance minister gave me an appointment during his lunch break. I could explain and convince him of the plight of my officers and men, i.e., our SHOs, who were expected to remain 100 per cent functional 24 hours and visit their family once in three to four days, and our beat patrolling staff, i.e., head constables and constables had to perform almost round the clock duties, which was adversely affecting their efficiency, performance and health. The finance minister was satisfied and in my presence he told the expenditure secretary over the phone to clear the Delhi Police proposal. If I remember correctly, the final approval of our upgradation proposal was received around mid-1994. The preparations to complete the formalities relating to promotions, updating of records of officers and men, holding of DPCs and other related works were undertaken at war footing to implement the upgradation by November 1994. Additional CP, administration, Shri V.N. Singh and his team deserve appreciation for their outstanding work in completing this difficult task perfectly and on time.

The upgradation of about 1,700 officers and men had created history in the Delhi Police. This had no precedent. SIs of nine batches, i.e., from 1977 to 1985 were promoted in one go. Each district DCP was given four extra ACPs to look after the public grievances, crime against women, special investigation unit, etc. All police stations were provided an additional SHO in the rank of inspector. This was a great morale boost for Delhi Police and energized our officers and men working in the field, i.e., constables, SIs and inspectors. These were the ranks that needed better motivation to face the challenges and to accomplish the arduous task entrusted to the police of the national capital. Their improved performance transformed the image of Delhi Police.

Before the above upgradation proposal, three vacancies came up for the rank of additional commissioner of police, but we could not fill the vacancies as the MHA's approval for promotion of eligible officers was awaited. Since this shortage of officers was affecting our work, I convinced the chief secretary and the LG to give higher rank (additional CP) to three senior-most DCPs, whose names had been sent to MHA for approval, so that the work at the supervisory level didn't suffer. It was also decided that till the MHA's approval, these officers would draw salary in the rank of DCP. The Delhi government issued orders giving them higher rank as suggested above. The chief secretary told me that while there was nothing wrong in doing it, it had no precedent. The officers who were promoted also could not believe it.

Few months after rejoining Delhi Police as CP, I had moved a proposal of ration money for the non-gazetted staff of the police force. I felt that we must create an environment which could motivate the force to put in the excruciatingly long hours of duties, go after criminals and risk their lives in the process. The force personnel must be in good health and fit to deliver the desired results. Before preparing my proposal, I had gone through all earlier proposals to find out as to why they had not been approved. When I took my proposal to the then home secretary, his immediate reaction was that this proposal had been rejected 11 times in the past and now it was the twelfth time. But I requested him to go through it so that I could make appropriate changes, which he thought was necessary. He told me that I appeared to be a very persisting type of a person. I very respectfully replied that it was a 'dharam yudh' for me. I added that while as a government it was his privilege to accept or reject it, I was convinced of the cause I was pursuing and would keep on chasing it till I get final approval. Thereafter, I again sent a revised proposal, but it was kept pending. Meanwhile, the home secretary changed and I had to restart the whole thing. While I could not succeed in this regard due to various reasons, I am glad to observe that Delhi Police was not a loser and one of my successors could get the ration money for our force. He successfully chased the old proposal and did what I couldn't. I am proud of him.

I left Delhi Police about two months after the implementation of the upgradation scheme. I felt contented and happy that I could contribute to the betterment of officers and men who had stood by me during this turbulent period.

24

CHECKING DISREGARD FOR LAW AND MISUSE OF POWERS

When I took over as CP, Delhi, the two immediate tasks before me were to restore the confidence of the people in the police and to create an atmosphere where the force could start having faith in themselves and their leadership. The core of any team and its success is faith amongst its members.

At that time, Sikh militants and J&K terrorists were disrupting peace in the city, communal tension due to the Babri Masjid dispute was at its peak, land mafia backed by UP gangsters were threatening the citizens and people's confidence in the police had been shaken up due to the dreadful strikes of the Bawarias and Pardhi gangs. We worked out a strategy and our sincere and persistent efforts resulted in successfully working out the sensational and heinous crime cases. Our specialized teams neutralized the land mafias and dreaded criminal gangs, including terrorist and militant groups, without any blot on the human rights credentials of the Delhi Police. Our well planned and firm handling of the communal situation in the aftermath of the Babri Masjid demolition ensured absolute peace in the walled city. In pursuance of the government's decision, the proposed mammoth rally of the BJP was not allowed. This created confidence in the people towards their police and the force also started having faith in themselves and their leaders.

Police Chief Prepares to Take on Disregards for Law

Reprinted from The Times of India, New Delhi, 15 February 1994

Once the law and order situation became a little normal, I thought that there was an opportunity to prepare the force to deal with other challenges, especially the growing 'disregard for law'. It was equally necessary to control the misuse of powers by the law enforcers as it was not only causing undue harassment to the common people but also tarnishing the image of Delhi Police. Our good work was being undone.

Police force must enjoy the trust of people it is serving.

The disregard for law had various manifestations, e.g., unauthorized encroachment on roads and pavements, violating traffic rules, especially at road crossings, and creating traffic congestion by wrong parking of vehicles, organizing dharnas on road crossings, gheraoing public and private authorities, taking out processions and organizing rallies without police permission. Criminals, exploiting gaps in the criminal justice system, managed obtaining bail in heinous crime cases and again indulging in committing offenses; absence of deterrent action against criminals encouraged lots of young men to commit crimes.

I held a meeting of senior officers and discussed the above issues to form a strategy to systematically control these illegal activities. I told them that the progress of the action taken by each district or unit would be monitored by the senior supervising officers at the police headquarter and I would personally review the progress in the weekly meeting.

Encroachments on pavements and roads by hawkers and roadside shopkeepers had become a big nuisance all over Delhi. Pedestrians were walking on roads exposing themselves to undue risk as pavements/footpaths were occupied by the vendors. At some places, even the central verge was occupied by the vendors. The Chelmsford Road connecting Connaught Place to New Delhi Railway Station was full of such encroachers. These vendors had the backing of the local politicians and there was the connivance of corporation staff and police. We selected several spots all over Delhi and on a selected day 'operation cleaning the roads/pavements' was launched and all encroachments were removed notwithstanding the protests. The SHOs, division officers and beat constables were made personally responsible to ensure that they were not reoccupied. Chelmsford Road was made completely free of encroachments. After a few days, we again launched this operation in other selected areas.

The next step in this drive was to clear two major roads—one connecting south Delhi to north Delhi and the second connecting east Delhi to west Delhi. In addition, all approach roads to railway stations and major hospitals were also selected for clearing of unauthorized encroachments. Strict action was also taken against unauthorized parking lots to reduce congestion. While this drive was highly appreciated by the people and the media, some local politicians felt annoyed as it dried up their regular source of income. I made its monitoring part of my monthly crime review meeting to ensure that both local police and traffic unit remain alert and gains of these drives are not frittered away.

If I remember correctly, sometime in 1993, I issued an order banning dharnas on road crossings, gheraos, mashaal processions and demonstrations at residences of people. These trends indicated disregard for law. Strict instructions were given to local police that any violation of the instructions would result in serious action against the local SHO and it would also reflect the poor supervision by the concerned senior officer. The reason behind these instructions was my experience during my deputation, of watching huge chaos caused by the prolonged dharna at AIIMS crossing during anti-Mandal agitations. Similarly, many instances of public transport buses being set on fire by people carrying mashaals had been reported. I also stopped demonstrations in front of the Supreme Court by a dissatisfied litigant, Shri Kalyan Singh, former UP chief minister, on the grounds that there was a legal procedure to convey their grievances to the court, i.e., filing an appeal. I also did not permit a protest march and rally that was being organized by the president of a national political party (Shri Mulayam Singh Yadav) for the release of a dreaded criminal, who was their party MLA. He was detained by me under NSA which was later confirmed by the Delhi High Court. Both these instances have been discussed separately in other chapters. Similarly, we told organizers of the kisan rally of Shri Mahinder Singh Tikait that their rally would be permitted only on the condition that they would not bring bullock carts, camel carts, raths and jugaads, etc., inside Delhi as it creates traffic jams; they were also asked not to carry lathis and batons more than four feet in length and a complete ban on carrying firearms was put in place. Protection to their leader would be provided by the Delhi Police. In the past, they used to bring about a dozen gunmen for the protection of their leader, which was not only inappropriate but was a little scary. They were told that the venue of their rally would be decided by the police and their rally would not be permitted inside the city. Delhi had had a very bad experience of Shri Tikait's earlier rallies. Our tough stand yielded results and the whole event went according to our instructions.

Our traffic units organized special drives in different parts of the city to curtail violations of traffic rules, especially at road crossings, jumping of traffic lights, over speeding, etc. The cooperation of public volunteers proved very effective. We also wrote to school principals to teach the importance of putting on seat belts in cars and using helmets on two-wheelers to their students with instructions that they, in turn, should persuade their parents and other elders to follow the same. This was a very friendly and effective way of enforcing road safety measures and disseminating information about the same.

Our close and regular monitoring of crime incidents

revealed that quite a few of these heinous crimes were being committed by hardened criminals who, taking advantage of the loopholes in the criminal justice system and also partly due to the connivance, managed to obtain bail. They utilized this opportunity not only to commit crimes but also to threaten the witnesses in criminal cases pending against them. Since this was a very serious trend, I ordered a study in this regard, which revealed that in recent months 17 such dreaded criminals had managed to get bail from the court and all of them again indulged in committing serious heinous offences. Fortunately, our police could arrest all these criminals again. We shared the results of our study with the district judge of Delhi and requested to take the required action.

To effectively control the incident of violent heinous crimes, it was decided to prepare a police station-wise list of all criminals who had committed offenses such as dacoity, robbery, snatching, extortion, knifing, etc., five times in the last three years and to ascertain their current whereabouts in the case that they had been successful in getting bail. If there was a reasonable suspicion of their involvement in fresh crimes, the court should be approached for the cancellation of their bail. The district DCPs were to report police station-wise progress during my weekly meeting. These lists were prepared by the police stations relying on their record and were vetted by the crime branch at the police headquarter. Such action had never been initiated in the past and it had a very deterrent effect on the criminals who were out on bail. Due to constant watch and checking by police, some of them got their bail cancelled and went back to prison. About three to four months after this, we prepared a second list of criminals who had indulged in three such crimes in the last five years. In these cases, local police had to only do their full verification, i.e., their residential addresses, their current occupation and verification of their reputation from the neighbours. These two crime preventive measures proved very effective and had the desired effect on the rate of crime. All these criminals, who formed quite a sizeable number, realized that local police were now not only alert, but were also keeping a close watch on them. This also created a deterrence in the minds of the new entrants in the crime world—that once you commit such a crime, you would be permanently under police watch. Shri N.K. Singh, director, Bureau of Police Research and Development, came to know about the scheme and was so impressed with its effectiveness and impact that he told the Union home minister about it, who called me for discussion. After going through the scheme, he desired that this scheme should be sent to Bombay Police.

During my interaction with members of public and also analysis of complaints received in the Vigilance Branch of police headquarter, I found that few areas where allegations of misuse of powers by police officers/men were normally made were arrests under Section 107/151 or arrests under section 186 & 353 of the IPC. Both these sets of legal provisions are very important—one for maintenance of peace and the other for ensuring the smooth functioning of the government machinery. But quite often they were misused for various reasons. To prevent the misuse, the SHOs were directed to report each arrest U/S 107/151 to his ACP, who after examining the reasons and satisfying himself, would give his approval. In case the ACP felt that arrest was not needed, he would direct the SHO to approach the ACP, designated to hear such cases of preventive action/arrests for his release. Earlier in case of any inquiry, some junior officials would be blamed. In case of action under Section 186/353 IPC, the case would be registered only after the ACP concerned had personally verified the facts and satisfied himself. What prompted me to initiate this action was the complaint of a doctor who was arrested under these provisions on the complaint of a DTC driver. The vigilance inquiry had established that the doctor had been wrongly implicated in the case. These two measures proved very effective and not only brought relief to victims from arbitrary arrests by police but also reduced the complaints on this count. These measures were also given publicity through the media for the general information of the public. The above measures proved very effective in fighting disregard for law and preventing misuse of powers by police. But this was only the beginning and a lot more was to be done.

I needed meaningful support and cooperation of people and a highly motivated and committed police force to achieve a higher level of public satisfaction. One thing that had always hit me hard was the general fear of people in going to the police station, even when they had a genuine complaint. They were scared of the institution which was meant to protect them. Police themselves had to look for their shortcomings. In this background, expecting cooperation from people was a distant dream. I always believed in and stressed on the 'friendly image' of police (Dost Police). In my various briefings to the force personnel, I repeatedly told them that they should conduct themselves in such a manner that the citizens should look upon them as a friend. They should be ready to help those who needed police protection. This would help us in getting their cooperation in preserving peace and maintaining law and order. A few months after my taking over as CP, I had launched Jan Sehyog Abhiyan to seek public support in policing the city and called it Jan Bhagidari. I also motivated police officers and men to be proactive and positive in dealing with people.

In order to reduce the gap between the police and the people, we initiated several measures. One important initiative was making police services accessible to common people at all field levels, i.e., SHO, ACP, DCP, additional CP and CP. I started to hear the people who were coming to police headquarter with their complaints, on a daily basis. My personal staff, with the assistance of the Vigilance Branch of the police headquarter, would take the complaints and note down the name, address and telephone number if any, and very briefly record the main allegations made in the complaint. After I had heard them, they would also record my directions in each case. If the matter was referred to any DCP, an appointment would be fixed with the DCP and the complainant would be informed. Instructions were issued that DCPs must honour these appointments and send very brief action taken reports, wherever required. A proper record of each complaint with proper follow-up action was maintained. Instructions were issued to all field officers to regularly hear people's complaints. We wanted to convey to the people that we are genuinely concerned about them. This system of hearing and redressing public grievances proved very effective and useful.

Once the system of personal hearing of grievances was settled, I started meeting larger groups of people, who were opinion makers, through their associations, such as those of lawyers, doctors, university students, teachers, etc. This has been discussed in detail in some other chapters. The success of these meetings gave me an idea to hold an open-house. The first 'open-house' event was organized in east Delhi covering the entire trans-Jamuna area. Delhi police gave wide publicity through media to the date and timing of the open-house and invited all professional associations of traders, industry owners, shopkeepers, hawkers, transporters, taxi and three wheeler unions, RWAs and the general public. About 2,000–2,500 people attended it. I had gone there with all my senior officers. I told them that the Delhi Police was accountable to them and thereafter reported the performance of Delhi Police in controlling crime and maintaining order in that area. We also discussed the issue relating to traffic movement and congestion, etc., which was a serious concern in that area. In this regard, certain decisions were taken at the spot in consultation with people and conveyed to them. A committee consisting of representatives of residents, shopkeepers and other road users was formed under DCP Traffic to sort out local traffic issues. Complaints relating to individual grievances were taken and they were assured that the written reply would reach them in 10 days. The open-house got a very positive response and the media welcomed it as a confidence-building and pioneering initiative.

Instructions were also issued to PCR vans to tow away stranded vehicles to a nearby safe destination during night time and assist passengers in getting a taxi or three wheelers for reaching their homes. All PCR vans were provided with ropes towing vehicles. The PCR would initiate this action on receiving a call from 100. The call could also be made by standard car owners or by anyone who noticed it. This facility was given sufficient publicity in the newspapers. Its benefit did not remain hidden from the masses. A *sankraman kaksh* [transit room] was provided in the front part of police stations for recording the statement of the witnesses to avoid their possible harassment inside the police station building. The objective was that except suspect or arrested persons nobody else should go inside the police station building, i.e., beyond the police duty room. Women of any age need not be called inside the police station beyond the duty room unless they were duly arrested for which there was a separate set of instructions. We could construct temporary sheds for sankraman kaksh in quite a few police stations. We also started the practice of sending a copy of FIR by post to the complainant's address; this was in response to a common complaint against the police that a copy of the FIR was not being given to the complainants. Initiative taken by the then DCP north, Shri Bhimsen Bassi, needs special mention in this regard.

The renewal of arms licences had been a source of harassment to licence holders everywhere for a long time. Delhi Police computerized the entire arms holder's record and made the date of birth of the licence holder as the renewal date for the license and started sending a reminder along with the renewal form to all arm licence holders a month before the due date. We also wished a 'Happy Birthday' to the licence holder at the time of renewal. This helped in creating a friendly image of the police.

Normally, curfew, irrespective of the justified reasons for enforcing it, causes a lot of inconvenience to the residents of an area. But we tried to transform it into a memorable experience for residents of Old Delhi, when we enforced curfew in some areas of the walled city in Delhi after the demolition of Babri Masjid in 1992. Three days after enforcement of curfew in the area, when the situation had started coming under control, I requested LG to direct MCD authorities in charge of sewage, etc., to use this opportunity to clean the drains/sewage in the entire area, which was not otherwise possible due to heavy movement of people and traffic. The roads, which had heavy layers of dirt settled on them, were cleaned with the help of machines. Similarly, electricity undertaking officers were asked to take advantage of the curfew and complete their long-pending work in the area. We also ensured, right from the first day, that there would be no shortage of essential commodities—vegetables, milk, LPG gas cylinder, etc., in the area under curfew. A system was devised to know the requirement of each area and supply arrangements were made accordingly. Police vehicles carried people to hospitals as and when ambulances were not available. This was a unique and pleasant experience for the residents of the area. An old lady came to me while I was standing outside the Jama Masjid police station and conveyed that the supply of essential items was never so easy even in the normal times and she gave lots of blessings to the police. We utilized this opportunity of curfew to earn goodwill for Delhi Police and create a relationship of trust between the common people and the police force.

Similarly, a lot of measures were initiated to motivate and create a sense of commitment in the force. In a uniformed force or any large organization where the lower ranks or junior staff do not come in contact with senior leadership every day, it is essential for maintaining their morale and commitment to give them confidence that in case of any problems, they had unhindered access to their leader and secondly that their leader has concern for them and their welfare. It is equally important to create trust that there would be objectivity in assessing their performance. In uniform forces, including the police, there is a system of 'orderly room', where force members appear before their seniors for redressal of their grievances. Normally, days for orderly rooms are fixed. But I made a few changes—in case of emergency, the force members could appear on any day and at any time and second, those who came to me for redressal of their grievance would come in my chamber on their own and would not be marched into the room as was the practice. This was done to help them retain their self-respect. I also kept one full day in a month for hearing the grievances of my men. On that day no other work was done including any official meeting. As the DG of the CRPF, I kept afternoon hours of every day for this work, since it was a very large force. It was given wide publicity in the force. No permission, as customary, was required to meet me. They would give their names to my staff officer, who would send them one by one. This enhanced the faith among the team members and the leadership.

The policy relating to transfer and promotion was made quite transparent and everybody who thought that he had been wrongfully denied his promotion was allowed to appear before me. Similarly, at the time of posting of SHOs they were clearly told that their tenure was for three years and if they are transferred before that they could appear before me. Right from the beginning, I followed the practice of calling all those who applied for voluntary retirement for a personal hearing. In case of anybody opting for voluntary retirement due to dissatisfaction with the department, I tried to look into the matter and if possible, provided them relief. I remember when I was additional CP, administration, in Delhi Police, Inspector Sadhu Ram Chowdhary, a very senior and efficient police officer applied for voluntary retirement. He was repeatedly overlooked for promotion to the rank of ACP on the grounds of a departmental inquiry pending against him. This inquiry had never been started for some reason or the other for seven to eight years. No action was taken on his repeated representations and therefore he applied for voluntary retirement. He was an excellent police officer and had been SHO of many important police stations. I brought the whole case to the notice of the then police commissioner and he asked me to review the case. As a result, he was promoted to ACP and his seniority was restored. In a uniform force, such stories spread very quickly and restore faith in leadership.

In Delhi Police, the non-gazetted staff gets one extra month's salary to compensate them for holidays and Sundays when they had to be on duty. Just before I took over, due to some indifferent handling of the matter by the Administration Branch of the police headquarter, a wrong report was sent to Delhi administration and the MHA that their additional salary was now not needed and order stopping it reached police headquarter. It was a Saturday (holiday) when I was entering the police headquarter and I heard some murmuring among the staff indicating resentment. I was surprised to find that due to some wrong reporting by the police headquarter, the benefit of an additional month's salary had been stopped. I immediately spoke to the then Union home secretary in this regard, admitted negligence on the part of police headquarter and requested him to intervene to stop the implementation of this order. On my request, the home secretary first stayed the order, which was then regularized in due course of time. Similarly, for removing stagnation in promotion, which was creating a lot of dissatisfaction especially in the ranks of constables, SIs and inspectors, we got sanction for about 1,700 posts in higher ranks by surrendering posts in the lower ranks and provided relief to the stagnating cadres.

A lot of rewards, including out of turn promotions, were given to policemen and officers, who had shown rare courage and had taken effective action against dreaded criminals without caring for the risk to their lives. Head constable Shri Krishan of PCR, who chased a hardcore terrorist resulting in his arrest despite suffering two bullet injuries, was given double out of turn promotion with the LG's approval; there was complete objectivity in giving this recognition. Media also helped in giving adequate publicity to these rewards.

In CRPF, I had to fight for getting better pay scales for the entire paramilitary forces, which was ultimately achieved. However, I had to pay the cost as I was transferred from the post of DG, CRPF, due to some mischievous propaganda against me. But even today the force remembers the DG for the benefits, which they got due to his persistent efforts. In CRPF, due to some inefficient accounting system, the field staff used to get their salary only in the third or fourth week of the month. This was a source of permanent grievance. For rectification of the procedure, I had to meet Comptroller and Auditor General (CAG) to obtain his approval for changing our accounting system. Now the salaries are credited to their account on the first day of the month.

My practice of meeting the force members both at the headquarters and during my tours yielded the desired results. During sammelans with the force, I would repeatedly tell them to come out with their grievances and tried to provide relief, wherever possible, on the spot. I also directed all senior officers of the force to hold such sammelans regularly. In some cases in the past, aggrieved members, due to mental pressure, had fired on their seniors. No such incident took place in my time. I also organized a welfare conference at the force level, where representatives of all ranks, such as cooks, water carriers, safaiwallas, lower and upper subordinates of the entire force had participated as delegates. The Union home minister himself presided over the conference and shared a lunch with all the delegates. The home minister also observed that this was the first time that he has seen such a welfare conference in any uniform force. He had been a very well-known labour leader of all India fame.

The force must feel assured that their leader has

confidence in their abilities to achieve the task entrusted to them. When LG Delhi suggested induction of Army after Babri demolition, I opposed it on the grounds that he was failing Delhi Police by not giving them a fair chance to prove themselves. I was confident that my force was competent to handle the situation. The LG very graciously agreed with me. Similarly, there should be a relationship of trust between the team members and their leader. The leader must, with his actions and initiatives, convince the team members that he has broad enough shoulders to carry their responsibilities and protect them for their bona fide performance of duties, including honest mistakes. The force members should also be confident that he has a large heart with no place for personal prejudices. A well-motivated and committed force achieves amazing results. My experience in Delhi Police, RPF and CRPF corroborate this.

25

SOME INTERESTING
INCIDENTS AND FACTS

1. Owning Responsibility

As deputy commissioner, security, in Delhi Police, I was responsible for the security of our VVIPs and a large number of protectees, including visiting foreign heads of state governments. This included His Holiness (HH) the Dalai Lama, who was permanently staying at Dharamshala, Himachal Pradesh. The protocol, as prescribed by the Ministry of External Affairs (MEA) required that during his visit to Delhi, HH the Dalai Lama was to be provided security of the level of head of state, which included escorting him from the point of entry in Delhi to his place of stay and protect him during the whole duration of the stay. The MEA had provided our security unit three foreign make old cars for escorting duties. These old cars had started giving a lot of trouble and our officer in-charge of the Motor Transport section (Shri Vijay Pal Singh) submitted in writing that considering the mechanical unfitness of these cars, we should instead provide Ambassador cars to escort dignitaries, which were available with the unit. This was accepted by me. However, during HH Dalai Lama's visit sometime in 1979, when our MT section in-charge provided an Ambassador car for escorting, the protocol people (MEA) insisted that only a foreign make car should be provided for escort. On their persuasion, the MT section in-charge supplied the vehicles desired by them.

As anticipated, this car created problem at the border, as it did not start. A police control room van, which we had arranged as a standby, escorted HH Dalai Lama. Surprisingly the MEA, ignoring the insistence of their protocol, made a complaint to the CP, who in turn asked for my comments. I gave him a detailed factual report including the fact that our MT section in-charge had given in writing about the mechanical unfitness of these old foreign make vehicles and also that it was provided at the instance of the protocol (MEA) people. The CP somehow did not accept our explanation, for reasons best known to him, and ordered that I should fix responsibility for this lapse. I tried to explain to him again, over the phone, but he was quite adamant stating that responsibility should be fixed.

As MT section in-charge had already given in writing that these vehicles were not fit for escorting duties, there was no justification for fixing responsibility on him. Since CP was insisting on it, I again wrote all facts in detail to him and mentioned that if it was considered necessary to fix responsibility on someone, then I, as head of the security unit of Delhi Police, take this responsibility. The very next day, CP Delhi conveyed his 'displeasure' in writing to me and also wrote that it should be placed on my record. I could have saved myself had I fixed responsibility on the MT section in-charge for providing unfit vehicles for escort duty, but it would have been quite unethical on my part. Besides, it would have damaged my reputation in the force, forever.

Meanwhile, my nomination for the Indian Police Medal for meritorious services, which had been recommended by CP and was under review with the Delhi government for onward transmission to the MHA, was rejected due to the the placing of displeasure on my record. I kept quiet. If I remember correctly, within three to four days of this, the CP had asked me during a meeting about the progress of my medal case and I had told him, without indicating any bitterness, that it had been rejected since there was a 'displeasure' on my record. CP immediately observed in front of the other officers that this was not his intention. He called his PS and dictated a DO letter to the chief secretary Delhi government stating that Shri Kaushal is an outstanding officer and there was no intention to damage his record. He also mentioned that the letter might be treated as withdrawn and a copy was also sent to MHA. In due course of time, it was rectified, but I missed my medal as the process of withdrawal and rectification of record took some time. The last date for submission of medal recommendations was over. The next time, CP made sure that my name was sent.

I don't know why CP Delhi was so adamant for fixing responsibility in the above case after all facts had been explained to him and he took rare initiative in withdrawing his displeasure and in admitting that it was not his intention to damage my otherwise good record.

I treat it as Almighty's blessings. I am grateful for whatever I got and do not feel embittered even if I lost something.

2. Did My Duty as Policeman

I was additional CP, New Delhi Range, and during one of my night rounds, when I was passing through Willingdon

Crescent (now named Mother Teresa Crescent) around 1.00 a.m., I noticed an elderly couple and a young woman standing near their car. They were waiting for help as the car seemed to have stopped working. Both women were wearing heavy jewellery and very expensive sarees. They were coming back from some relative's wedding. The place where they were standing was absolutely deserted—as on one side was the Rashtrapati Bhawan compound and on the other side was the ridge. They were also looking a little scared, but felt assured seeing a police vehicle. I got down from my car and on my asking, the elderly gentleman informed me that they were staying at Kalibari Marg and were looking for a ride to reach home. As a police officer I realized that if I leave them there, even if it is for a short while, it was a readymade case for robbery. Besides the ladies were quite scared, so I advised them to sit in my car and told my driver to drop them at their residence in Kalibari Marg and come back to pick me up. I also informed the SHO, Mandir Marg, to get the car towed away to a nearby petrol pump or to his police station from where they could collect it the next day. They were looking quite surprised with the turn of events. The gentleman politely asked for my name and thanked me before sitting in my car. After their departure, I along with my operator waited for about 20–25 minutes on the roadside for my car. The local SHO also arrived in his vehicle along with my car. After instructing the SHO that the car of the stranded persons should be returned to them without any problem, I proceeded further on my night round.

After about two or three days, my office orderly informed me that a family of about six persons had been waiting to see me. I told him to call them. When they entered my chamber, I could immediately recognize the elderly gentleman, whom I had met at Willingdon Crescent during my night round. As I asked them to take their seats, the elderly gentleman started saying that the persons accompanying him were his son, son-in-law, daughter and daughter-in-law, who were staying in the UK. He added that his wife narrated the incident when they were stuck up on the lonely road at midnight and how a senior police officer helped them reach their home safely in his own car and also arranged for towing of their car to a safe place; they couldn't believe that this could happen in India. The elderly gentleman very proudly told them that though they always praised London Bobby, Indian policemen are very good and helpful too. They had come to thank me for helping their family.

When I took over as CP Delhi, relying on this experience, I ordered all police control room vans to carry proper ropes as part of their equipment, to tow the stranded cars during night time and this was given wide publicity in newspapers and on television for public awareness.

3. Small Goodwill Gesture

During my tenure as CP from 1992 to 1995, the Delhi Police on average would approximately receive a little more than 100 complaints daily in their Vigilance Branch. Some of these complaints which were addressed to CP, an average of about 20–25, would come to my office. Either my staff officer or my PS would put up them to me. I would pick up about 10 complaints daily and go through the allegations contained in them and then talk to the complainant on phone. I would normally inform them that I had gone through their complaints and also about the proposed action, i.e., to whom it was being sent for inquiry and the approximate time by which they would be informed about the results—I followed this routine throughout my tenure of three years. The remaining complaints were sent to the Vigilance Branch of the police headquarter for appropriate action

During this routine exercise, I saw a complaint written by one Mrs Singh on her pad in which she admitted that though her car had crossed the 'stop' line at Kotla/Defence Colony crossing, she had stopped much before the traffic light. She added in her complaint that the traffic policeman on duty spoke to her very rudely and made some unpleasant remarks. I told my PS to direct the traffic inspector of the area to go to the woman's and apologize to her on behalf of the traffic police and also on my behalf. Thereafter, I spoke to the complainant and told her that I had seen her complaint and that I had no reason to doubt her version. I apologized for the misbehaviour of my constable and told her that I had directed the traffic inspector to meet her. I also mentioned to her that while I am not justifying the behaviour of my constable, the area from where constabulary is normally recruited, that was the way they generally spoke. To my surprise, Mrs Singh checked twice with me whether I was the CP. She probably never thought that I as CP Delhi, would respond to her complaint.

I think, quite a few years after that, I was attending a colleague's daughter's wedding at the Air Force auditorium lawns in Dhaula Kuan and I saw Shri M.K. Narayanan, former director, IB, talking to a lady. Since I wanted to talk to Shri Narayanan, I waited at some distance. Shri Narayanan, who saw me waiting, said a little loudly, 'Kaushal, just wait for a while.' This alerted the woman, who asked Shri Narayanan whether I was the same Kaushal, who was CP Delhi a few years back, and after he confirmed this, she requested him to call me. Shri Narayanan introduced the lady to me. She was Mrs Singh, wife of former foreign secretary Shri S.K. Singh, whom I had met earlier. Then she narrated the whole incident to Shri Narayanan and also said that at first she had not believed that CP Delhi, had himself rung her up and also felt sorry for the misbehaviour of his constable. She also said that she had narrated this incident to many other people. Shri Narayan looked happy.

Sometimes small gestures earn a lot of goodwill.

4. Meeting Lawyers' Association

During my tenure as commissioner of police, Delhi, I was meeting everyday with people to hear about their grievances and suggestions. This gave me a good insight into our functioning and also about people's expectations from the police. I devised a system, where my staff officers were maintaining a brief record of each complainant, i.e., full name with address and telephone number, date and time of meeting, brief of complaint in one or two lines and action taken there on. The appointment of the complainant with the concerned DCP were fixed and he was informed about it. The DCPs were also directed, in case of serious allegations, to send a brief action-taken report. This was being reviewed from time to time. I had also directed DCPs to honour the appointments without fail. Instructions were also issued to all field officers to regularly meet complainants, who came to them directly with their grievances.

After about six months in office, I started meeting big groups of people like lawyers, university teachers, students, doctors, etc., through their professional associations and groups like RWAs, etc. These people were opinion makers. In the past, same sort of conflict had existed between the police and some of these groups on some occasions. I thought that since there was no conflict at that time, I should meet them. I invited the lawyers' association of the New Delhi and Tis Hazari courts (Old Delhi) for a meeting. The lawyers came in good numbers, including most of their officer bearers. During tea, their president started introducing their office bearers to me. The atmosphere was quite pleasant. One of the senior lawyers, while thanking me for the hospitality, asked me why I had invited them. I told them in a lighter vein that in the past we had history of occasional clashes between lawyers and police, resulting in lawyers' strike and some inquiry into the matter. Since everything was normal then, I thought we should meet and peacefully appreciate each other's problems and devise some mechanism/procedure to be followed in case of any incident. This would avoid any possible clash and consequent strike, etc., in the future. The lawyers were extremely happy to hear this and lauded me for this gesture. This created an understanding between the two sides and established a communication channel, which proved very useful. Fortunately, no clash occurred between the lawyers and police during my tenure.

Thereafter, I met other groups like university teachers, students, medical association, etc. This helped us create a better perception of the police and removed a lot of misgivings.

5. Permitting Demonstration at Police Headquarter during Prohibitory Orders

The Babri Masjid demolition at Ayodhya on 6 December 1992 was followed by communal riots in different parts of the country. The communal situation was quite fragile and the central government, along with the concerned state governments, were keeping a very close watch on the developments. Sometime in the second or third week of January in 1993, the BJP declared their intention to organize a rally on 25 February at the Boat Club lawns at Rajpath. Their application for permission mentioned that they would be mobilizing about 10 lakh BJP supporters for the rally, which would be addressed by Shri Atal Bihari Vajpayee, Shri L.K. Advani and other important leaders of the party. A lot of posters and hoardings had come up in Delhi and in other important towns of the country. The posture and attitude of the BJP was quite aggressive.

After lot of deliberations, it was decided in the meeting held on 31 January 1993, at the PMO that keeping in mind the prevailing communal situation, the proposed rally of the BJP should not be allowed. I was the main initiator of this move. As commissioner of police I was entrusted with the responsibility of implementing the decision. Delhi had been an old stronghold of BJP and preventing their rally in Delhi was a very challenging task. It needed very meticulous and massive police arrangements. In pursuance of our efforts, sometime in the second week of February 1993, I, in my capacity as commissioner of police, promulgated orders under Section 144 CrPC for the entire UT of Delhi banning rallies, processions, collection of five or more persons, etc. But the unique feature of the prohibitory order was that I had exempted the road in front of the then Delhi Police headquarters in IP Estate from the scope of this order. This is a small road between Bahadur Shah Zafar Marg and the Ring Road with a divider in between. I had done this deliberately, since I believed that in a democracy, people had the right to convey their grievances and lodge their protest against the executive authority. In this case, since the prohibitory orders were issued by me, I thought it appropriate to allow protest against me. Not only my officers, but the media was also quite surprised to see this order. In a meeting held in the home minister's chamber in connection with the rally, I was asked as to why I had made this exception; my explanation was simple: since I had issued the prohibitory orders for the entire UT to maintain order, therefore, I allowed people to protest against me. I also assured them that with our security arrangements and intelligence apparatus, nothing untoward would happen.

Two small demonstrations, including one by Delhi University students, took place in front of the police headquarters during this period. The traffic on the road was regulated and both demonstrations remained peaceful. The student's delegation, which met me to handover their memorandum, also asked me the same question, as to why I had made this exception. I only said that had I not made this exception, they wouldn't have been able to talk to me.

For quite some time, this order was mentioned in the media and our gesture earned lot of goodwill for Delhi Police. We were viewed as a friendly force, one that accepted peaceful demonstrations.

6. Persuading a National Leader to Change His Party's Decision

In 1980–81, when I was additional CP, New Delhi Range, the BJP called for a protest march and 'courting of arrest' by their supporters in front of Regal Cinema in Connaught Place. Delhi Pradesh BJP had put up posters all over the city stating that the protest march would be led by their top leaders, namely Shri Atal Bihari Vajpayee, Shri L.K. Advani and others. The main organizers were Shri Vijay Kumar Malhotra and Shri Madan Lal Khurana of Delhi BJP. Normally, these protest marches led to Parliament Street and protesters would be arrested, if required, either at Patel Chowk or Jai Singh Road-Parliament Street crossing. The BJP shifted the venue to make their protest more prominent and since Connaught Place was a commercial centre, it would get them better publicity.

Shri P.S. Bhinder, who was the police commissioner at the time, asked me to meet and persuade Shri Atal Bihari Vajpayee to shift the venue of protest from Connaught Place to Jai Singh Road-Parliament Street crossing. His argument was that since Connaught Place was a popular market area, a lot of people including foreigners were always moving in the area and the likelihood of the protest march, especially the courting of arrest, turning into a law and order situation or a riot cannot be ruled out. I told CP that Delhi Pradesh BJP had already publicized the venue a lot and might not agree to shift it. Shri Bhinder observed that I was good at persuading people and that there was no harm in trying.

I had met Shri Vajpayee, who was the leader of the Opposition in Parliament, on two or three occasion before this. So I rang up Shri Shiv Kumar, special assistant to Shri Vajpayee for an appointment and he asked me to come that evening. While going to his residence, I was trying to figure out what should I tell him to make him agree to our proposal for shifting the venue of arrest. Quite a few options were coming to my mind. Finally, I decided not to suggest a shift of the venue straight away and decided to approach the conversation in such a way that the suggestion to shift the venue could come from him.

Both Shri Vajpayee and Shri Advani were known for being courteous. When I met him, he ordered for tea and then asked me the purpose of my visit. I normally used to talk to leaders/organizers of rallies and protest marches, etc., about the police arrangements which were being made for regulating their rally. This always helped in reducing the tension between the two sides. I had spoken to Shri Vajpayee too before. So I told Shri Vajpayee that I had made adequate police arrangements for their event and sufficient number of buses would be there to carry all those who would be courting arrest. I was setting the foundation for raising my issue. Shri Vajpayee observed that Delhi Police always made satisfactory arrangements. At this juncture, I told him that on this occasion, the situation was a little different because of the change in the venue. Connaught Place is a very popular commercial area and a large number of people, including women and foreign tourists were always present in the area. Since the process of courting arrest might create some commotion, the situation could get disturbed and anti-social elements would then try to take advantage of the same. The possibility of damage to commercial properties, even attempts to molest the women present in the area could not be ruled out. We would be deploying force overseen by very experienced police officers, but we would need cooperation and support of some party volunteers to regulate and control the protest march and the subsequent courting of arrest. Shri Vajpayee immediately said the organizers should have anticipated this possibility and why should they insist on courting arrest in front of Regal Cinema; It could be done a little ahead on Parliament Street. He asked his special assistant Shri Shiv Kumar to connect him immediately with either Shri Vijay Kumar Malhotra or Shri Madan Lal Khurana. He told Shri Malhotra that the venue for courting arrest selected by the Pradesh Party was not appropriate and would cause a lot of inconvenience to general public and possibility of damage to commercial properties could not be ruled out. He clearly conveyed to them that venue should be shifted to some point on Parliament Street beyond Connaught Place. All pleas of Shri Malhotra and later on of Shri Khurana, including the fact that a lot of publicity had already been given to the venue, could not change Shri Vajpayee's decision.

My job was done. I expressed my gratefulness to Shri Vajpayee and also thanked him for averting the possibility of an ugly situation. The consideration shown by Shri Vajpayee for the convenience and safety of the general public is a lesson for all political leaders.

7. Delhi Police Day 'Ceremonial Parade' and 'At Home'

When I took over as CP Delhi, one of my missions was to take Delhi Police to new heights and raise its status. It required Delhi Police to put up an outstanding performance in controlling crime and maintaining order and it also needed Delhi Police as an institution to connect with top official leadership and constitutional authorities, along with a meaningful engagement with media and the people. In pursuance of this I decided to organize an 'At Home' on Delhi Police Day, i.e., 16 February, on the pattern of Army Day and invite the president of India, vice president, prime minister, home minister and other VIPs to attend the function. Such a function had never been organized in the past. Earlier, only a ceremonial parade used to be organized on this day. I also decided to invite the prime minister to take salute on the Delhi Police Day parade on the morning of 16 February. I knew that if we succeeded in organizing these two functions, it would take the Delhi Police up by quite a few notches. We had to put on the best show.

When I was appointed as CP Delhi, Delhi Police had been facing quite a difficult time. However, my officers and men had put up a great performance in 1992 by demolishing well-established land mafias, liquidating the dreaded criminal gangs and successfully foiling the attempts of Sikh and Islamic terrorist groups to disrupt the peace in the national capital. When in the aftermath of the Babri Masjid demolition serious communal riots engulfed important towns of northern India, the firm and well-planned handling of the communal situation by Delhi Police had kept the entire walled city absolutely peaceful with the exception of a riot in a trans-Yamuna locality, which was contained very effectively within two to three days. While the government was extremely pleased with our performance, it also restored the people's confidence in their police.

With this background, I launched the preparations for the two ceremonial events. I sent a formal communication to the president of India inviting him and the First Lady to grace the occasion of Delhi Police Day 'At Home' with their presence, which would immensely boost the morale of their police force. A copy of the communication was also sent to the Union home secretary. I requested the president's PS that he fix an appointment for me so that I could personally request the president and the First Lady to accept our invitation. When I called on the president, he very gracefully accepted our invitation and agreed to attend the function, along with the First Lady. Thereafter, I took an appointment with the PM and requested him to attend both the functions, i.e., take salute in our ceremonial parade in the morning and for attending 'At Home'. A formal communication was addressed to the prime minister with a copy to the Union home secretary. The PM was kind enough to accept both the invitations.

Thereafter, I personally called on the vice president, the home minister and LG, Delhi, to invite them for the 'At Home'. I also invited the two ministers of state for home, Chief Justice of India, chief election commissioner and Union home secretary. Personal invitations were sent to former CPs of Delhi to grace the occasion. I also requested director, Intelligence Bureau, and all chiefs of central police organizations to attend the function. All of them graced the occasion with their presence.

While our preparations for celebrating Delhi Police Day were in full swing, I got a phone call from Shri Kashyap, informing me that all the three service chiefs had called on the President to request him to change his decision to attend the event. Their argument was that it was only a state police and it would not be appropriate for him to attend their official function. He also told me that the president had heard them, but had not communicated his decision. Probably, the military secretary to the president had informed the three chiefs. I immediately requested Shri Kashyap to get me an appointment with the President, which was arranged. I informed the President, which was arranged. I informed the president that the entire Delhi Police was feeling grateful to him for accepting their invitation and looking forward to the day when the president, along with the First Lady, would bless them with their presence. I also mentioned that Delhi Police was his police as it was guarding the national capital and also looking after his security. The president told Shri Kashyap to officially communicate his acceptance of our invitation.

On the morning of 16 February 1993, the PM's helicopter landed at Delhi Police sports ground at Kingsway Camp. I received the PM and escorted him in his car up to the saluting base, where he received salute at the ceremonial parade of Delhi Police. Thereafter, the formalities of the parade were completed and the PM gave medals to the awardees of gallantry medals and President's Police Medals for distinguished service. The PM then addressed the officers and men of Delhi Police and appreciated their excellent performance. He expressed confidence in Delhi Police that they would continue to maintain their high standard of work.

I introduced my senior officers to the PM and thereafter he briefly joined us for tea. This was after a long time that the PM had taken salute at Delhi Police parade. The media, who were present in a large number and was quite excited, congratulated me and gave very good coverage to our event.

The venue of the 'At Home' was my residence at 12, Lodi Estate. All special invitees and guests had arrived in time before the arrival of the president of India. I, along with my wife, received the President and the First Lady on their arrival. The Delhi Police band played the national anthem. I first introduced my senior officers and gallantry medal awardees to the President and then introduced the former police commissioners of Delhi and chiefs of central police organizations. Meanwhile, Mrs Kaushal introduced the wives of senior police officers to the First Lady.

The vice president, prime minister, home minister, Chief Justice of India, LG, Delhi, chief election commissioner, former Delhi Police commissioners and other VIPs had graced the occasion. All officers of Delhi Police up to the rank of DCPs, including some senior retired officers of the ranks of ACPs, who had rendered outstanding service to the Delhi Police also attended the function. After all guests had left, I thanked my officers for their contribution in earning laurels for Delhi Police by effectively controlling crime and managing law and order situations, which gave us opportunity to organize these two events at this level.

It was a great day for Delhi Police.

Since 1993, the two events of Delhi Police day, i.e.,

ceremonial parade and the 'At Home' are regularly celebrated and the president of India, vice president, prime minister, home ministers and other VIPs have been gracing the occasion.

8. Convincing the Home Minister to Revise His Decision

After the Government of India sanctioned additional 225 battalions for augmenting the strength of the central paramilitary forces, including the Rashtriya Rifles and India Reserve Battalions for strengthening the state police, secretary, National Security Council (NSC), an Indian Foreign Services (IFS) officer, met the home minister and convinced him that since most of the Central Para Military Force (CPMF) were deployed at the country's borders, the defence ministry may be entrusted with the responsibility of framing rules regarding command, control and deployment of these forces. The home minister agreed with him and told the home secretary to take the required follow-up action. The home secretary tried to oppose this decision, but the home minister was quite adamant and clearly told him that his decision was final.

The home secretary, before initiating any further action, called me (secretary, IS) and joint secretary, police, for a meeting to discuss this issue. He briefed us about the developments and also that the home minister was quite firm on implementing the decision. He suddenly asked me to persuade the home minister to change his decision. Naturally, my first reaction was that if he had refused to listen to the home secretary on this matter, there was no possibility of his hearing my views. But both the home secretary and joint secretary, police, insisted that since I was good at persuading people, I must try to convince the home minister to change his decision. The home secretary booked an appointment with the home minster to discuss an important matter. Since Parliament was in session, our appointment was fixed at the Parliament office of the home minister.

When we reached the home minister's chamber, we found that secretary, NSC, was already there. This could be a coincidence. The home secretary asked me to initiate the subject. The moment I mentioned that we wanted to discuss the issue of framing of rules relating to command and control of CPMF being entrusted to the Ministry of Defence, the home minister immediately cut me short and with little annoyance told me that he had already taken a final view on the matter and that there was no need for any further discussion. This also alerted the secretary, NSC. I immediately said that we were not asking him to change his decision, which he must have taken after considering all aspects of the issue, and that we had only come to bring a few facts to his notice. After receiving his nod, I told him that the MHA's main responsibilities were to look after the internal security of the country, including maintenance of law and order, and the second relates to the maintenance and deployment of Armed Forces of the Union (CPMFS). As regards maintenance of law and order, generally, we play an advisory role, since it is a state subject. It was for the state to decide whether and to what extent they would accept our advice. The only subject which was totally under our control was the AFU and if we hand over that too to the defence ministry, we would be virtually left with nothing. This argument clinched the issue and the home minister, without losing any time, immediately told the secretary, NSC, that what I had said was correct and that he had decided to reverse his earlier decision. Now this job would be done by the MHA. The secretary tried to oppose it, but the home minister was very clear that the MHA was the appropriate authority to do it.

A very important issue, which had far-reaching implications for the functioning of the MHA, was settled in our favour because we had decided to take a stand for what we thought was right. We later on learnt that the defence forces had lobbied for it with the secretary, NSC.

9. Anti-Corruption Branch in Action

On 31 October 1967, after my return from Himachal Pradesh, I was posted as SP in-charge of the anti-corruption branch of the Delhi administration. Sometime in February–March 1968, a woman with her husband met me and complained against the conduct of the director of education, Delhi administration. She wanted an assurance from me before filing a complaint that proper follow-up action would be taken on her complaint. After she and her husband felt assured, she informed me that she was a trained teacher and had applied for a job vacancy advertised by the Directorate of Education, Delhi Administration. During the recruitment process, she was contacted by the director over the phone who had asked her to meet him in a restaurant in Connaught Place. When she met him, he assured her that she would get her appointment and in return demanded a sexual favour from her. He also told her that if she was agreeable, she should inform him over the phone and then he would tell her the meeting place. At this stage, she had come to report the matter to me. I was quite disturbed after hearing about the incident.

It was decided that she would be talking to the director as desired by him and we would record their conversation on tape. The tape recorder, which they had brought, was tested and found working to our satisfaction. She herself suggested that she would be conveying her consent in response to what he had said during their last meeting and then see how their conversation went. This was a task that required one to be extremely careful. The director naturally felt very happy and said a few more incriminating things. He invited her to come to his office on the coming Sunday. I very discreetly surveyed his office room after work hours and found that unlike other officer's rooms, his room had double curtains and one of them was of a very thick material. I met the chief secretary and after hearing the tape he congratulated me for a job well done. But he told me that the director of education was well known to the LG as they had attended university together. He also told me that the director was on extension and was likely to become chairman of the board of secondary education (I am not very sure of the name of the educational body). He felt that instead of organizing a raid, he would personally bring it to the notice of LG. I accompanied him. After hearing the tape, the LG immediately told the director to proceed on leave and his extension was terminated. His further nomination for the chairmanship of the educational body was alsowithdrawn. A senior IAS officer from the cadre was posted as director.

Despite the fact that this was a very discreet enquiry, some facts of the incident leaked. The fact that director of education, who was considered quite influential, had suddenly proceeded on leave till retirement further corroborated the story. This was probably for the first time that action for misconduct was taken against a senior government official—that too a head of the department—on the report of the anti-corruption branch of the Delhi administration.

A few months after this, we conducted a raid on the government distillery, where the excise department, in collusion with their contractor, were producing illicit liquor. Around 10,000 bottles of such liquor were recovered, along with lot of other unauthorized material, which was being used for packing these bottles. The manufacturing cost of one bottle of excise paid desi liquor was ₹13, but as per the contract, the contractor was selling it for ₹10. To compensate his loss, he was on an average producing two extra bottles on which no excise duty was paid. This was the point where the excise department was conniving with the contractor. The chief secretary personally conveyed the government's appreciation to me.

The above two incidents enhanced the prestige of the anti-corruption branch of the Delhi administration. We tried not to let anyone escape the law, irrespective of their influence and power.

10. Refusal to Avail Exemption from Enquiry

Sometime in 1969, when I was working as SP in-charge of anti-corruption branch, the chief secretary, Delhi administration, under whom I was working, called me to inform that the CBI had asked his permission to conduct an inquiry against me on the complaint of a brother of an assistant sales tax officer (ASTO), who we had trapped and against whom a case under the Prevention of Corruption (POC) Act had been registered. The complainant had alleged that I had demanded some illegal benefits from him. I was shocked and surprised as the complainant had met me about one year back. The chief secretary wanted to know the facts of the case. I told him that my branch had, on the basis of a complaint, laid a trap and arrested the ASTO while accepting the illegal benefits from the complainant, who was a shopkeeper in Mehrauli market. A month or two after that I got a call from Shri Ved Marwah, under whom I had worked as ASP, to hear the ASTO's brother in connection with the criminal case pending against his brother. Shri Marwah also told me that the matter had been referred to him by Shri Natwar Singh, IFS, who was his old friend. Shri Ved Marwah did not make any recommendation and he only wanted me to hear him.

The ASTO's brother came to see me, without any prior appointment, on a Sunday. I was staying in a court lane police flat near Raj Niwas. I did not call him inside and met him outside in the foyer area of the staircase. I scolded him for coming to my residence and that too without any appointment. After hearing him for about five minutes, I told him clearly that nothing could be done in the case as his brother had been arrested red-handed while accepting the money and we would be filing the charge sheet on completion of the investigation. The meeting lasted for about 15 minutes. Thereafter, nothing happened for almost a year, when Shri R.D. Singh, DIG Range of Delhi Police, under whom I had done part of my training, rang me up to inform me that the complainant of the aforementioned trap case of the anti-corruption branch had been arrested by the south district police at Mehrauli. He had some doubts about the authenticity of the case as he suspected some connivance with the local police. The DIG wanted me to visit the spot and find out the facts. I visited Mehrauli, along with my investigating officer, met the local SHO and the family members of my complainant, who had been arrested. On my return, I reported my findings to DIG on call. While I had only made informal preliminary enquiries, the connivance of local police was quite obvious. The ASTO's brother had not made any complaint for almost one year after meeting me. He filed his complaint only after my visit to Mehrauli for enquiry.

After hearing the details of the case, the chief secretary,

who was a very strong person, told me that he would not give permission to the CBI to conduct the inquiry and would be speaking to the director of CBI. I thanked him for his trust, but told him that as SP, anti-corruption, I did not want any exemption from the inquiry as it might create some doubt about me. My only request was that the CBI should call me and record my statement before conducting any further inquiry. At that time, I had just completed six years of my service and I don't know how this wisdom dawned on me. The chief secretary, Shri Verma, was also surprised with my reaction, but agreed with me. In fact, he was very happy, which he conveyed to me later on.

After the chief secretary spoke to the CBI, I was called by Shri Choudhary, DIG, CBI, Delhi branch. When I met him, he asked me to fill up a questionnaire. On this, I told him that his questionnaire would be based only on the information available with them and instead I could tell them all that I know about the case and after that I would have nothing to say. He agreed and I narrated the entire story as I had told the chief secretary. I also told him that the chief secretary, who was not inclined to give permission, had agreed for the inquiry only on my request. Shri Choudhary was quite happy and told me that I had given more information than what they had asked for in the questionnaire. He also informed me that both Shri R.D. Singh and Shri Ved Marwah had spoken to him on the phone and confirmed what I had said in my statement. Both of them had also said a few good things about me. I told Shri Choudhary that I had not spoken to either Shri R.D. Singh or to Shri Ved Marwah. It was out of their sheer goodness that they had spoken to him.

Shri Choudhary, DIG, CBI, was absolutely satisfied with my statement and told me that no further enquiry would be conducted and that he would be closing the matter. He also mentioned that the Delhi administration would be informed.

I am still surprised that with only six years of service, I got the wisdom and courage to refuse exemption from an inquiry against me on a false but a serious charge and also how quickly the matter was closed. Probably, it was Lord Almighty's special blessings.

This also reaffirmed my faith in doing what I considered right, irrespective of the difficulties that one may have to face.

11. Breakfast with Hunger Strikers

In 1984, I was on deputation to RPF and was working as director, security, in the Force Headquarters at the Railway Board. Since the post of IG, Eastern Railway, an important railway, was vacant, I was given the additional charge along with my duties at the Force Headquarters. I used to shuttle between Delhi and Calcutta. Once when I was travelling from Delhi to Calcutta in Rajdhani, the divisional security officer met me at the Asansol station and conveyed DG, RPF's message for me to get down at Asansol and immediately proceed to Rourkela (on another railways—Southeastern Railway) to sort out the problem created by the RPF association, which had gone on a hunger strike to protest against the arrest of some of their colleagues in a murder case by the local police. The train had reached Asansol quite early in the morning. My security officer had made arrangements for saloon services in the train proceeding to Rourkela, which enabled me to freshen myself for the meeting at the destination.

At Rourkela, DIG in-charge of South Eastern Railway, along with his staff, was waiting for me at the station and had arranged for breakfast. I told them that I would have my breakfast with the jawans who were on hunger strike and then proceed for RPF staff barracks, the venue of protest. An important leader of the RPF association SI Uma Shanker Jha, who was behind the strike, was also present at the barrack. Normally union/association leaders utilize such opportunities to create tension for increasing their influence and importance. I had some experience of handling both the association office-bearers of the RPF and the force personnel.

Initially, I asked one of the jawans on hunger strike to explain their grievance to me, but as soon as he started speaking, an association office-bearer intervened to say that he would give me the facts. I stopped him and said that let the jawan on hunger strike, who had first-hand knowledge of the events, complete his version and thereafter I would listen to him. Such interventions help in dominating the situation. After hearing from the jawans on hunger strike and the association office-bearers about the facts of the case as understood by them, I told them that before I speak they must know that I am one of them and it was not just the problem of the jawans who had been arrested, but it was my problem too. I would be taking it up with the highest local police authorities. But since legal action had already been initiated, it could be sorted out only by following the legal process. I would be able to say anything only after meeting the police authorities for which my appointment with IG police, Rourkela, had been fixed. At this juncture, I told the jawans how my journey to Calcutta had been cut short and diverted to Rourkela and that I hadn't had a chance to have breakfast. I told them that if they agree, we could have our breakfast together in the barrack and thereafter I would proceed to meet the police authorities. By this time, I was in control of the situation and the jawans agree to have breakfast, which was arranged by the local RPF officers. The association office-bearers were looking a little lost and I invited them to join us too.

Meanwhile, IG, Rourkela, Shri Shyam Narain Tewari, who was my batchmate, came to know about my arrival and conveyed a message that he was waiting for me in his office. He had also invited me for lunch.

When I had asked for the appointment, I had not been aware that my batchmate was the local IG. This changed the entire atmosphere.

After breakfast with the hunger strikers, I left for IG's office. Before leaving, I assured them that after talking to the IG, I would come there to inform them about the developments. Since there was no direct evidence about the involvement of the RPF jawans in the case and they were taken into custody only on the basis of circumstantial evidence, the IG assured me after talking to the DSP and the inspector concerned, who were investigating the case, they would not oppose bail. I came back to RPF lines as promised and spoke to the force personnel, who were satisfied and happy. The DG was informed that the hunger strike was over.

I left for Calcutta by the evening train.

12. Out of Turn DG

In 1988, I was working as executive director, security, and IG, HQ, in the RPF at the Railway Board. DG, RPF, Shri S.P. Bannerjee, was due for superannuation on 22 February1988, but no orders regarding his successor were issued till 21 February. It was presumed that Shri Raja Sreedharan (IPS, 1957, MP), CSC, Eastern Railway, who was the senior-most IG in the RPF, would be either asked to temporarily officiate as DG or might be posted as regular DG. His batchmates had been promoted as DG in other central police organizations. But on the morning of 22 February, to everybody's surprise including me, the railway ministry issued orders directing me to officiate as DG, RPF. This naturally shocked my senior colleagues in the force, which included Shri Raja Sreedharan, Shri Anantachari (IPS, 1958), Shri Ramalingam (IPS, 1960) and my batchmate Shri Subhash Tripathi.

Immediately after I got the orders, I first met the chairman of the Railway Board and then railway minister Shri Madhavrao Scindia. I tried to convince them that in a uniform force, it would be quite embarrassing for me, with three seniors present in the organization, to function as DG which involved issuing supervisory instructions and directions, etc. I further told them that while I can manage the work, the fact that I was junior to those who would be working under me, might make it a little difficult for them. The railway minister, who had a lot of trust in me, observed that he was fully aware of these facts and had knowingly taken this decision. He added in a lighter tone that as the railway minister it was his privilege to decide who would be the DG, RPF; his decision had conveyed his confidence in me and had also made my functioning in the Railway Board very smooth.

My senior colleagues, who had come for the DG's farewell, met me a day after I took over as DG. They were full of resentment and two of them (I would not like to mention their names) told me to refuse this appointment in writing. I told them about my meeting with the chairman, Railway Board, and the minister and their replies to me. I also told them that this was the ministry's order and I had no option but to comply. I suggested that if they were so unhappy with the decision, they could go and meet the minister and convey their objection. Shri Raja Sreedharan, the senior-most among them did not say anything and instead advised them to accept the orders. He told them that I had no role in getting these orders issued.

I officiated as DG, RPF, for about five months. But for this entire period, as a routine, I would call Shri Sreedharan, IG, Eastern Railway, the senior-most among us, every day to briefly inform him about what I was proposing to do. I consulted him on almost all the important issues, in spite of him repeatedly telling me that it was not needed. This was to maintain propriety. There were some misgivings about Shri Sreedharan that had come in the way of his promotion. Since Shri Scindia had a lot of confidence in me, I persistently made efforts to sort out issues relating to Shri Sreedharan and ultimately succeeded. He took over as DG on 9 July 1988 and I continued as his IG, HQ, till I went on promotion to my cadre as CP Delhi. We had excellent relations which continued for a lifetime.

While it was quite a task to manage these seniors, I learnt a lot during this short tenure. It was an important experience. I was attending meetings, both in other ministries and in the Railway Board as DG, RPF. I think I was getting advance training for my future assignments and it gave me a lot of confidence. As head of an AFU, you experience a different kind of sense of responsibility. On the plus side, I was provided a gold pass, which entitles you to the highest level of privileges available on the railway system, including an AC saloon for travelling. I availed this privilege on two or three occasions.

It is true that late Shri Madhavrao Scindia had a lot of faith in me and had trusted me with important responsibilities in the past. But it is still a mystery to me as to why he ordered me to officiate as DG for five months, while there were three officers senior to me in the force. What did he see in me that he couldn't see in my seniors?

Anyway, it was a thrilling experience and I enjoyed being a short-term DG.

13. An Encounter with Hardcore Terrorists

Under pressure from Punjab Police, Sikh terrorists were escaping to Delhi, considering it a safe hideout as it was easy for them to merge here with the local population. However, Delhi Police was very vigilant and the first encounter, in which four Sikh militants were killed, took place in April 1992 in south Delhi's Kailash colony. In this encounter, the alert beat constables had spotted the terrorists in a park in front of the Kailash market and had challenged them. During the chase through the colony lanes, all the four militants were killed during an exchange of fire. The local residents had witnessed the chase and the firing by both militants and the police. This had happened two months after I had taken over as CP Delhi. The recognition and reward given to these brave constables infused new enthusiasm in the force, which led to a very daring and amazing performance by our men. Bravery and courage are at times infectious and have far-reaching effects.

In the last week of July, our Special Cell arrested three militants during an encounter in west Delhi. Their interrogation revealed that they were part of a terrorist outfit which had various cells based in west Delhi and they were planning terrorist strikes in the city. The only relevant clue they could provide was that the outfit had a black Yamaha motorcycle. Thorough and consistent inquiries by the Special Cell in the suspected area led to the tracing of the motorcycle. It was found parked near DDA flat no. 396, pocket GH-8, Paschim Vihar. The police team took positions at strategic points. While the survey was still on, one of the terrorist came down and suspecting that he was being watched, fired on the police party. He was chased by an officer of the cell, but being a congested locality he succeeded in escaping. The Special Cell then tried to raid the suspected flat, when an explosion from inside the flat injured two members of the raiding party. The injured policemen were immediately taken to Deen Dayal Upadhyay Hospital and since their injuries were serious they were shifted to AIIMS.

I was being kept informed about the developments, but when I learnt about the injuries of two constables and also the fact that the venue of the encounter was a thickly inhabited cluster of LIG flats, I issued instructions for urgently moving additional reinforcement of commando units and quick evacuation of surrounding flats by requesting the residents to immediately shift from there. I also advised the Special Cell and other senior officials present at the spot to move cautiously. I also directed Shri P.R.S. Brar, additional CP of the neighbouring range, a very daring officer who had experience of conducting such operations, to meet me at the spot and I left for the venue along with DCP, Crime, Shri Neeraj Kumar. My main concern was that the venue was a congested locality requiring extra precautions and our two policemen had suffered bullet injuries.

When we reached the venue, we found that many local residents had assembled there without realizing the risk they had put themselves in. The local police officers were directed to remove them immediately. After talking to the officers who were handling the encounter, we realized that we were neither sure about the number of terrorists who were inside, nor had any idea about the quantity and quality of their weapons. Our direct storming into the flat could have caused casualties to our raiding police party. It was decided that if we could create suffocation in their room by pumping a lot of tear gas through a hole in the roof, they would be forced to come out. We also placed shooting parties in the flats opposite to the targeted flat.

Additional CP Brar, an officer who was very daring and always prepared to accept the challenges, took four to five constables with some hammers and moved towards the staircase of the adjacent block to reach the top of the building and then shifted to the roof of the targeted flat. I realized that I had exposed Brar and those policemen to great risk and therefore I should accompany them. We together went upstairs and then walking on a nine-inch-thick connecting wall between the blocks reached the top of the targeted flat. We succeeded in our efforts to create a small hole in the roof and pumped lot of tear gas inside the flat. The suffocation created by the tear gas forced the militants to leave the room. They came out firing their weapons, but our shooting parties shot them down. There were two militants, including a woman. From the search of the premises, one AK56 assault rifle, 351 live rounds, 36 empty cartridges and four magazines were recovered. Combing operations were launched in the locality and nearby colonies to locate the militant who had escaped. A photograph of me and Brar moving on top of the nine-inches-broad connecting wall came out the next day in the newspapers. We had successfully managed to eliminate dreaded armed terrorists without causing any injury to anyone living around.

The residents of the area assembled and thanked the police for saving their lives. No one except the two policemen got injured in the incident. After posting some police pickets at strategic points in the area and deploying additional beat patrolling to restore the confidence of the residents, we left for our office.

This incident got a lot of publicity. Minister of state in the MHA Shri M.M. Jacob made a detailed statement in Parliament about the encounter and assured the House that the government was determined to curb the terrorism and provide full protection and security to citizens.

Our fight against terrorism continued and we achieved a lot of success.

14. Himachal Outing

On my first promotion as SP, I was transferred to the Union Territory of Himachal Pradesh with direction to report to IGP at Shimla. I reported at Police HQ, Shimla, on 9 December 1966. I called on the IGP, who after a short briefing gave orders posting me as SP, Central Striking Reserve Force, at Junga in erstwhile Mahasu district. This was a striking reserve, which had been brought back from the Indo-China border and stationed at Junga.

Next day morning, I left for Junga, which was about 22 kilometres from Shimla, to assume the new charge. It was a kaccha hilly road. After travelling for about 11–12 kilometres, the driver turned onto a mule track instead of proceeding on the regular road. He told me that remaining half of the road normally remained blocked due to regular landslides, therefore police vehicles adopt mule track for travelling to Junga. Except police vehicles, only one public transport bus occasionally went to Junga, subject to road clearance. Negotiating about 10 U-turns on the mule track was quite an experience. Since there was very little space on the U-turns, either it would take two to three attempts or otherwise one had to drive first on back gear and then on front gear.

Anyway, on reaching Junga, I was received by Shri Atmaram Thakur, DSP, one of the most interesting persons I have met in my life—a live wire, without whose presence my 11-month stay in that jungle would have been very difficult. I was told that Junga had no electricity and water supply. There was a natural stream near the village, which was the only source of water, and for light, lanterns were being used. The local population beside my force was about 500. After Delhi, it felt like moving backwards, but was a learning experience nonetheless. All around Junga, there was electricity and water supply. The reason for this special blessing was that the local MLA was a fiery Opposition leader Shri Hira Singh Pal. My residence was an old abandoned house belonging to the forest department which needed a lot of repairs to prevent snakes from creeping in through the mud walls. I took leave to bring my wife from Lucknow.

My short tenure of about 11 months in Himachal would always remain as the most unforgettable on two counts—first relates to my posting and second to raising an unsanctioned armed police battalion. Unlike today, in those days, transfer implied delay of two to three months in receiving salary, as transfer of Last Pay Certificate (LPC) used to take a lot of time. In this case, it was transfer from one Union Territory administration to another which was expected to take a little more time. I had reconciled that I would be getting my salary in about three to four months' time. When after about three months I checked with my accountant, I was told that sanction of my post was awaited from the government. I was surprised and told him that I had taken charge of this post in pursuance of a regular order issued by the police headquarter. When nothing happened for about four months, I went to Shimla and to my surprise I was told by the AIG, Shri Govind Singh Mehta, that police headquarter had posted me in December against a post which had been abolished in last September. I met IGP, who without expressing any regret for what had happened, told me that he was trying with the government to get my posting regularized.

On 1 November 1966, as a consequence of reorganization of the state of Punjab and Union Territory of Himachal Pradesh, four new districts were added to Himachal, which had caused a lot of chaos in the administration and, unfortunately, I fell victim to this mismanagement. IGP told DIG, CID, to give me ₹500 from the secret fund for my expenses, which I immediately refused. Finally, it took almost 10 months to adjust me against a sanctioned post and I got my salary and arrears of pay just a month before my transfer back to Delhi in the third week of October. Police headquarter had transferred me to snow-bound district of Lahaul-Spiti without knowing that the MHA had already issued orders transferring me back to Delhi. I was relieved on 28 October by the Himachal administration with direction to report to chief secretary, Delhi.

As if this was not enough, another whirlpool of trouble was brewing. A month after my assuming the charge, I received orders from the police headquarter to raise the first battalion of Himachal Armed Police (HAP 1) and complete the recruitment process in about two months' time. I constituted recruitment teams, which were sent to different districts of Himachal for recruitment. If I remember correctly, sometime in May, the recruits started arriving at Junga and by middle of June about 600 recruits had reported for training. Initially, we met the expenditure on ration, etc., from the existing mess fund and then ration was taken on credit. I needed regular funds from the government to give salaries to the recruits and for providing uniform and other requirements of a newly raised battalion. My officers were finding it difficult to get credit from the market for purchasing rations. As far as clothing was concerned, I used old condemned uniforms in our clothing stores for training of jawans. My letters to police headquarter in this connection were not getting any response. Since it was becoming difficult for me to manage ration from the market on credit and also to answer queries from the new recruits regarding their salaries, I went to Shimla to meet the IGP. What I learnt was more astonishing than what had happened in case of my own posting. The battalion was raised without any sanction, hence no funds were available for paying salaries to jawans and their clothing, etc. I told them that it was not possible to manage 600 jawans without any payment of salary. Purchasing ration was an immediate necessity. The possibility of a strike or a demonstration could not be ruled out. The chances of the media playing it up were also there. Since the Junga MLA was from the Opposition, there was also likelihood of the issue being raised in the Assembly. I was surprised that our CID had not taken any cognizance of it. I told police headquarter to find some solution in a month's time.

Meanwhile, I kept them busy in various activities besides their tough training. A gymnasium was built through *sramdan* [physical labour] and foundation of a temple was laid in the lines. The police lines and the force office were decorated by transplanting trees from the nearby hills with the assistance of the local forest department. A welfare canteen, with nominal profit, was also established and cheaper ready-made clothes were obtained from Delhi for the jawans. I also organized a cultural competition among the jawans from different districts and it became very popular. In about two months' time, the police headquarter, which could not manage sanctions for the new battalion, ordered the adjustment of these recruits against the existing vacancies in different districts and units with instructions to complete their training at Junga. This adjustment and payment of salaries almost took a month and a half.

The new recruits had gradually come to know about the problem, but the various activities that I was organizing throughout this period besides their training, had created a special relationship between us. At one stage I had to tell them that the reorganization of states had created this chaotic situation and even I was not getting my salary. But I kept on assuring them that their jobs were secure and they would get their salaries with arrears. Before I left Himachal, I had ensured that they get their regular appointments and salaries.

I treat my short tenure in Himachal as a great learning exercise in man-management. I also experienced staying in tough conditions without essential facilities of electricity and water and completely cut off from any kind of social life. This was especially significant because this happened during the fourth year of my service, which included my training period.

15. 'In' and 'Out' of Delhi Police

I reported to Delhi Police for the first time on 12 April 1965 for my district training after completing my initial training at the National Academy of Administration, Mussoorie, Central Police Training College, Mount Abu and Punjab Police Training College at Phillaur. During my entire service, I had been in and out of Delhi Police three times and on 4 January 1995, I bid it a final goodbye after completing my tenure as commissioner of police. I still continue to be a proud member of the Delhi

Police family. I am writing about these three occasions, which is otherwise a routine matter in the UT cadre (now Arunachal Pradesh-Goa-Mizoram and Union Territory), since something unusual and interesting happened each time.

After my initial induction in Delhi Police in April 1965, I left it for the first time on 1 December 1966, when I got orders to report on promotion to IGP, Himachal Pradesh, in Shimla. It was then Delhi-Himachal cadre of IPS. On 1 November 1966, four districts were included in Himachal Pradesh from erstwhile Punjab state under the state reorganization plan and in the resulting confusion I was posted by the Himachal government in December 1966 against a post which had been abolished in September 1966. Sometime in October 1967, by the time my posting was regularized and my pay was released, I was also handed transfer orders by the Himachal government posting me to snow bound district of Lahaul-Spiti. They were not aware that the MHA (my cadre controlling authority) had already issued orders posting me back to Delhi police. Finally, I was relieved on 28 October 1967 for Delhi. During this period I had received a phone call from SP, Central District, Delhi, Shri D.K. Agarwal, informing me that Delhi administration had decided to post me as SP, central district, and he wanted to know when I would be reporting back to Delhi. However, when I reached Delhi and reported to IGP Delhi, I learnt that at the last moment, posting orders were changed and I was posted as SP in-charge, anti-corruption branch, under Delhi administration, in place of Shri Ravi Kant Sharma (on deputation from Punjab), who was sent as SP, central district. Although I had temporarily lost the chance to do a district posting, I treated it as a routine service matter.

On the second occasion, when I completed my tenure as IGP Goa, my transfer orders to Delhi contained the direction to report to IGP Delhi for posting. But before I left Goa, Shri P.V. Jaikrishnan, deputy secretary, MHA, who had come to Goa in second or third week of January 1976, had told me to meet him before joining Delhi Police. During our meeting, he informed me that there was some reluctance in Delhi administration/police headquarter to accept me and therefore he would advise me to go on deputation. This was surprising since only in November 1975, Shri Om Mehta, MoS, Home, in the Union Cabinet and a very powerful minister at that time had visited Goa and pressed the local government for my early release for Delhi Police. The MHA had already issued orders for my transfer to Delhi Police. The minister also told me about it and had advised me to report to Delhi Police at the earliest. Besides, the then LG, Delhi, Shri Kishan Chand, had known me personally for more than 15 years and had visited my residence two to three times when I was posted in Delhi. I later on learned that the objection had come from the 'power centre' dominating Delhi government at that time. Anyway, I accepted the deputation to RPF, Railway Board, as AIG for a period of four years.

I had just completed a year in the RPF, when one of my senior colleagues in Delhi Police, Shri R.K. Ohri, who met me at a dinner sometime in early March 1977, told me that there was a likelihood of my coming back to Delhi Police. He did not elaborate it further. Meanwhile, I had planned an official tour to Faizabad and Lucknow in second or third week of March. Since my train was in the afternoon, I went to my office in Rail Bhawan to collect a few papers regarding my tour. There I found the IG's personal secretary desperately looking for me as IG wanted to see me. When I met IG, Shri R.D. Singh, he directed me to cancel my tour and report that day to IGP, Delhi, for posting. I was quite shocked and surprised as only a year back Delhi administration/police headquarters were reluctant to accept me and now they wanted me to rejoin without any notice. There had been no change in their set-up. My IG, RPF, also told me that while formal orders of my transfer were yet to arrive, the home minister had requested the railway minister to relieve me immediately. I was relieved on that day itself without any formal order from the MHA with direction to report to IGP Delhi. It was later that I learned that quite a few officers and men (inspectors and other ranks) of Delhi Police had been arrested in a murder case and the needle of suspicion was pointing towards some senior officers also, which had demoralized the police force. One or two other cases with similar allegations were likely to be registered. Under these circumstances, the MHA was looking for some officer who had a popular image and wide acceptability in the force. This search ended with my name and hence I was transferred back to Delhi Police. Look at the way life works: from an unwanted, I became the most-wanted officer. These are the ways of destiny. This was my second entry in Delhi Police. As regards the events connected with my transfer to Goa, I have already described them in the chapter 'Left for Goa, Despite Opportunities to Stay Back'.

In May–June 1983, I again left Delhi Police to proceed on deputation to Ministry of Railways. In fact, my name, which was on the offer list for deputation, was picked up by CRPF, Ministry of Petroleum and Railway Protection Force. I was keen to go to RPF as I could not complete my deputation with them during my earlier tenure. I served the RPF for a record period of eight years and eight months in this tenure. In fact, the railway ministry had written to the MHA and the cabinet secretary that in view of my contribution to the railways they would like to retain me as long as Government of India could spare my services.

However, in September 1991, my name came up for consideration for the post of commissioner of police, Delhi. Since it was a highly prestigious police assignment, lot of pulls and pressures came in action in the next few months. Names of some senior officers from other states were also considered. This being a very important and coveted assignment of Indian police, a lot of political pressure was at work. Finally, the proposal was put up to the PM (chairman of the ACC) along with the recommendations of the ministry, and my name was approved. I received orders posting me as CP Delhi, on 12 February 1992, and I joined Delhi Police once again on 18 February. This was naturally my last tenure with Delhi Police and I handed over my charge on 4 January 1995.

My different tenures in Delhi Police were a great experience and taught me a lot. I consider these opportunities to serve the Delhi Police as a privilege and will always cherish them.

26

...AND MY TEAM DID IT!*

There is no better indicator to assess the effectiveness of the police than the level of public satisfaction achieved at any given time. The task before the police has increasingly become complex and challenging in the last three to four decades. Managing law and order in Delhi, the national capital and the political drawing room of the country, has always been a very daunting task—it is like walking on a razor's edge.

In mid '80s and early '90s, Sikh militants and terrorist groups from J&K were disrupting the peace in Delhi. Coinciding with this was the communal tensions due to the unresolved Ramjanmbhumi–Babri Masjid dispute was at its peak. The land mafias backed by gangsters from UP were threatening the citizens of Delhi, whose confidence in police was already shaking due to dreadful strikes of criminals belonging to Bawarias and Pardhi tribes. Those were particularly difficult days. It required a highly motivated and committed

---

*This article was written for the proposed coffee-table book of Delhi Police during the tenure of Shri B.K. Gupta, when he was CP Delhi.

force, meaningful cooperation from the people and proper understating by the media to retrieve the situation and restore people's faith in Police. Delhi Police rose to the occasion and once again proved that it was capable of achieving the highest standards of policing.

Police functioning has always been a team effort. Therefore we started open-house deliberations at different levels of the force and chalked out the future strategy. While on the one hand, we committed ourselves to work out the sensational and heinous cases of recent murders and dacoities, we also simultaneously formed special teams to chase terrorist groups and land mafias. This together with close monitoring at senior levels gave excellent and tangible results. Since most of the encounters with terrorists and dreaded criminals happened in public view, there was no blot on the human rights credentials of Delhi Police. We were informing the National Human Rights Commission regularly. The initiatives taken by Shri R. Tewari, Shri P.R.S. Brar, Shri Neeraj Kumar, Shri Deepak Misra and their teams deserve special mention.

Our officers and men meticulously prepared a detailed plan to meet any possible communal riot in the walled city due to the Ramjanmbhumi–Babri Masjid dispute, which in fact ensured total peace in the walled city in the aftermath of Babri Masjid Demolition on 6 December 1992. This was a great effort by Delhi Police at all levels and boosted their own confidence and morale. When the then LG Delhi, a very experienced administrator, told me that he wanted to call the Army for assistance, I firmly opposed it and requested him to trust Delhi Police and give it a fair chance. This was accepted. The honour of Delhi Police had to be defended. My officers and men took it as a challenge and ensured that the situation remained under complete control. There was not even a minor incident of communal nature in the walled city in the following 50 days after 6 December 1992. This was a great effort by Delhi Police at all levels and boosted their own conviction and spirits.

In one of the meetings in the PM's office to discuss police arrangements to prevent the proposed mammoth rally of the BJP on 25 February 1993, the then MoS, Home, Shri Rajesh Pilot, observed that the PM felt that after the Babri Masjid demolition, people's perception was that there was no government and we had to dispel this impression. Delhi Police, successfully, without any major incident, managed the challenge. We could achieve a seamless interface between intelligence, operation and law and order machinery. This surprised not only the authorities both at the Centre and the Delhi government, but also the media. These police achievements started restoring people's confidence in their police and the force developed faith in their leadership at different levels.

It is difficult for me to list out the names of senior officers, as a whole lot of them gave their best and made this success possible. Time has nonetheless proved that they are leaders of the force in their own right.

The force had started realizing that the senior police leadership had broad enough shoulders to carry their responsibility and protect them for their official actions including honest mistakes. While appearing before the Privilege Committee of the Lok Sabha in connection with privilege motions served on me and some of my officers, I appeared before the committee and told them that for all the alleged omissions committed by the police force on 25 February 1993, I alone was responsible. My statement left a big impact on the committee headed by Smt. Vijay Raje Scindia,

MP and senior vice president of the BJP, and they decided to drop all privilege notices against Delhi Police.

In another instance when under pressure from some central ministers, my seniors, both political and official, asked me to transfer the then SHO Jama Masjid, Inspector Vedpal Rathi, as the then Shahi Imam was uncomfortable and annoyed with him, I refused it on the grounds that he had only been carrying out my orders. Ultimately, the PM personally spoke to me and I explained my stand which he appreciated. I took his permission to post inspector Rathi to another equally important police station within the walled city. The same thing happened with the transfer of the then DCP, Northeast Delhi, and the PM again intervened. However I could protect my officer and posted him to a better district. The accruing advantage was that thereafter no political person asked me for posting/transfer of any police officer.

By now, the force at all levels had developed a sense of collective responsibility and started taking initiatives to show results as they were being given credit, recognition, publicity, rewards and, in some cases, out of turn promotions. Big photographs of our brave heroes were displayed at the entry point of police headquarters with the caption '*Dilli police ke bahadur sipahi ...ek se barrhkar ek* [The brave officers of Delhi Police, better than the best]'. Head constable Shri Kishan of PCR, who chased a dreaded terrorist even after suffering two bullet injuries on his body and finally fell unconscious, was given a double promotion, probably the first ever, and was appointed SI with the LG's approval. Shri Kishan's incident was a manifestation of a larger sense of responsibility and leadership emerging at different levels. All this had put the force in one mode, i.e., of showing good performance and created a team spirit with commitment. I will always remember the night of 24 February 1993, when preparations for preventing BJP's protest rally on 25 February were underway, it suddenly started raining. The CPWD labourers, who were putting concertina wire ran away. Our officers, DCP Sundari Nanda, ACP Tarlochan Singh Bhalla and Inspector Gurcharan Singh, without caring for the rain on a winter night, started putting wires on the railings with the help of their men. One could not have expected more. The daunting task before the police started looking manageable. The image of Delhi Police was becoming larger than the challenges before it.

The performance of the Delhi Police earned us a lot of goodwill with the government. The president of India, vice president and PM agreed to attend our Police Day Reception at the CP's Residence, which was a great honour for Delhi Police and boosted our morale and status. This happened despite some opposition from senior defence officials. The PM also took salute at the Police Day parade in the morning and addressed our men. Both these events had happened for the first time. The central government was also gracious enough to accept our proposal for about 1,700 upgradations/ promotions in different ranks including 120 posts of ACPs and about 441 posts of inspectors which cleared a huge stagnation. The Balakrishnan Committee report, which had made recommendations against the police commissioner system in Delhi, at the instance of some interested officials in the MHA, was opposed by us and finally consigned to record.

We believed that meaningful public cooperation is the basic requirement for ensuring effective policing. Our officers up to the SHO level made conscious efforts to make themselves available to people with proper follow-up actions on their complaints. In some cases, senior officers started contacting complainants directly over the phone about their grievances.

'Jan Sahyog Abhiyan' meetings in different districts created a sense of participation in people. An 'open-house' public meeting of the residents with the CP along with senior officers in the trans-Yamuna area was a pioneering initiative and earned a lot of goodwill for the police. Adverse news items appearing in newspapers and electronic media were attended to in the daily afternoon meetings of CP with the senior officers and follow-up actions were taken. An effective 'encroachment clearing drive' of some important road corridors and roads leading to railway stations, big hospitals, airports, etc., had a direct impact on the people. When prohibitory orders under Section 144 of the CrPC were clamped in Delhi to prevent the BJP's proposed mammoth rally, only one exception was made. The area in front of Delhi Police headquarters was consciously excluded to allow protest against Delhi Police and in fact, the Delhi University students had organized a demonstration during that period. We also took advantage of the curfew in some police station areas during that time and requested the MCD to clear the sewage and clean the roads, which was not otherwise possible in the congested area. The residents highly appreciated this friendly gesture of the police.

We had meetings with the lawyers' association and DU students to discuss issues that had strained our relations in the past. This created a better understanding with them. The Delhi University Police Station (Maurice Nagar) was designed to merge with the university ethos and did not have a boundary wall. Initiatives like sending a copy of FIR to complainants through post, sankraman kaksh for talking to witnesses, reminding arms licence holders about the renewal along with forms, assistance by PCR vans to car owners for towing their stranded vehicles to the nearest petrol pump or police station during night time, etc., were taken. People also liked that we almost totally stopped dharnas on road junctions, gherao's, demonstrations at the residence of people, masaal processions and also demonstrations at Rajpath. A proposed demonstration of about 30,000–40,000 people led by the head of a national political party in support of a gangster was not allowed to enter Delhi and disturb the peace and normal life of the city. All this was possible due to people's support.

I will always be grateful to the media for showing a good understanding of the challenges faced by the Delhi Police. They appreciated the handling of the situations varying from crime waves to terrorist activities, encounters and arrests of hardcore criminals to effective and firm police action in the aftermath of the Babri Masjid demolition and preventing BJP's proposed protest rally immediately after it, etc. We must also understand that finding out news and chasing it is a professional requirement of the media and the best way to deal with it is to provide them news and in time. In fact, any effort to hide it is acting like an ostrich. The media should be engaged meaningfully and with understanding.

My force was my strength and support. For me, serving the Delhi Police was a great experience and education and I have always deemed it as a privilege that I got this opportunity.

Delhi Police has the advantage of getting some of the most outstanding officers of the IPS to lead it and during their tenure, they have taken it to new heights of both performance as well as public service. The leadership in the recent past and present are tirelessly working to take it further in the same direction and I am confident that they will bring many more laurels to Delhi Police.

27

TWO ELECTIONS IN J&K

The militancy in J&K started around 1989–90. Large scale corruption, poor administration, rigged elections, active prompting and support by the intelligence agencies of Pakistan were some of the reasons for this. But the governor's decision to dissolve the legislative assembly in January 1990 became the ignition point. What followed was an unprecedented spurt in the militancy, killing thousands of innocent people. This created a general sense of insecurity and the Hindu section of the population, especially Kashmiri Pandits, a dominating community, were forced to migrate from the Valley, leaving behind their properties. The authority of the state government had almost collapsed. The terrorist organizations stepped up their activities and increased their area of operations extending it to some portion of the Jammu region. Pakistan's strategy was to recruit and train Kashmiri youth as a terrorist, supply them arms, communication equipment and communalize the society to destroy the secular fabric of the state. The state could not hold the general elections to the country's Parliament in 1991 and for this, the law had to be amended. There was no possibility of holding fresh elections for the state assembly.

While the number of incidents of terrorist violence, the number of civilians and security personnel killed and attacks on security forces did not decline, the security forces, by the end of 1994, had become dominant and the state government started resuming its normal functioning. The additional deployment of paramilitary forces including the Rashtriya Rifles and disenchantment of the local population with prolonged terrorist activities were reasons behind the improvement in the situation. This encouraged the Government of India and the state government at the beginning of 1995 to think about the conduct of the elections to the state assembly. In early 1995, chief election commissioner of India, Shri T.N. Seshan visited Srinagar along with the home secretary to make the spot assessment of the situation for conducting the elections to the state assembly. Thereafter, the state government started preparations for holding elections to the 87 constituencies of the state assembly.

At this stage, the MHA appointed me as the chief coordinator for the J&K elections. This was done on the specific recommendations of the chief election commissioner, who was extremely happy with my performance during the Bihar Assembly elections in February–April 1995, where elections were conducted without any incident of booth-capturing—a hitherto regular feature of elections in Bihar. The task of coordination included working out the force required for the election, its deployment according to the security needs of the area, liaison with the state government for accommodation, transport and other logistics, coordination with MHA for equipping the troops to deal with the disturbing situation in the state, coordination with other paramilitary and state police forces regarding their deployment and logistics, arranging and providing civilian personnel for election duties and assessing the vulnerability of sensitive and hypersensitive polling stations, etc. The total number of polling stations worked out to approximately 6,500 in 14 districts of the state—six each in the Jammu region and Kashmir Valley and two in the Ladakh region. Meanwhile, the MHA also appointed Shri A.S. Gill, IPS, as IG, CRPF, J&K, to assist me.

I landed in Srinagar on 9 May 1995. It was Eid. The holy shrine of Charar-e-Sharif and the nearby township, not very far from Srinagar, had been occupied by terrorists headed by the Afghan war veteran Mast Gul and his associate Abu Jindal. On 9 May, they set the town on fire and destroyed about 600 houses and 100 shops. The very next day, they set the shrine on fire. In the encounter which followed between the terrorists and security forces, about 20 terrorists were killed. While Abu Jindal was arrested, their leader Mast Gul escaped. The people in Srinagar kept on firing AK47s throughout the night to celebrate Eid. This was our initial welcome to the Kashmir Valley.

I started planning for the elections with the assistance of IG Shri A.S. Gill. We first listed out the issues which needed immediate attention and prioritized them. To start with, an ad hoc working set-up was created with a control room in one of the battalion headquarters at Srinagar. Meanwhile, about 30–35 DIGs, ADIGs and commandants reported at Group Centre (GC), Bantalab, Jammu, for election duty. I came to Jammu along with Shri Gill to meet and brief them about their task. When I saw them first, I noticed lack of enthusiasm, anxiety and uncertainty on their faces. They were suddenly directed to report at Jammu for elections, their duration of stay was uncertain as election dates had not been finalized yet. The terrain and the situation in which they had to work were quite difficult and unfriendly. Most of them were in their 40s and, naturally, had the usual family issues. I realized that my first priority was to create confidence in them and also assure them that their personal issues, including their visits to their family, would be looked after. This unexpected start to the meeting suddenly changed the mood and one could notice the enthusiasm and smiles coming back on their faces. Timely appreciation of their anxieties and its assured redressal helped me motivate them and get their absolute cooperation. They were now willingly prepared to take ownership of their responsibilities.

I do not intend to give all the details of the progress and conduct of elections as it would take up a lot of space. However, I propose to give a broad picture of all that we did to ensure the successful completion of the election process, including some interesting incidents and developments that took place during that period.

We started working out the force required for the state assembly election. The force deployment was to be made in three phases—the pre-poll phase, the force for the actual conduct of elections and the force required for maintaining peace and providing security to certain vulnerable people after the election process was over. This was in addition to the deployment of CPMF, already available for area domination, road opening duties and security of important persons and installations. The additional force for pre-poll deployment started arriving. But sometime in June, after the visit of CEC Shri Seshan, it was revealed that elections were postponed to October–November 1995. It was mainly due to the opposition of the political parties, which had been conveyed to the CEC during their meeting with him. However, the pre-poll force of 176 companies of CPMF were retained and the remaining force was sent back. The preparations for elections continued. As chief coordinator, I informed the MHA sometime in August or September that our preparations were complete and we were ready to conduct elections. However, the full election commission (all three members) again visited J&K in 1995. After consulting the state political parties, state administration, central security and intelligence agencies, they returned to Delhi and recommended to the government that the ground conditions were not conducive for holding elections. Once again, the de-induction of central forces started and even the pre-poll force level was reduced to 112 companies.

On 9 March 1996, the election commission announced the schedule for the parliamentary elections for the country. It also included elections to the six parliamentary constituencies of J&K in three phases, i.e., on 7, 23 and 30 May 1996. The state government was keen to hold assembly elections along with the parliamentary elections, but the election commission did not agree as the major political party of the state, i.e., the National Conference, had refused to participate in the election. With the postponement of assembly elections and the election to parliamentary constituencies being confined to three phases, the force requirement needed to be reworked. Finally, after a lot of detailed discussions and consultations, it was decided to induct additional 550 companies of CPMF and other state police forces. The main component had to come from CRPF and BSF and the remaining force was provided by ITBP, RPF, Sashastra Seema Bal (SSB), CISF and Punjab Armed Police. The responsibility for the coordination of all activities relating to the outside forces was also entrusted to me as the chief coordinator. This included their induction, movement, deployment, logistics, accommodation, provision of equipment and finally the de-induction. During parliamentary elections, we did not deploy J&K police for election duties.

When elections were postponed in November 1995, an interesting incident took place. Lieutenant General Saklani, advisor (home) to the governor, ordered that the CRPF companies, which were retained in the Valley be attached to the police stations for duty and they would be shifted to tent accommodations near the police station. I opposed it as unlike other CPMF deployed in the Valley, such as ITBP and BSF, we had no Arctic tents and the local police personnel were either staying in their homes or barracks. Staying in ordinary tents in harsh months of winter from November to March was very risky for the health of my jawans. When Lieutenant General Saklani insisted, I wrote to the Union home secretary that in case the J&K government did not agree to provide us with pucca accommodation or Arctic tents, I would withdraw my force to Jammu and would remain available there for duty. But I could not put the health of my men at risk by shifting them to ordinary tents during severe winter. Thereafter, the General kept quiet.

The force induction during the election and later the deinduction was planned in detail to avoid inconvenience to the residents of major towns of J&K and also small towns falling on the way. At the entry point itself on the Jammu border and also at the railway stations in the Jammu region, bus and trucks carrying the force were given printed instructions about the route they had to follow and the location of various parking lots on the way. CRPF had also provided auto workshops and canteens on the way for the convenience of the force. This had earned appreciation from the local media. Some troops were also brought by air.

Providing accommodation to the large force was another major task. We needed accommodation during transit and then at each district location. Transit accommodation was provided at Jammu, Udhampur and Srinagar. The accommodation at district headquarters was provided by our nodal officers with the help of district authorities, who were given suitable instructions by the state government. Similarly, camp accommodation was also provided for some distant polling stations.

The induction and movement of such a huge force during the entire election period required the requisitioning of a large number of commercial vehicles and also arranging POL for them. The scale of vehicles required for each company was fixed and conveyed to the state government. This was provided by the state government in consultation with us. These vehicles were handed over to the force on their arrival at railway stations and airports. Most of these vehicles were requisitioned from outside the state.

All items of ration were purchased one month in advance and distributed to the force on arrival. The force had to be equipped with other items of operational and administrative necessities. Our GC at Bantalab in Jammu was given responsibility for storing and distributing these items to the force. It included operational levels of arms and ammunition, BP jackets, night vision devices, generator sets, flexi tanks, tentage, etc.; a lot of it was purchased by the CRPF directorate and some equipment like sleeping bags and Arctic tents were obtained from the Army.

Initially, the Army headquarter did not respond favourably when approached by the MHA. After informing the Union home secretary, I made an appointment to see the vice chief of the Army Staff, Lieutenant General Moti Dhar and met him to request supply of the equipment. He was very courteou, but politely expressed his inability to meet our requirements on the ground since they had to equip their Rashtriya Rifles battalions and some other Army units. I told him that he was the best judge to decide his priorities, but I thought it necessary to inform him that both the PM and the home minister had made statements in Parliament that elections would be conducted in J&K. This matter had not only national but international importance too. The CRPF which had been given the responsibility to coordinate and conduct the election-related activities in J&K could not do anything without the equipment. The situation could turn quite embarrassing for the Government of India. The General immediately assured me that all our requirements would be met and deputed two Major Generals to coordinate with my officers and supply the entire equipment. A little effort at a personal level sorted out an important issue.

From an operational point of view, we divided the entire state into zones mainly comprising of two districts each, and each zone was put under the charge of a DIG or ADIG. Doda district, which was heavily infested with terrorists and had difficult terrain, especially in the Kishtwar area, was made a separate zone and put under an outstanding IPS officer, Shri Amranand Patnaik. One CRPF commandant was appointed as a nodal officer at each district headquarters. Officers of the level of deputy commandments and assistant commandments were nominated as Assembly segment officers. While zonal officers kept liaison at a senior level with state authorities, Army, other CPMFs, the nodal officer arranged the camping sites for the force deployed in their area in coordination with district authorities, its logistics, transport, etc. They were also made responsible for the movement and deployment of the force and the polling parties to the polling stations and back. They kept liaison with the Army and other security forces for area domination during their movement and also coordinated with district authorities. An information folder was given to each company commander containing the entire scheme of deployment for his company during the entire period, details of polling stations, where it was to be deployed, names of district and CRPF officers in their area, intelligence about the area, logistics and transport.

An operational headquarters for the CEC was established at Srinagar with a control room. IG, CRPF, A.S. Gill, assisted me in planning, organizing and implementing all the election arrangements. We had appointed ADIG-level officers in charge of transport, logistics and operations (election deployment and planning). A senior-DIG-level officer Shri P.P.S Siddhu, IPS, was stationed at Jammu for coordinating the movement of the force and for providing the required equipment and transport. Officers were also selected for coordinating with state authorities, state police, electoral office, other CPMF and central intelligence agencies.

We introduced a system of periodical review of the arrangements and made the required additions and alterations as needed.

While each CPMF, except CISF, had their fully equipped medical teams, the state government formulated a detailed action plan for this purpose. The Army also provided the support of their hospitals.

Since it was clear that the state government personnel would not be available for polling duties, about 11,000 government employees were brought from outside. While some employees, especially Urdu knowing, came from neighbouring states, about 10,000 government personnel were airlifted from Delhi to Srinagar and Avantipora airfields. They were given two days of election training in Delhi. On arrival, they were welcomed by CRPF and state government officials and were given tea and snacks. Each one of them was provided a bulletproof jacket, a lunch packet and was handed over to the district nodal officer of the CRPF to go to the camping site with sufficient escort. During the entire election period, none of them fell ill or got injured except one person from Najafgarh, Delhi, who had developed a minor heart ailment and was admitted to the Army hospital. When the CRPF nodal officer asked him if he wanted to be sent back by air, he refused saying that he might not get the needed medical care at home. These civilian personnel, who were not used to working in conditions of militancy, had to discharge the important responsibilities of conducting elections. It required a lot of understanding and a very careful handling.

Paramilitary forces and the state police were adopting, as a counter-terrorism effort, an exercise called 'cordon and search' to flush out hiding terrorists from a particular locality. In this, a locality or an area would be surrounded by the force and all the residents would be ordered to come on the road and then the search would follow. This caused a lot of annoyance and protest. There were complaints of molestation, theft and harassment of old and sick people. I wrote to the MHA that while I would fight and chase terrorists in case of confrontation and take strict action, including encounters against them, CRPF will not conduct 'cordon and search' operations as they had to go in all localities during elections and at that time their number would be very small. We do not want to unnecessarily annoy the people and earn their ill will.

During the entire pre-election period, at least twice to thrice a week, IG A.S. Gill and I would visit one of the district headquarters or some remote or sensitive polling stations either by helicopter or by car for meeting and briefing the security force personnel and officers. This experience gave us first-hand knowledge of almost all important areas. We were able to visit all sensitive and remote polling stations in Kupwara, Baramulla, Anantnag, Srinagar, Pulwama, Budgam, Doda, Rajouri, Poonch and Udhampur. During our visits, we realized that there were some polling stations, which were not only at a long distance, but were also critically located, and in case of an ambush, or any other difficulty, it would have been difficult to provide them any assistance. We requisitioned a round-the-clock NSG unit with helicopters and devised a system to provide immediate protection to our stranded polling parties. This type of air protection to polling parties was provided for the first time. We got a special sanction of MHA to provide special food packets for our polling parties who had to travel a long distance.

Our personal rapport with the two Corp commanders, i.e., Lieutenant General Dhillon of 15 Corp at Srinagar, and Lieutenant General Dinesh Singh of 16 Corp at Jammu proved extremely helpful. Lieutenant General Dinesh Singh knew me from his childhood. On our personal request, not from the ministry, they provided area domination, road opening parties, anti-sabotage checking of polling stations and camping sites for polling parties. They also provided protection, of course, from a distance, to our polling parties returning with the ballet boxes. After the elections, IG A.S. Gill and I personally met them to convey our gratitude.

The entire planning was done so meticulously, taking into consideration the minutest possible details, that once the actual election process had started, it went like clockwork. There were no major incidents and none of the CPMF officers and men, including election personnel, received any serious injury. There were also no complaints about human rights violations.

The voter turnout for the state was 49.2 per cent. Out of a total electorate of 44.51 lakh, 21.82 lakh voters cast their votes. Similarly, the overall percentage of polling during the state assembly elections, which followed parliamentary elections, was 43.28 per cent. This happened despite the call for boycotting the elections given by the Hurriyat Conference and threats of terrorists. It was also revealed that Hurriyat's hold was confined to Srinagar town and some areas in Anantnag and Pulwama.

Since the central government wanted credit for the elections to go to the state government, a press conference after each phase of election was held by the state chief secretary and DGP, even though the central forces had actually conducted the entire elections.

The Government of India was extremely pleased with the successful conduct of parliamentary elections in J&K. The Union home secretary congratulated me on call and also conveyed to me the Union government's appreciation in writing. The letter said:

These elections were held amidst intense international interest and scrutiny and in the presence of national and international media, which creates additional complexities and challenges...all the above arrangements and requirements called for an extremely high quality of planning, mobilization, movement, coordination and utmost professionalism...an extremely complex and difficult task has been performed by rare perfection... the challenges posed by the terrorists and secessionist elements were effectively pre-empted and neutralized. I am aware of your pivotal role in contributing to the success.

In my case, every success had been generally followed by an anti-climax. My batch was expecting a promotion to DG's rank in Government of India and I was informally told by the home secretary that I would be posted to CRPF as DG. After a few days, the government issued a notification promoting officers of a batch senior to us, leaving a few vacancies unfilled. When I met the home secretary during the morning walk in Lodhi Gardens, before I could say anything, he told me that the PM was very happy with the success of parliamentary elections and desired that the same team should be deputed to conduct the assembly elections in J&K. The state government was also keen on the assembly elections. I told the home secretary that nothing could be predicted and if anything goes wrong with the assembly elections, it might affect my promotion. But he just made a pleasant observation that 'nothing untoward would happen with you as in-charge of the election arrangements and you would get your promotion on the same day'.

The home secretary kept his promise and on the last day of assembly elections, i.e., 30 September 1996, I was at Nawapachi in Kishtwar, Doda district, when I got the message about my promotion. Since the elections were over, I flew to Delhi and took over as DG, CRPF, on the same day.

An interesting development took place in early September. The home secretary told me that the government had agreed to promote Shri A.V. Liddle, my batchmate and a good friend, who had only 18 days left for his superannuation and he would like to adjust him in CRPF as DG. I was informed so that I do not get unnecessarily worked up, as I had already been told about my posting as DG, CRPF. To his surprise, I told him that I was very happy for Liddle that he could get the promotion as DG and I would wait for my turn. I took Liddle to Srinagar for a visit and organized a grand farewell there.

I will fail in my duty if I do not recognize the great effort put in by CRPF officers and men in making these two elections a great success. They went the extra mile, which made it memorable for me. Shri Rakesh Chandra, my staff officer, was a big support to me during this period. Shri Amranand Patnaik, who was prepared to accept any challenge, did outstanding work in Doda, a very difficult area to work in. But my main support came from my IG Shri A.S. Gill, who most unassumingly exhibited qualities of planning, organizational and operational abilities and exemplary leadership. He proved to be an asset to the organization

The state of J&K got its democratically elected government after seven years.

28

FIGHTING FOR BETTER
PAY SCALES FOR CRPF & OTHER
CENTRAL ARMED FORCES

n 1996, the Union government announced the 5th Pay Commission for the central government employees. Various government employees' unions and service associations started preparations for presenting their case before the commission. The process of consultation with members of the association was started. I do not recollect the exact date, but sometimes either towards the end of 1996 or the beginning of 1997, a meeting of the IPS Association was held in the auditorium of the National Museum. I also attended the meeting as an ordinary member of the association. As a matter of principle throughout my service, I never accepted any post in any service association or in any other civil society organization. I always thought that I should devote all my energy and efforts to the role officially assigned to me. At that time I was working as DG, CRPF, and was probably among the few senior-most IPS officers in the country.

During the meeting, a very senior IPS officer working with

the MHA, who was heading the cell preparing the case for the IPS Association, presented a very well-deliberated proposal emphatically projecting all aspects of pay revision, including difficult service conditions, sacrifices made by police officers, their contribution in ensuring the unity and integrity of the country, etc. Thereafter, members of the service were asked to give their suggestions. At this juncture, I intervened. But before I could speak, the presiding officer and other officers on the dais insisted that I should take a chair on the dais and give my views.

I told the meeting that while putting forth the case of IPS officers, we had mentioned the sacrifices made by different ranks of police forces, including the Armed Forces of the Union (paramilitary forces), but we were not taking up the pay revision case of officers and men of these forces. Unlike other all India services and central services, we were leaders of these forces and it was our responsibility to look after their interests. We should, therefore, include their case in our proposal. If we do not do this, we would be, by default, pushing them to either form some sort of association or seek help from political leaders. Both would have an adverse effect on the discipline and culture of the forces. I also said that so long I was DG, CRPF, I could not support any proposal, which did not include the pay revision proposal regarding officers and men of the central forces. A few senior officers, whom I do not want to name, did not agree with my point of view and insisted that our association should take up the case of only IPS officers. But the majority of the IPS officers, especially, middle-level officers and some junior members present there, got up one by one and supported my views. Ultimately, it was decided to revise the already prepared proposal and put up a fresh proposal where the case of officers and men of central forces would also be included. Two young IG-level officers, Shri Kamal Kumar, who later on became director, NPA, Hyderabad, and Shri Anami Roy, who later became CP, Mumbai, and DG, Maharashtra, were entrusted with the responsibility of preparing the revised proposal. It was for the first time that the IPS Association took up the pay revision case of the entire police force working under the central government. This also gave me a lot of satisfaction as I had been able to take up the cause of officers and men of the Armed Forces of the Union.

The revised proposal of the IPS Association was submitted to the Pay Commission for consideration. The developments were being monitored and pursued by the association. The Pay Commission finalized its report and submitted it to the government. The report neither made any special recommendation for the IPS, nor gave any additional benefits to officers and men of Armed Forces of the Union. General upgradation in pay scales was done with reference to pay grades implemented after the 4th Pay Commission. The recommendations made by our association based on difficult service conditions, such as separation from family, risk to life, sacrifices made by force personnel, contribution towards national security, etc., were not given any consideration. Again, a meeting of the association was held and it was decided that a delegation of the DGs of paramilitary forces and some other senior police officers should take up the matter with the home minister and PM. The recommendations of the commission regarding police service were once again thoroughly examined and a list of issues to be discussed with the home minister and PM was worked out.

In the meeting with the home minister, both cabinet secretary and home secretary were also present. After my other colleagues had spoken, I took up the issue of abolition of the post of DIG from the police hierarchy and post of naik in paramilitary forces as these posts had lost their relevance and were unnecessarily delaying promotion to the next rank. I also took up the issue of giving a higher pay scale, which was already being given to Delhi Police, to the constables of paramilitary forces. I thought that this was an opportunity to do something substantial for the force, so I was very emphatic in pleading my case. Home Minister Shri Inderjit Gupta was a very calm person and had been a seasoned trade union leader. He told us that he would be considering our case sympathetically and, if required, he would take it up with the PM.

After taking clearance from the home minister, we approached PMO for an appointment. Our meeting with the PM was scheduled at the PM's office in Parliament House. All of us reached there half an hour before the appointed time. About 10 minutes before we were to go in, the leader of our delegation called me aside and without giving any reason told me that I need not go with the delegation. I was shocked. Later on, I learned that he had been briefed in this regard. I had always been a disciplined police officer so I did not raise any objection, but the two young officers, Shri Anami Ray and Shri Kamal Kumar, who were also part of the delegation, told the leader clearly that if I was not going with the delegation, they would like to withdraw. They said that only Kaushal Saheb could argue the case forcefully. The leader, who was a very senior police officer, was taken aback as he had not expected this and finding no other option he again requested that I accompany the delegation.

The home minister, cabinet secretary and home secretary were also present in the meeting. After the discussion started and when my turn came, I first look up the case of abolition of DIG's rank from police hierarchy. The cabinet secretary immediately intervened and said that the Army would object to this as they had a corresponding rank in their hierarchy. I promptly replied that when benefits were given to the defence personnel, no such consideration had been shown to us. I cited the case of ration money and requested that this should not be a ground to reject our proposal. The PM intervened and the discussion was shifted to another point, i.e., higher pay scales for sepoys of paramilitary organizations. I told the PM that with due respect to the defence forces, our sacrifices during that period had been more than the Army. The paramilitary forces are on the front lines on international borders and as per the Geneva Convention, fighting insurgency and militancy in different parts of the country and were responsible for guarding the internal security within the country.

During the PM's meeting, an interesting development took place. At one stage, when I was speaking, the cabinet secretary suddenly intervened and said, 'Sir, I have assured Kaushal that the various demands given by the IPS Association will be considered sympathetically.' I immediately realized that there was something behind this as there was no justification in mentioning any assurance being given to me (in fact, nothing like this had happened). I immediately said that there was no need to give me any assurance, as the cabinet secretary's words were enough for us. I also mentioned that when I was taking up the policemen's cause, I was only discharging my duty as DG of the force. At that time, I hadn't realized that there had been a game at play and a wrong impression was being created about me. The PM assured us that our case would be considered sympathetically, and the meeting was closed.

I think two to three days after this, I got a call from Shri Vijay Shankar Mathur, IPS, special secretary, IS, in the

MHA, informing me that the home minister wanted to see me immediately. Vijay and I had done our master's (English Literature) together at Lucknow University. I reached the MHA and met Vijay, who told me that the PM had entrusted the entire matter of revision of pay scales of policemen to the home minister for final settlement and it had also been decided to discuss the matter only with DG, CRPF, i.e., me. No other senior police officer or DG had been called. Suddenly, a big responsibility had come on my shoulders. He also told me that the home minister would be proposing three advanced increments in the old pay scale instead of two which were given after the last Pay Commission and if it was acceptable to us, he would be obtaining the cabinet approval for it. Vijay advised me to accept it, as the home minister had shown special consideration for my efforts. It was a moment of great pressure for me. I had to take a view on a matter which would affect the pay scales of all paramilitary forces (AFU) for the next 10 years. I also knew that the fact that the decision regarding the revised pay scales had been taken in consultation with only me, would also be known to all paramilitary forces. This was a rare opportunity and honour, but had put immense responsibility on me. Different options were coming into my mind and I told Vijay that we should go to the home minister's chamber. I felt that this was a great chance for me to make some valuable contribution to the police forces, whom I had served all my life. I decided, just before entering the home minister's chamber, not to accept the home minister's proposal and request for reconsideration of our earlier demand for a higher pay scale. I also thought that my insistence could annoy the home minister and it might damage my career in the last lap of my service. But the desire to do something for the betterment of the forces was foremost on my mind.

After Vijay informed the home minister that he had briefed me about his proposal, I first expressed my gratitude to the home minister for choosing only me among all the DGs for this important discussion and I also thanked him for his special consideration for the paramilitary forces by proposing to give them three advance increments. Thereafter, I stopped for a while and then very politely told the home minister that since he had been gracious enough to only call me for this discussion, he would not mind if I did not accept the offer. I told him that I had been pleading for higher pay scales for the forces in view of their extremely difficult service conditions and the sacrifices that the forces had made, and that I was convinced that they deserved it. The home minister also knew that some murmuring had been going on among the forces. I added that if our request was not accepted, I would have to hold a Sainik Sammelan of the force personnel to inform them that we had tried our best, but our efforts had not succeeded. As soon as I finished speaking, the home minister wasted no time and directed the special secretary that all paramilitary forces should be given the higher pay scale as requested by them.

I had apprehended that the home minister might get annoyed with me for being adamant and send me off. Therefore, the home minister's decision came as a pleasant surprise to me and Vijay as well. I just could not believe that we had achieved what we wanted. Approval of higher pay scales for sepoys resulted in an increment of about ₹500 (including DA) in the monthly emoluments of the constables and a consequential rise in the pay scales of other ranks. The post of naik, as proposed by us, was also abolished, which gave immediate promotions to a large number of existing naiks and accelerated promotions in the future. I came back to my force headquarters and the news spread like wildfire among all paramilitary forces. Everybody was delighted and congratulated me.

This was followed by a bombshell. I got my transfer orders posting me as special secretary in the MHA. Some of my friends in the service, who were not happy with the importance that had been given to me during the settlement of the Pay Commission issue and earlier due to my successfully conducting the two elections, parliamentary and assembly, in J&K, succeeded in creating a wrong impression about me that I was trying to assume leadership of the police forces and with the active support of a very senior bureaucrat had got my transfer orders issued. Since they knew that the home minister was happy with me, he was told that as I was one of the senior-most police officers, whose services would be very valuable in the ministry. This was revealed to me by the home minister himself when I called on him after joining the MHA. As was my habit, I had immediately handed over the charge of the post of DG, CRPF, and had joined the MHA. The charge given to me included branches which hardly had any important work. Since the home minister had come to know about the game played in this matter, he conveyed his annoyance to all concerned. Mr Arun Mukherjee, IPS (Retd), former director of the CBI, who was an advisor to the home minister, spoke to me from abroad and provided clarifications. Since I have never bothered about these things, I told him to forget it. Within a fortnight, a new post of special secretary, in-charge, Department of J&K Affairs, was created and I was posted.

This further strengthened my faith that if one does what he thinks is correct and makes sincere efforts with the right intentions, they are appreciated by everyone and it leads to a lot of professional satisfaction.

When you fight for protecting other's interest, the Lord Almighty comes to your rescue.

29

ACTION PLAN FOR HANDLING MILITANCY IN J&K

On 1 December 1997, I took over as special secretary, in-charge, Department of J&K Affairs, in the MHA. The problem of militancy in J&K was reigning high in the country's internal security agenda for a decade. The induction of foreign mercenaries in the Valley at an unprecedented scale, upgradation of terrorist weaponry and determined efforts to bring in new areas in the Jammu region in the vortex of militancy had lent new urgency to the militancy problem in the state.

Given this, a high-level meeting was convened by Union Home Minister Shri L.K. Advani at Vigyan Bhawan, New Delhi, on 18 May 1998, to review and formulate an effective strategy to meet the serious internal security threat posed by Pakistan-sponsored militants in J&K. Besides the home minister, the meeting was attended by the defence minister, governor and chief minister of J&K, cabinet secretary, principal secretary to the PM, Chief of Army Staff, home secretary, secretary (R), director, IB, director generals of BSF, CRPF and J&K and me.

There was a consensus among the participants that there had been no let-up in Pakistan's covert offensive to destabilize the situation in J&K through armed mercenaries to achieve its political and strategic objectives. The singling out of soft targets in the hinterland and heightened insecurity among the members of the minority community were some of the issues which needed a resolute response. It was felt that there was an urgent need to re-evaluate the manifestations and implications of the threat posed by Pakistan in the context of internal security and to suggest an appropriate strategy to fully and effectively counter the threat. This was to be followed by working on, within the broad framework of the agreed strategy, a time-bound and deliverable 'action plan' to tackle militancy in J&K. This action plan was to identify the problem areas, suggest remedial measures, fix a time frame for completion of various tasks and make recommendations about additional resources wherever required to augment the capabilities of various organizations in the counter-militancy exercise. To achieve these objectives, a multidisciplinary special group headed by me (special secretary, J&K) was constituted. The membership of the group was as under:

1. Shri M.B. Kaushal, special secretary, J&K Affairs, chairman, MHA
2. Lieutenant General Inder Kumar, DG, military operations, Army headquarters, Military Operations, Army HQs
3. Shri A.S. Dulat, special director, IB
4. Shri E.N. Rammohan, General, BSF
5. Shri Gurbachan Jagat, DGP, J&K
6. Shri Rakesh Hooja, joint secretary, Department of J&K, member secretary, Special Group

The group held a series of discussions amongst themselves and with officials of different departments (both from the Centre and the state) engaged in counter-militancy operations. We also visited J&K, where we confabulated with the governor and the chief minister to acquaint ourselves with their perceptions and suggestions to improve the ground situation. We also held meetings with the chief secretary, General Officer Commanding-in-Chief, Northern Command, the DGP, J&K, the two Corp commanders, home secretary, J&K, besides officers of intelligence agencies, JKP, BSF and CRPF posted in J&K. The group also had joint deliberations with representatives of all agencies to have a composite appreciation of the ground situation and thrash out the areas of conflicting perceptions. During this tour of J&K, the group also visited some of the security force locations in Rajouri and Poonch, where various ground-level problems were deliberated upon with the local formation commanders, police and district officials. The group also held a series of consultations with the representatives of the Army, CPMFs, state government, intelligence agencies and some divisions of the MHA on its return to Delhi.

The core elements and priorities of the new strategy were identified as—(1) curbing infiltration, (2) countering militancy in the hinterland, (3) protection of the minorities, (4) tackling alienation of border population, (5) enhancing intelligence capabilities, (6) demolishing the processionist base, (7) greater functional integration through institutional framework of operational and intelligence groups at Unified HQs and field levels. For this, upgradation of technological components of the counter-insurgency operations through improved technology, gadgetry and equipment for the security forces were also considered.

I have not included details of the action plan as they are confidential. I submitted the final report of the group containing a time-bound action plan at the macro level, which could be used as a framework by the two Unified HQs to work out the location-specific details for their respective jurisdictions. Keeping in view the fact that challenges thrown up by the militancy change over time, we recommended that strategies, tactics and actions outlined in our report need to be reviewed from time to time as a part of the dynamic planning exercise. I must acknowledge the support and assistance given by the various officers of the central and state governments, especially, Shri Rakesh Hooja, my joint secretary and member secretary of the group in preparing and completing this report in time.

The report of the special group was submitted to the home minister and the PM for their perusal and approval, which was received in less than a week. The required financial sanction was also obtained in a short time.

The action plan was sent to all concerned for immediate implementation. It was a matter of great satisfaction to me that an important strategic project of national importance, involving the functioning of the different wings of the central and the state government, was entrusted to me and I could, with the support of my colleagues, complete it in time and to the satisfaction of the senior-most of the land.

30

MISSION CHENNAI–
ARREST OF UNION MINISTERS

t was around 11.00 p.m., on 30 June 2000, I had just returned with my wife from a dinner, when my RAX started ringing. Home secretary Shri Kamal Pande was on the line and without briefing me about the matter, he just said that he was speaking from the PM's residence and I should speak to him (Shri Atal Bihari Vajpayee was the PM then). The PM came on the line and in his usual easy style told me that two central cabinet ministers namely Shri Murasoli Maran and Shri T.R. Balu had been arrested by Chennai Police, along with former CM Shri K. Karunanidhi. This had happened under the instructions of the new CM of Tamil Nadu, Jayalalithaa. The PM desired that I should immediately proceed to Chennai and an ARC plane had been arranged for me. If I wanted any other officer to accompany me, I should indicate it to the home secretary. He also told me that the governor of Tamil Nadu had been briefed about my visit and she would be making the required arrangements. Naturally, I asked the PM for the brief for my visit, i.e., the purpose and the task I was supposed to perform. The PM, in his most inimitable style only said, '*Kaushal ji, aap samajhdaar afsar hain, Chennai jayein aur situation dekhein* [Kaushalji, you are a seasoned officer. You visit Chennai and assess the situation for yourself].' I was told to submit my report by 12 noon for consideration of the Union cabinet. I told the home secretary that I would like Shri O.P. Arya, joint secretary, police, who was working with me in the MHA to accompany me. Thereafter, I left for the airport, where Shri O.P. Arya had already reached. Around 1.00 a.m., we left Delhi.

Meanwhile, I learned the details of the incident which took place in Chennai. On 29 June 2000, commissioner, Chennai Corporation, had lodged a police complaint alleging corruption in the construction of mini flyovers in the city causing huge financial loss to the government. During the investigation, the Chennai Police arrested the former chief minister and head of the DMK, Shri K Karunanidhi, on 30 June at 1.30 a.m., for his involvement in this case. He was allegedly manhandled when he resisted arrest. Minister at the Centre Shri Murasoli Maran, who had reached the spot and had opposed the arrest, was also arrested for obstructing public servants in the performance of their duties. Later, another minister at the Centre, T.R. Baalu, came with many DMK party workers and protested. He was also arrested. While Shri Baalu was sent to Vellore prison, Shri Murasoli Maran, who was a heart patient and had a pacemaker, was arrested and kept in custody at Apollo Hospital, Chennai.

Our plane landed at Hyderabad Airport for refuelling and since this was taking time, I started walking on the tarmac. Shri O.P. Arya observed that while everybody was sleeping on the plane, I was awake; he wanted to know the reason. I told him that Ms Jayalalithaa, the new Tamil Nadu CM, was a very intelligent and sharp person and might question our visit on the grounds that the matter was within state jurisdiction and the central government need not interfere. I was thinking of an appropriate reply. After a while, I told him that I had decided that if asked, I would say that since two Union cabinet ministers had been arrested, the central government had deputed me to visit and check their welfare and to find out if they needed anything.

We reached Raj Bhawan a few minutes past 6.00 a.m. and found governor Fatima Beevi waiting for us in her office. Chief secretary P. Shanker, the home secretary, DGP, CP, Chennai, and a few other senior officers were also present at the Raj Bhawan. After having a cup of tea, we were ready for the meeting. I told Shri O.P. Arya that while I would be busy talking to different persons, he should make notes of the discussions so that we send our report in time. We first met the governor in her chamber. She virtually narrated the version given by the local government and had not made any efforts to verify the facts. She had not consulted any other political party or leader or any mediapersons who had been present at the venue to know more about the incident. She had also not consulted any expert to check the legality of the action taken by Chennai Police. She had formed her opinion based only on the facts given to her by the officials of the state government.

Thereafter, we met other officers including Chief Secretary Shri P. Shanker, the DGP and the CP, Chennai. The chief secretary briefed me about the facts of the case and the stand taken by the state government. The police officers, especially, CP, Chennai, showed us the FIR and other related documents and a video clip covering the entire incident, including the violence that had occurred at the time of Shri Karunanidhi's and Shri M. Maran's arrest. Both Jaya TV and Sun TV (owned by the Maran family) had also covered the entire incident. I was very careful and took the governor's permission to meet Shri Maran, who was in custody, but admitted to Apollo Hospital, and also requested that some senior prison officer should accompany us. Additional DG, prison, was deputed for the purpose.

We met Shri Maran at Apollo Hospital. His wife had been allowed to be with him in the hospital. He gave his version of the incident. A DSP of Tamil Nadu Police, who was in the arrest party, alleged that Shri Maran had punched his face and he was hurt by the ring he had been wearing. Shri Maran explained that he had never worn any jewellery item in his life after his marriage and refuted the allegation of punching the DSP. He was satisfied with the medical care taken by the Apollo medical team. When we were coming out, some members of the press, including Shri Sunil Prabhu of NDTV had reached the hospital, but we very politely refused to speak to them. Thereafter, I and O.P. Arya went to Raj Bhawan for completing the remaining work. Since we learned that members of the press were waiting for us at the main entry gate of Raj Bhawan, we entered the place through the back gate. The chief secretary was still there and he invited us for coffee. I sought some clarifications from the chief secretary, which he provided. We completed our work quickly as we had to send the report to Delhi. After informing the officials we left. From my interaction with the officials, I learned that contrary to our impression, Jayalalithaa was a little nervous and was anticipating an adverse report from the central team. Her subsequent conduct confirmed this—she had visited the Guruvayur temple on the same day to make the offering of an elephant.

I asked O.P. Arya to quickly prepare an aide memoir for sending the report to Delhi. I told him, in brief, my impression of the whole incident. Chennai Police had taken action against the former CM on a duly registered FIR and arrested the two Union ministers correctly for obstructing public servants in the performance of their duties. There was nothing legally wrong with their action. But it was also true that the whole incident smacked of vengeance. The hurry with which the 78-year-old former CM was arrested at midnight, within three to four hours of the registration of the FIR and the rough treatment given to him and Shri Maran during the arrest, were evidence of the vengeance. It was a case of corruption and there was no possibility of the former CM disappearing; the arrest could have been done at any later stage. In jail, he was kept in the same cell in which Jayalalithaa has stayed. But on the face of it, there was nothing illegal. The Tamil Nadu government had justified their action on the grounds that the former CM, Union minister and some DMK supporters had resisted arrest and had tried to assault the police arrest party. The governor had believed the state government's version of things as facts and had taken no initiative to verify the facts of such an important incident, with far-reaching political implications. She had not interacted with any other political party, legal experts or media representatives, some of whom had witnessed the incident.

We requested Delhi for a short extension in time. A report was prepared and sent to Delhi on the basis of facts noted during our interaction with the governor, other officials and Shri Murasoli Maran. We could not meet Shri Baalu, another Union minister, as he was being kept at Vellore jail. Since I did not have any specific brief, I had sent a factual report. We reached the airport for our return journey, where we learned that the governor of Tamil Nadu had been transferred. Our report had been considered by the Union cabinet in its meeting.

We landed at Delhi Airport around 6.00 p.m., with message from Shri Arun Jaitley, law minister, informing us about an urgent meeting at his residence. Since we had been travelling for the last 20 hours, we requested a small break to freshen ourselves. A little before 8.00 p.m., we reached the law minister's residence in Kailash Colony. Additional Solicitor General Shri Kirit Rawal was also present.

Shri Jaitley started with a bombardment and said that my report had disturbed quite a few of his cabinet colleagues, especially Shri Nitish Kumar, who had questioned why I had been sent. During the discussion that followed, it was indicated that the report needed some amendments to meet the expectations of the ministers, who were not happy with my report. I very clearly told the meeting that the PM had sent me without any specific briefing. He had only asked me to see things for myself and send a report. Therefore, I had sent a factual report after interacting with the governor, other officials of the state government, including the top brass of the state police and Shri Maran. I also told them that both sides had video recorded the whole incident and while preparing the report, it had been like walking on the razor's edge for me. I added that if the government thought my report was not satisfactory, they could reject it and accept the report of NDA Convenor Shri George Fernandes, who had also visited Chennai on the same day for reporting on the same incident. On this, Shri Jaitley observed that it was a question of credibility. I immediately intervened that if my credibility is more acceptable then why was I being asked to change the report. On this, Shri Kirit Rawal, additional solicitor general (who later on become solicitor general), observed that there was nothing wrong with my report and it should be accepted. On this, Shri Arun Jaitley said that the PM had also appreciated my report and had agreed with it. This encouraged me and I said that if the PM, who had deputed me for this task had appreciated my report, why was I being asked to make amendments to my report and added that I was not concerned with the reactions of other ministers. The meeting ended and the report submitted by me was accepted.

But the story did not end here. The lobby which wanted to settle a score with CM Jayalalithaa and was not satisfied with my report convinced the home minister that the two senior officers of the Tamil Nadu Police, i.e., the DGP and the CP, Chennai, should be taken on deputation in the central government so that departmental action could then be initiated against them. An official note to this effect was prepared under instructions from the home secretary and was put up through me for onward transmission. As I was not consulted, I was shocked to see this attitude. The fact was that since nothing could be done against Ms Jayalalithaa, it was decided to punish the officers who acted upon her orders. I had never agreed with such an approach and I recorded that the central government is the highest executive authority in the country and should not be seen acting in vengeance. I was not aware of the developments since the file had not been routed through me during its return journey.

The deputation orders of the two Tamil Nadu Police officers were issued. In response, the Tamil Nadu government requested that as these officers were holding important posts, they should not be called on deputation. The state government also mentioned that they were not in a position to spare the services of the two officers. No response was given. In the meanwhile, the MHA received a notice from the Madras High Court asking reasons for insisting on the deputation of these two officers. This created a problem and a meeting was held in the home minister's chamber to find a way out. At this stage, I was called to suggest a solution. I told them that I had opposed the action from the beginning and if now the case was allowed to proceed, it might result in embarrassment to the central government. The High Court might ask for the MHA's file for inspection, which could cause immense embarrassment to the government due to information recorded on it. So if we decide to close the deputation matter, a way out could be suggested for consideration. On getting the nod, I suggested that we had not responded to the state government's request to cancel the transfer, which we could do now. We should write to them that on reconsideration, the central government had decided to accept the request of the state government and had decided to close the deputation case of the two Tamil Nadu Police officers. A copy of this letter could then be sent the next day to our additional solicitor general based in Chennai to inform the court with reference to their notice that the matter had been closed by the central government.

The central government was thus saved from embarrassment.

31

HANDLING TRADE UNIONISM IN CRPF

The concept of an 'Armed Forces of the Union' has no place for trade unionism. The officers and men of the uniformed forces are trained to follow strict discipline, obey and implement orders without any question and are bound by a very tough code of conduct. They function under a single chain of command, which does not permit any interference from any outside agency. While trade unions and service associations are not part of the official set-up, they exercise a lot of influence on the functioning of the organization and are a constant source of interference. A heavily armed force cannot afford the luxury of any type of unionization. Any relaxation in this respect could have very serious implications. However, denial of the right to form a union or association to convey and present their demands casts a very heavy responsibility on the state and force leadership to unequivocally ensure that the benefits and advantages that have been extended to other government employees are simultaneously made available to Armed Forces of the Union or paramilitary personnel. Besides, they have to be adequately compensated for the extremely tough and arduous nature of their duties, i.e., long hours of duty, the likelihood of being posted anywhere in the country on short notice, strict code of discipline, separation from family, the risk to life and limbs, etc. It must be accepted that while in the last 10–15 years the government had done reasonably well in this regard, a lot more was required to be done given the prevailing challenging security environment.

Before I mention the incident about which I propose to talk, I am reminded of another very interesting one that happened a few years before it. I was posted on deputation as IG, headquarter, in RPF at the Railway Board. Before RPF became an Armed Forces of the Union in 1985, the force had very active and strong associations of force personnel in each zonal railway, which had become a nuisance and had very adversely affected its functioning. These zonal associations had virtually created a parallel hierarchy, which did not allow the force officers to function. The indiscipline in the force was quite widespread and there were quite a few instances of force personnel going on strikes. We convinced the then railway minister, Shri Madhav Rao Scindia, to convert the RPF on the pattern of other central armed forces, as AFU, which besides other advantages, will put a total stop to the activities of the force associations. My main argument was that a force armed with weapons cannot be permitted to have associations which create a parallel chain of command in the force. The consequences could be disastrous. I was entrusted with the responsibility of drafting the Bill, which became an Act in 1985. A very high level of secrecy was maintained during the drafting of the Bill. The former office bearers of the RPF Association immediately filed a case in the Supreme Court of India against the Union of India, Ministry of Railways and also named me as one of the respondents. Then onwards they kept on making serious efforts to revive their association with the help of various political leaders. The most vocal among them were Shri George Fernandes and Shri Basudeb Acharya. The former RPF Association leaders convinced both these political leaders that so long I was in the force, there was no chance of revival of the association. Both of them separately wrote to the railway minister for my repatriation from the force. The ministry did not respond to their request.

But in 1989, the complexion of the government at the centre was changed and in the new government, Shri George Fernandes became the railway minister. As per normal protocol, all heads of the departments at the Railway Board were calling on the minister and briefing him about their subject. When our turn came, I told the then DG that my days in the RPF seemed to be over, especially given his (Shri Fernandes) recommendation about me in the recent past and therefore it would not be appropriate for me to accompany him for the meeting. However, on DG's insistence, I attended the meeting which lasted for about 45 minutes and the minister raised a few questions. Both the DG and I were shocked as the railway minister had not mentioned about the association even once. It was just unbelievable, but it happened. Throughout his tenure in the railways ministry, he neither discussed the subject of RPF Association with us, nor did anything to revive it. In February 1992, I went back to Delhi Police as CP Delhi, and after completing my tenure in 1995, I joined CRPF, where I was made election coordinator for central and other state police forces for Bihar assembly elections. During this period, I had an opportunity to travel with Shri George Fernandes in the same train coupe (two berths) while travelling from Patna to Delhi. We had some informal pleasant conversation. But I could not resist my temptation to ask him as to why he had not discussed the RPF Association issue during our meeting at the Railway Board, especially considering his views on the subject which he had repeatedly conveyed in his letters to the railway ministry in the past. He kept quiet for some time and then very coolly said that as a minister, he had to run the railways; we did not discuss this issue any further.

The important point is handling of the association matter in an armed force as and when it occurs. However, it would defer from situation to situation. In all cases, force leadership has to exhibit a lot of understanding and exercise restraint, but handling has to be firm, effective and humane. It should not even remotely indicate any vengeance. This matter should always be tackled on top priority since it has the potential of a wildfire. The following incident relates to one such situation.

While I was posted in the MHA, I learned that a few officers of the CRPF (an IG, a DIG and five to six commandant-level officers) had formed an association under the leadership of IG, Shri P.N, Rama Krishnan, who was from the CRPF cadre. The objective was to fight for making the CRPF cadre an 'organized service', including the betterment of service conditions like promotions, preventing induction of outside officers, especially from the police. The association functioned only for a short period and was dissolved by its promoters. However, these developments were reported to the MHA, which took a very serious view of the matter. It was decided to deal with these officers departmentally for a major penalty.

It was at this stage that I got involved in the matter. All these officers had worked under me during my tenure as DG, CRPF. Some of the officers, including the IG, who were facing an inquiry, met me and requested that I persuade the government to close the matter and save their career.

They also mentioned that the association had not initiated any activity and now stands dissolved. They also knew that in the departmental proceedings, if the charges were proved against them, which was most likely to happen, they could be dismissed. I told them that I will be examining the matter. Thereafter, I thought it proper to discuss the entire matter with the then DG, CRPF. While I always had a very firm and clear view that activities like an association could not be permitted in an armed force, this situation was a little different. An association was formed and without initiating any untoward activity it had been dissolved in a short time. The officers involved had also expressed their regret.

I weighed various options. The first option was to allow the department proceedings, which had already been ordered, to be completed and since there was sufficient evidence on record, their dismissal from service was almost a certainty. This would have been very harsh for the officers, who had an otherwise good record, especially in view of the fact that their association existed only for a very brief period and did not indulge in any objectionable activity except the formation of the association. While dismissal could have closed the matter and given a very stern warning to other members of the force, scars of such an incident would have lasted for a long time in the minds of force personnel. The other option for the government was to take a view on the initial replies of the defaulting officers in response to the notices served by the inquiry officer Shri Ganeshwar Jha, IG, CRPF. If they accept the charge and plead guilty, the disciplinary authority, i.e., the government, could have taken a generous view because of the special circumstances of the case and closed the proceedings. This would have settled a very serious issue with far-reaching implications on a happy note. However, it could be argued against this option that closing the matter without any exemplary punishment might encourage others to repeat it. But I was convinced that under the circumstances, especially after regret expressed by the involved officers, showing forgiveness was a better option and would have a desirable effect.

But this option had two important conditions—one, that all the charged officers must agree to plead guilty and thereby give up their option to proceed further with the inquiry and second, that the government must give some informal indication that it would take a lenient view and might close the case. As regards to the officers, it involved a huge risk since if they accepted to plead guilty, the possibility of their dismissal could not be totally ruled out. The government on their part could not have given any open assurance about their final decision. It was also necessary that before the government took a final view in the matter, the officers must plead guilty. Meanwhile, I had discussed the case in detail with both the home secretary and the home minister and they had agreed with my proposal. I had also told them that I would be informally conveying their view to the concerned officers.

These officers were very keen to get the matter settled, as they knew that I had to superannuate in the next three months. I called the officers and informed them about the developments. In fact, they had discussed the matter among themselves before coming to me and took almost no time to convey their decision to plead guilty in the inquiry. This suddenly put a very heavy burden on me—they were putting their entire career at risk solely on their faith in me and my ability to persuade the disciplinary authority to take a favourable view in the case. I must confess that at that point, I felt a little uneasy and asked them to reconsider their decision as nothing could be ruled out. But the officers were very clear in their mind and once again expressed their faith in my efforts. I told them to wait for my clearance as I wanted to discuss the matter once again with the home secretary and home minister and again obtain their oral assurance. I probably did this to give myself confidence.

Meanwhile, a very interesting thing happened. When I was discussing the matter with the home secretary, a very senior IPS officer of DG's rank (I am deliberately not mentioning his name) also came to meet the home secretary. Since he knew about this case, we continued our discussion. As I conveyed to the home secretary that the defaulting officers had agreed to plead guilty, the senior IPS officer intervened and very emphatically observed that with his experience, he was sure that none of these charged officers would plead guilty as they knew that it could result in their dismissal. He said in a light vein that he was prepared to have a bet with me on the matter. Normally, such things had never disturbed me and since I had conveyed the latest position to the home secretary, I left the room. Thereafter, I again discussed the matter with Shri Advani, the then home minister, who agreed with me that if they pleaded guilty, the government could consider taking a lenient view in the matter. After I conveyed the informal assurance to the concerned officers, they pleaded guilty before the enquiry officer (EO) and submitted their written replies.

The report of the EO came to the MHA through DG, CRPF, for decision. As secretary, IS, I recommended that since all the officers had pleaded guilty and their association, which had now been dissolved, had not indulged in any untoward activity during its short existence, the government might consider taking a generous view by forgiving these officers and the case against them could be closed. This would settle a bad incident on a happy note. The file was sent to the home secretary for onward submission to the home minister for decision. That was my last week with the government and I reminded the home secretary two to three times to send the file to home secretary. But he kept on assuring me that since we had already agreed he would be doing the needful as promised. I once again reminded him on the last day. However, on 2 or 3 January 2002, after I had retired from service, I was told that the defaulting officers have been given notice for censure. I must admit that I was shocked and quite disturbed. This was a complete breach of faith. I contacted Shri Advani and reminded him of his assurance in the matter and also asked him what had happened. He said that he had seen my detailed note and signed the file in agreement. He had missed the one one-line of the home secretary recommending censure. The home minister was also quite disturbed. However, the mistake was rectified by the home minister on my request, and the decision to censure the officers was dropped. The case against the defaulting CRPF officers was finally closed.

I later on learned that while the IG and DIG, charged in this case, retired peacefully with honour in their rank, out of the five commandants, two retired as additional DIG, two as DIG and one of them, Shri Madan Singh Raghav, retired as additional DG a few years back.

An incident, which had all the potential to damage the careers of so many officers, had a happy ending and a controversial matter was settled amicably in the larger interest of the force.

32

AS NEGOTIATOR

D uring my tenure of a little over four years in the MHA, the government entrusted me with many important and sensitive responsibilities and handling of certain critical situations. This also included conducting negotiations with militant groups, insurgents and leaders of violent movements.

1. Negotiations with Hizbul Mujahideen

Hizbul Mujahideen (HM), meaning the party of Holy Warriors, is a separatist militant organization active in the state of J&K that seeks its integration with Pakistan. The organization has claimed responsibility for carrying out multiple terrorist attacks in J&K. It had been designated as a 'terrorist group' by the US, the European Union and India.

Founded by Muhammad Ahsan Dar in September 1989, it is considered as one of the most important players that evolved the narrative of the Kashmir conflict from nationalism to the religious lines of the radical jihad. Some view it as the military wing of Jamaat-e-Islami. The outfit is supported since its inception by Pakistan's intelligence agency, Inter-Services Intelligence (ISI). Its headquarters are located at Muzaffarabad in Pakistan-occupied Kashmir (PoK) and has a liaison office in Islamabad, Pakistan.

HM is the largest cessationist group in the state. In 1998, the organization claimed a strength of over 10,000-armed cadre, most of whom were trained across the border. It has the best network in terms of the logistics and manpower. The outfit has both field and intelligence units all over J&K. Its first major strike is deemed to be the assassination of Maulvi Farooq, then Mirwaiz of Kashmir.

Around 1998–99, the group started to fragment as the ISI pushed foreign mercenaries and Punjab militants into Hizbul. Rivalries developed in the group, often leading to violence. Several Hizbul leaders were displeased with the manner in which the ISI was treating Kashmiris, putting them on the sidelines.

Between April and August 2000, the conflict of Kashmir came once again into sharp focus. Around April 2000, Abdul Majeed Dar, the Kashmir commander and other top leaders of Hizbul, were having parleys with central government officials in Delhi and at other venues that led to the build-up of a ceasefire offer. Consequently, offensive counter insurgency operations against the group were reduced. On 24 July 2000, Abdul Majeed Dar with four other Hizbul commanders made an unconditional declaration for ceasefire for a span of three months from the outskirts of Srinagar. They asserted that they had surveyed and it had the backing of the local people. Dar had visited Pakistan before the announcement for consultation with the Hizbul Mujahideen's central command. The ceasefire was welcomed and was immediately ratified by the Pakistan-based Hizbul chief commander, Syed Salahuddin.

The Pakistan government ordered its forward posts on the LOC to abide by the 'no shoot first' policy. The Hizbul Mujahideen's announcement of ceasefire came as a surprise to people both in India and Pakistan. In India, the response was of universal approval with media treating it as a window of opportunity for a solution; the response in Pakistan was not so positive.

The Muttahida Jihad Council (MJC) severely criticized the ceasefire next day and called it a betrayal. From 31 July, a lot of killings took place in Kashmir, including killings of 31 Amarnath pilgrims and their porters while they were going for darshan to the holy shrine. Nevertheless, the Government of India stated that it would pursue the home minister's ceasefire offer and would not let terrorism succeed in derailing the peace process.

On 1 or 2 August 2000, Government of India decided to appoint me as their representative for carrying out negotiations with Hizbul Mujahideen. At that time, I was special secretary, IS, and was not handling the Kashmir portfolio. Probably considering my experience relating to Kashmir and trusting my abilities as a negotiator, I was entrusted with this responsibility. Senior intelligence agencies officials briefed me about the background of the ceasefire and the possible issues that could be raised during the negotiations. On 3 August, formal talks were held for the first time, where the home secretary, Shri Kamal Pandey, told them that Government of India would be represented in the talks by Shri M.B. Kaushal, special secretary, MHA. The Hizbul Mujahideen nominated a four-member team led by Khalid Saifullah. The objective of the talks was to settle the modalities of the ceasefire.

During the talks, which were being held at the heavily guarded Nehru Guest House at the foothills of Zabarwan, Srinagar, all the four representatives of the Mujahideen had covered their faces and only their eyes were visible. After introduction, I initiated the talks by observing that while they knew to whom they were talking, I only knew their names and could see only their eyes. I said this in a very pleasant tone to make a friendly start and the Mujahideen delegates immediately responded by removing their masks. They also said, 'Kaushal Saheb, there is no purdah with you'. We had a very meaningful and friendly discussion with them and they showed a lot of understanding and appreciated our point of view. While it would not be appropriate to give details of the talks we had with them, I mention an interesting observation made by Khalid Saifullah while discussing the modalities of the ceasefire. He said that if they accepted all the conditions which Government of India was suggesting, their followers would get the impression that they (Mujahideen delegates) were sold out. I immediately intervened and told them that their credibility was very important to us and it would be our responsibility to ensure that it was maintained. Thereafter, I suggested in detail how we would go about including what they could tell their people and media. On our part we would be making only positive and restrained statement. Our talks were held smoothly with an understanding that we would be meeting again soon. A friendly cricket match was also played the next day between the Indian Armed Forces and the Hizbul.

Meanwhile Hizbul's chief commander issued an ultimatum from Islamabad that India must agree to tripartite negotiations in which Pakistan was to be included. This was promptly rejected by India as it was not part of the unconditional talks envisaged in the original ceasefire offer, which had clearance from Salahuddin. Still, India continued to make positive confidence-building overtures to the Mujahideen. On 6 August, after a good survey, the Mujahideen issued a statement that talks would continue. Dar, in an interview with BBC Urdu Service, on the night of 7 August, declared his wish that talks should continue, pointing out that the first round of talks with the representative of Government of India had shown 'a ray of hope'.

However, on 8 August 2000, Syed Salahuddin announced the withdrawal of ceasefire offer on very flimsy pretexts. It was reported that Syed Salahuddin was under house arrest and was pressurized by the ISI to issue the withdrawal statement. The ceasefire offer was made from the outskirts of Srinagar and its withdrawal was issued from Islamabad.

2. Negotiations with Naga Undergrounds

After declaration of ceasefire by the National Socialist Council of Nagaland (Isak-Muivah Group), both sides, i.e., Government of India and NSCN (IM) finalized a set of ground rules in December 1997 to undertake steps for effective unambiguous implementation of the ceasefire in Nagaland. This was a set of 11 ground rules covering various aspects of engagement between the two sides, for example, no offensive operations against the NSCN (IM) by Indian Army, preventive patrolling, protection of convoys and roads by Indian forces, the NSCN (IM) would not carry out any offensive operations and would not do any parade or march in uniform, there would be no road blocks or disruption of developmental activities, no forcible collection of money and no forced recruitment. The implementation of these rules was to be monitored by a group. The ceasefire was for four years. But the experience was that the Naga insurgents outfit followed these rules, mostly in violation.

The Government of India decided to review the ground

rules of the ceasefire and drafted more stringent and specific rules. This was to be discussed with the Naga outfit. Although I was not dealing with matters relating to the Northeast, the government decided to nominate me for leading the official team for negotiating the revised ground rules with the representatives of NSCN (IM). Joint secretary, Northeast Division, Shri G.K. Pillai, briefed me in detail about the background of the matter, various points likely to be raised during the discussion and the official stand.

Two meetings were held between the two teams, i.e., the official MHA team and the NSCN-IM delegation. The first meeting was held in January 2001 at Hotel Kanishka, in which all these ground rules were discussed in detail. As expected, the Naga team did not agree and the meeting ended without any result. But it was agreed that the next meeting would be convened in the near future. The second meeting was organized in June 2001. After a long discussion, we decided to close the meeting as the Nagas were not prepared to accept the proposed ground rules. While dispersing, I told Shri Gopal Pillai, the then joint secretary, Northeast, that I had a gut feeling that the Naga team, which was looking less rigid than the last time, might accept the proposal if we give them another chance.

So we decided to stay for the lunch. In the dining hall, we again met and indulged in some pleasant conversation. I told them that while we are parting without any settlement, we are friends and would find out some solution in the near future. Suddenly, the Naga leaders expressed their willingness to meet again for discussion after lunch. Our patience had shown the results. We met again and after a short discussion, they agreed to accept the ground rules proposed by us. Both teams thanked each other for their understanding and consideration. After the ground rules were agreed upon, the four-year ceasefire was extended by one more year.

The intended objective had been achieved.

3. Negotiations with Subhas Ghisingh, the GNLF Leader

Subhash Ghisingh was the leader of Gorkha National Liberation Front (GNLF), which he founded in 1980. The Gorkha movement started with the demand for a separate state of ethnic Gorkha (Nepali) in Darjeeling district of West Bengal. The GNLF led the movement which resulted in massive violence between 1986 and 1988 leading to a large number of killings. After two years of violent agitation, the Government of India and the state government of West Bengal agreed on granting a semi-autonomous administrative body to Darjeeling Hills. In July 1988, the GNLF gave up its demand for a separate state and in August 1988, the Darjeeling Gorkha Hill Council came into being. Subhash Ghisingh became its first chairman after winning the council's elections.

After some time, Subhash Ghisingh started pressing the central government for granting the Sixth Schedule Tribal Council for Darjeeling Hills. Government of India was not inclined at that time to accede to this demand. In this connection, he wanted to meet the Union home minister. It was decided in the MHA (I do not recollect the exact date and year—it was either in 2000 or 2001) that the meeting should be held at secretary level and thereafter, if considered necessary, he could meet the home minister. Subhash Ghisingh was informed. Although I was not handling the Northeast division of the MHA, I was asked to lead the negotiations. The Joint Secretary, Northeast, Shri G.K. Pillai, briefed me about the background of the matter, issues likely to be raised by Subhash

Ghisingh and our official stand on the matter. The meeting was scheduled in the conference room of the MHA.

I, along with Shri Pillai and other officials, reached the conference hall a few minutes before the scheduled time for the meeting. Lot of members of the press including photographers were waiting outside the conference hall. Subhash Ghisingh with his team entered the conference room at the scheduled time and to our surprise announced that he had decided to walk out of the meeting. All of us were shocked as this was the most unexpected development. Before Ghisingh could leave the room, I drew his attention and told him that the media was waiting outside the conference hall and it would be quite embarrassing for him to say that he had boycotted the meeting since our talks had not even started. I suggested that he could avoid this situation, if he stayed in the meeting room for 15–20 minutes and leave thereafter. He understood the point and realized that it would save his position before the media. He agreed to stay and I ordered beverages to be served. I told him that if he was not interested in discussing the issue, we could talk about something else. And this became our starting point for the discussion, which continued till lunch time. We had a very meaningful discussion with him and he was satisfied. We had not conceded his demand for inclusion in the Sixth Schedule. After lunch, I went with him to meet the home minister, where he conveyed his satisfaction with the talks.

The issue was settled for quite some time.

33

UNPRECEDENTED SANCTIONS

K eeping in view the post-Kargil War situation, the central government constituted a Groups of Ministers (GoM) to review the national security system, especially, the security arrangements at the country's borders and the internal security. The Cabinet Committee on Security (CCS) considered the recommendations of the GoM and in its meeting held on 2 March 2000 directed the setting up of an Inter-Ministerial Group (IMG) to draw a five-year plan for augmenting the paramilitary forces (CPMF), including the Rashtriya Rifles. While as secretary, IS, I was assisting the two GoMs, the government constituted the IMG under my chairmanship consisting of representatives from different ministries and departments i.e., DG, BSF; DG, CRPF; additional secretary, expenditure, Ministry of Finance; principal director, DGS, cabinet secretariat; joint secretary, defence; joint secretary, Northeast; joint secretary, J&K; financial advisor, MHA; and joint secretary police (member-secretary).

The internal security scenario in the country during the last decade had been a matter of serious concern. The militancy in Punjab had been brought under control after a great deal of efforts and sacrifices. Towards the end of 1989, the militancy started in J&K and the situation quickly deteriorated due to Pakistan's policy of proxy war by infiltrating foreign mercenaries, arms, ammunition and funds. A marked improvement in the situation came in 1996, when Government of India installed a democratically elected government in the state. To counter this, Pakistan stepped up the proxy war and, finally, it culminated in the summer of 1999 in intrusion and a war. Thereafter, the situation in J&K had undergone a big change. Pakistan started sending 'suicide squads' for targeting security establishments with a view to tie down the security forces so that they could not undertake operations against the militants. The security forces in J&K were under great pressure and the challenge both within the state and at the borders needed to be met squarely.

The situation in the Northeast at that time particularly in Manipur and Tripura was quite disturbing. The security forces there were targets of insurgents, who were also indulging in the smuggling of arms, ammunition, narcotics and extortion from local people. Insurgency in Assam also required serious consideration. Left-wing extremism had affected Andhra Pradesh, Maharashtra, Orissa, Bihar and Madhya Pradesh. A concept of 'revolutionary zone' from Nepal down to Andhra Pradesh was being propagated. The possibility of the spread of Left-wing extremism in other adjoining areas was there. The ISI was extending its activity on the Indo-Nepal border, where a large number of madrasas had come up on both sides of the border. This border was also being used by the ISI for smuggling arms, fake currency and infiltration. Various states also needed assistance from the central government to handle serious communal situations and caste riots.

The group looked into the 'approach paper' prepared

by the MHA regarding the futuristic requirement of CPMF and also considered the prevailing security scenario. The parametres on which the futuristic requirements could be assessed were also discussed. The group felt that it should take an overview of the security situations that is likely to prevail in the next decade.

The growth of the state police force including their armed police was quite slow during the period of 1991–99. It was also noticed that the state armed police were not trained and equipped to face the modern terrorists and militants and this led to the tendency of the state governments to depend more on central assistance. It was felt that the central government must indicate the conditions and situations when it would provide assistance to the states.

The group also took into consideration the deployment of CPMFs at that time. The CRPF was 100 per cent deployed and their rotational training was almost finished. Out of 157 battalions of BSF, 45 battalions had been diverted for internal security duties by thinning their deployment at the border. The border management group had suggested the requirement for the Indo-Pak and Indo-Bangladesh border as 179 battalions. Eleven companies of ITBP and five companies of CISF were also withdrawn and deployed on internal security duties. All reserves of these forces had been pressed into service and even nine battalions of SSB, which was at that time under the cabinet secretariat, were also deployed.

The nature of militancy, which was prevailing in J&K warranted active deployment of the Army to fight the proxy war waged by Pakistan. About 30 battalions of Rashtriya Rifles that were being manned by the serving Army personnel were also deployed in J&K. Similar situation existed, to some extent, in the Northeast.

The security concern of the country had to be addressed and whatever augmentation of CPMF was necessary had to be considered. While there had been intermittent sanctions of paramilitary battalions, the situation that developed in the last decade rendered the available force totally inadequate. This led to the diversion of the task-specific forces like BSF, ITBP and CISF to internal security duties and also the deployment of the Army.

To put an end to the culture of dependence on central assistance, i.e., CPMF, it was decided to strengthen the state armed police to meet the enhanced threat of terrorism and militancy in various states. In this background, the MHA in their note had proposed the creation of 50 India Reserve (IR) battalions for the states. Before raising these IR battalions, it was necessary to obtain the consent of the concerned states to meet the recurring expenditure of the new battalions. It was also felt that to maintain a uniform level of preparedness, the new IR battalion should be raised, trained and equipped on the lines of the CPMF, mainly the CRPF. Under the IR battalion schemes, the first charge of the utilization of these battalions rests with the central government for the first five years.

With the fencing of the Punjab border, Pakistan's ISI made Nepal its new base for carrying on its anti-India activities, i.e., smuggling arms, ammunition, circulation of drugs and fake currency and infiltration. Since it was an open border, the ISI found it easy to operate through this route. The requirements of the Indo-Nepal border were not taken into consideration by the IMG while considering the strengthening of border policing at other international borders.

At that time, 59 battalions of BSF/ITBP/CISF were deployed on internal security duties by withdrawing them from their specific duties. Similarly, Army units were deployed in big numbers in J&K and in Northeast states for counter-insurgency duties. In case of hostilities, the Army had indicated that they would withdraw their 60 units. The shortfall in the deployment in various states for internal security duties was about 71 battalions. The total requirement for internal security duties, if the presently deployed task-specific forces had to return and the army withdrew its 60 units for dealing with hostilities, would be around 190 battalions. This would include the requirements of various states too.

The border management group had examined the requirements of the Indo-Pak and Indo-Bangladesh border and had recommended an additional 22 battalions for the BSF. This was mainly required to insure reduction in inter-border out posts distances in the eastern sector mainly to prevent infiltration from Bangladesh. A committee set up by the MHA in 1996 had recommended an additional nine battalions for the Assam Rifles to man the Indo-Myanmar border. The overall assessment of the futuristic requirement of CPMFs was 225 battalions.

The total initial cost of raising these battalions was estimated to be ₹7,584 crore. Besides these one-time costs, there would also be a recurring expenditure of about ₹1,882 crore towards salaries, ration, etc. The question of technology and manpower trade-off was also considered by the IMG in detail. The group felt that while technological upgradation would improve the effectiveness of these forces, it would not result significantly in lowering the manpower requirements.

To cut cost, it was decided to add more manpower in each existing battalions, that is, instead of six companies, each battalion would have seven companies and the newly created battalions would also have a strength of seven companies. This saved the supervising set-up and the office expenditure of about 55 battalions. Similarly, CRPF Group Centres would have five battalions instead of four. Since this was likely to affect the professional capability of the forces, it was decided to treat it as a temporary measure to be restored in future. The strength of Assam Rifles was restructured and strength for five new battalions could be provided by reducing the strength of existing battalions. Similarly, the requirement of Rashtriya Rifles was reduced from 37 battalions, as proposed by the Ministry of Defence, to 30 battalions. The IMG also recommended a schedule of additional raising over a period of five years starting from 2000–01. The cost reduction measures also resulted in substantial savings, which was around ₹2,600 crore in the non-recurring and the capital cost and also ₹250 crore in the recurring cost.

To sustain these additional battalions, there was a requirement of supporting and supervisory elements so that the forces could be effectively commandeered and supported. The estimated cost of this was ₹141 crore as recurring expenditure and ₹470 crore towards non-recurring and capital costs.

The requirement of the Indo-Nepal border was not covered by the IMG. Since the full potential of the SSB, which was with the cabinet secretariat, was not being utilized, I, later on, moved a proposal to shift the administrative and operational control of the SSB from the cabinet secretariat to the MHA, which was accepted. The MHA renamed it as SSB and deployed it on the Indo-Nepal border. This border is now being guarded by this force very effectively. This step was taken after the hijacking of IC 814 and Government of Nepal was informed.

A cabinet note was prepared based on the IMG report for the consideration and sanction of the Union cabinet.

Since this was on the instructions of the CCS, its approval was received in time.

The sanction of such a large number of battalions in one go had no precedent. It made the country's security apparatus more formidable and effective. It was a matter of great satisfaction for me that as in-charge of IS in the MHA, I got the opportunity to assist the two GoMs in reviewing the security arrangements at the country's borders and internal security and also helped them in formulating their recommendations. I also got the privilege of heading the IMG which made the proposal for creating such a large number of battalions to augment the strength of almost all CPMFs and the state police organizations and obtained the approval of the government. The SSB was also added to the list of CPMFs under the control of the MHA.

In this entire exercise, the valuable contribution made by my Joint Secretary, Police, Shri O.P. Arya, deserves special mention. He had a very positive approach and was always concerned about the welfare of the police and the paramilitary forces.

On 31 December 2001, I bid adieu to government service and superannuated as a happy and content person with sweet memories of the people with whom I had had the privilege of working with, of incidents that had happened, the challenges that I had faced and the bountiful blessings of God which gave me strength to sail through this long and enriching journey.

www.ingramcontent.com/pod-product-compliance
Lightning Source LLC
Chambersburg PA
CBHW022032020426
42338CB00032B/1802/J